PSYCHOTHERAPY
OF THE
SUBMERGED
PERSONALITY

COMMENTARY

"*Psychotherapy of the Submerged Personality* is the most significant theoretical and therapeutic contribution to psychotherapy and psychoanalysis since Kohut. The theoretical explanation is clear and convincing (makes one think 'Of course! Why didn't I think of it?'). Detailed case histories by six therapists carefully illustrate, in step-by-step fashion, how the theory guides the therapeutic process. A must for all psychotherapists and analysts."

—Clifford Sager, M.D.

"If the '70s and '80s were the time of the borderline personality, then the '90s appear to be the time of the submerged personality. Drs. Wolf and Kutash have rightly refocused on the exceedingly difficult patients who are appearing in the office of the psychiatrist and psychotherapist, whose primary difficulty appears to be not in their perception of reality, but in submerging their individuality. In many areas such as cult affiliation, multiple personality disorder, gender and sexual orientation, and work with minorities . . . this is a book that will inspire the therapist to rediscover his art."

—David Halperin, M.D.

PSYCHOTHERAPY
OF THE
SUBMERGED
PERSONALITY

edited by
Alexander Wolf, M.D.
and
Irwin L. Kutash, Ph.D.

JASON ARONSON INC.
Northvale, New Jersey
London

Production Editor: Judith D. Cohen
Editorial Director: Muriel Jorgensen

This book was set in 11/14 Berkeley Oldstyle
by Alpha Graphics of Pittsfield, New Hampshire, and
printed and bound by Haddon Craftsmen of Scranton, Pennsylvania.

The author gratefully acknowledges permission to reprint poem number 435 from THE COMPLETE POEMS OF EMILY DICKINSON, edited by Thomas H. Johnson. Copyright © 1914, 1929, 1935, 1942 by Martha Dickinson Bianchi; Copyright © renewed 1957, 1963 by Mary L. Hampson. Reprinted by permission of the publishers, Little, Brown and Company and the Trustees of Amherst College from THE COMPLETE POEMS OF EMILY DICKINSON edited by Thomas H. Johnson, Cambridge, MA: The Belknap Press of Harvard University Press, Copyright 1951, © 1955, 1979, 1983 by the President and Fellows of Harvard College.

Library of Congress Cataloging-in-Publication Data

Psychotherapy of the submerged personality / edited by Alexander Wolf,
    Irwin L. Kutash.
        p.   cm.
    Includes bibliographical references (p.   ) and index.
    ISBN 0-87668-644-7
    1. Personality disorders. 2. Ego (Psychology) 3. Self.
4. Parent and child. I. Wolf, Alexander, 1907–   . II. Kutash,
Irwin L.
    RC455.4.E35P78   1991
    616.85′8—dc20   90-1234

Manufactured in the United States of America. Jason Aronson Inc. offers books and cassettes. For information and catalog write to Jason Aronson Inc., 230 Livingston Street, Northvale, New Jersey 07647.

This book is dedicated to our memory of
Emanuel K. Schwartz—
challenging student, magnificent teacher,
and beloved friend.

Contents

Foreword

A young woman who was vulnerable to extreme states of self–other confusion opened the first session of her analysis with the words, "Doctor, I turn into anyone I meet. You won't let that happen, will you?" (Stolorow et al. 1987, p. 155). This patient's utterance captures the central theme of this volume. This is a book about a spectrum of disturbances of self-differentiation—derailments of the developmental process of becoming a demarcated and distinctive human being with a unique affective life and an individualized array of personal values and aims. A critical requirement for the child's attainment of individualized selfhood is the presence of caregivers who are reliably able to recognize, affirm, enjoy, and pridefully treasure the unique affective qualities and independent aspirations of the child. When a parent cannot recognize and affirm the child's central qualities and strivings because they conflict with the parent's own self-organization requirements, then the child's self-delineating efforts will be seriously compromised.

The derailment of the self-differentiation process occurs when central affective states associated with the emergence of individualized selfhood are consistently not responded to or are actively rejected. A fundamental psychic conflict thereby becomes enduringly established between the requirement that one's developmental course must conform to the emotional needs of caregivers, and the inner imperative that its evolution be firmly rooted in a vitalizing affective core of one's own. Several outcomes of this basic conflict are possible. The child may abandon or sacrifice central feelings and aspirations in order to maintain indispensable ties. This is the path of submission and chronic depression, as the child feels compelled to "become" what the parent requires and thus to subjugate any striving to develop according to his own separate design. Accordingly, he may construct a negative ego (Wolf 1957)—retitled submerged ego and dual pseudo-ego by Kutash (Wolf and Kutash 1984), and currently termed the submerged personality, a defensive "false-self" (Winnicott 1960), and an "identity theme" (Lichtenstein 1961)—that serves the needs of the parent at whatever cost to authentic self-experience (Miller 1979). In contrast, the child may attempt to preserve and protect his core of individualized vitality at the expense of emotional ties by adopting a pattern of resolute defiance and rebellion. This is the path of isolation and estrangement, undertaken, as Kohut (1984a) has pointed out, in the service of psychological survival. A third alternative is a life of relentless, tormenting ambivalence, of being endlessly torn between inner aspirations and needed relationships that seem irreconcilably opposed. This is the path of wrenching indecision and noncommitment.

Wolf, Kutash, and their associates have described a group of psychological constellations that combine all three of these pathways into a complex configuration termed the submerged personality, which is the product of a defensive adaptation to a narcissistically exploitive parent, usually the mother. Essentially, the child perceives that any expression of his own distinctness that frustrates his mother's need for him to serve as her self-extension results in the loss of her love. In the hope of regaining that love, he submerges his offending feelings and aspirations—that is, his "true self"—and becomes the compliant "pseudo-self" in harmony with his mother's narcissistic needs. However, since such subjugation threatens the child with self-extinction, he develops a second pseudo-self characterized by compulsive rebellion that serves to counteract the compliance.

Through rich clinical discussions and illustrations, the authors show how the submergence of the true self and the constant tension between the two defensive pseudo-selves can be responsible for a broad range of psychopathological symptoms and painful states. Their treatment approach, developed over the course of nearly fifty years of clinical experience, combines individual psychoanalysis and psychoanalysis in groups in a systematic attempt to facilitate the liberation of the patient's affective aliveness and creativity and, concomitantly, to weaken the grip of the pseudo-selves on the patient's experience and conduct.

I began these brief remarks with a patient's query. In this volume, Alexander Wolf, Irwin L. Kutash, and their associates supply an implicit answer: "You may indeed turn into me, but I will help you to refind *yourself*." Many patients and their therapists will surely be grateful for the detailed guidance this book provides as to how this goal can be achieved. The concept of the submerged personality and the dual pseudo-selves (compliant and rebellious) is an important contribution to the understanding of the self.

Robert D. Stolorow, Ph.D.

Preface

Contained in this volume is a detailed description of a type of disorder first contemplated in the early 1930s, verified by clinical experience through the 1940s and early 1950s, first written about in 1956 (Wolf 1957), and refined by the two of us in the 1980s (Kutash 1984b, Kutash and Greenberg 1986, 1990, Wolf and Kutash 1984a, 1985). Because it is a disorder encountered in a great number of patients, we believed that the diagnosis needed a book devoted to it to disseminate our findings to other clinicians. This disorder is the submerged personality (di-egophrenia).

For years before undergoing his own analysis (1930–1937), Wolf made notes indicating his conviction that all pathological mental states represented the incorporation of destructive forces prevalent in society at large. After he entered his own treatment, he became more familiar with how parental psychopathology shaped and reshaped the minds and perceptions of infants and children. Nevertheless, he never outgrew his early sense that society at large continued to impose a profound and noxious influence on individuals. From 1942 to 1946, he filled notebooks with evidence to confirm these impressions.

In 1938, when Wolf began practicing psychoanalysis in groups, his focus was largely in the intrapsychic area. He observed the interpersonal distortions of patients, and in trying to bring them to more objective perceptions, he was made more aware of how their experiences in society continued to exert destructive pressures on them. Despite this, many of his patients became increasingly able to cope with their socially imposed difficulties. Others relapsed in the face of these obstacles.

In the 1940s Wolf became aware of what was then called *pseudoneurotic schizophrenia* and was subsequently named *borderline personality*. This disorder was first alluded to in the 1949–1950 publication, *The Psychoanalysis of Groups*. In 1956, in a discussion of a paper by Gustav Bychowski on latent schizophrenia, Wolf suggested that Bychowski's patients were not "latent schizophrenic" or borderline. Rather, they were suffering from a suppression of intact egos and were functioning with what was then termed a negative ego, an ambivalent introjected parental ego, which the individual complied with and rebelled against. Wolf proposed the term *submerged* as a more appropriate descriptor for these patients. This was further refined by Kutash and termed the *dual pseudo-egos*. The introjected and therefore compliant parental pseudo-ego and a second rebellious pseudo-ego, in opposition to it, were formed as a defense by the intact submerged ego, a kind of antibody response to the parental ego introjections.

In the 1970s Kutash, in the "Equilibrium–Disequilibrium Theory of Stress Induced Anxiety," described a model of mental health based on the level of stress one was experiencing in the four environments in which one lives: the interpersonal environment, the physical environment, the mental environment, and the physiological environment (Kutash 1980). This theory stressed the effect of external and internal forces on the individual ego. After attending Wolf's 1980 Karen Horney Memorial Lecture ("Di-Egophrenia and Genius"), Kutash felt that Wolf's ideas helped explain the impact of the interpersonal, parental, and societal environments and how they could affect the emerging ego. This concept could be understood in terms of "pseudo-egoality." The two authors began to collaborate, and this book, along with earlier articles on submergence, is the culmination of this association.

The influence of the parent is clarified in Chapter 1, along with the social forces that entrench the pathology. The placement of the disorder within the diagnostic spectrum is described in Chapter 2. Chapter 3 describes the treatment approach to be used with these patients. In Chapter 4, the concepts of the authentic ego and the pseudo-ego are explored, providing further implications.

In Part II, the treatment of various kinds of submerged patients is presented, including homosexual, depressed, schizoid, paranoid, oedipally conflicted, and dually diagnosed borderline/submerged personalities.

We are greatly indebted to our associates, whose creative and scholarly contributions have enlarged our understanding of this disorder. Without their originality and thoughtfulness, this book would not have been possible. We would also like to express our appreciation to our supervisees and patients, whose penetrating questions and interactions with us enhanced and shaped the evolution of our thinking.

Alexander Wolf, M.D.
New York, New York

Irwin L. Kutash, Ph.D.
Livingston, New Jersey

Contributors

Alexander Wolf, M.D.

Private practice of psychotherapy and psychoanalysis in New York City. He is a senior supervisor, training psychoanalyst, and faculty member of the Postgraduate Center for Mental Health and the New York Center for Psychoanalytic Training. For twenty-five years he was an associate clinical professor of psychiatry at the New York Medical College, and a training analyst, supervisor, and faculty member in the psychoanalytic division there. He received his M.D. in 1932 from Cornell University Medical College. Dr. Wolf originated the practice of psychoanalysis in groups in 1938. In 1957, Dr. Wolf received the Adolph Meyer award from the Association for Improvement in Mental Health "for his contributions to psychoanalysis in groups," and in 1963 he received the first Wilfred C. Hulse Memorial Award from the Eastern Group Psychotherapy Society for outstanding contributions to the practice of group therapy. Dr. Wolf received the Distinguished Writer's Award of the New York Center for Psychoanalytic Training in 1985.

Irwin L. Kutash, Ph.D.

Private practice of psychotherapy and psychoanalysis in Livingston, New Jersey. He is a clinical associate professor of mental health sciences at the New Jersey College of Medicine and Dentistry, and a senior supervisor, training psychoanalyst, and faculty member of the New York Center for Psychoanalytic Training and the Institute for Psychoanalysis and Psychotherapy of New Jersey. He is also a field supervisor at the Graduate School of Applied and Professional Psychology of Rutgers University and a psychological consultant to the New Jersey Department of Institutions and Agencies. Dr. Kutash received his Ph.D. in clinical psychology in 1972 from the Institute of Advanced Psychological Studies of Adelphi University and holds a postdoctoral certificate in psychotherapy and psychoanalysis from the Postgraduate Center for Mental Health, where he received a ten-year service award in 1982. He also holds a diplomate in clinical psychology from the American Board of Professional Psychology.

Dr. Kutash served as president of the Society of Psychologists in Private Practice in New Jersey, as president of the New Jersey Academy of Psychology, and as a board member of the New Jersey Association for the Advancement of Psychology and of the New Jersey Psychological Association. Dr. Kutash is past president of the section on group psychotherapy of the psychotherapy division of the American Psychological Association and is the editor of the *American Journal of Group Psychotherapy*, the journal of the Group Division of the APA. Dr. Kutash received the Distinguished Writer's Award of the New York Center for Psychoanalytic Training in 1988.

Steven Dranoff, Ph.D.

Psychoanalyst in private practice in Clifton and Livingston, New Jersey. He received his Ph.D. from Fordham University in 1981 and certification in Psychotherapy and Psychoanalysis from the Postgraduate Center for Mental Health in 1989. He is past director of the Clifton

Mental Health Services. Dr. Dranoff is a field supervisor at the Graduate School of Applied and Professional Psychology at Rutgers University. He is a member of the American Psychological Association and the New Jersey Psychological Association, and is both a trustee and a member of the executive board of the New Jersey Academy of Psychology.

Jeffrey Greenberg, Ph.D.

Clinical psychologist in private practice in Livingston, New Jersey. He received his Ph.D. in 1982 from the University of Georgia. He has worked as a staff psychologist for the Essex County Guidance Center and for New Jersey's Employee Advisory Service (Employee Assistance Program). He is currently serving as a consultant to the New Jersey Employee Advisory Service. Dr. Greenberg is a trustee and member of the executive board of the New Jersey Academy of Psychology.

Daniel P. Juda, Ph.D.

Psychoanalyst in private practice in New York City. He received his Ph.D. from the New School for Social Research in 1980. He is currently an associate professor at the John Jay College of Criminal Justice and is on the faculty of the Postgraduate Center for Mental Health, where he graduated from the psychotherapy and psychoanalysis program in 1983, and from the training program in supervision of the analytic process in 1987.

Michael Lindenman, Ph.D.

Private practice of psychotherapy and psychoanalysis in New York City. He received his Ph.D. in 1970 from New York University. Formerly on the faculty of Montclair State College, he is currently a member of the training faculty at the Institute for Contemporary Psychotherapy, the Training Institute for Mental Health, Beth Israel Hospital, Department of Psychiatry, and the Postgraduate Center for Mental Health, all in New York. He received his certificate in psychoanalysis from the New Jersey Institute for Training in Psychoanalysis in 1987 and his certificate in group therapy from the Postgraduate Center in 1988. Dr. Lindenman is currently associate editor of the journal, *Group*.

Arnold Wm. Rachman, Ph.D.

Psychoanalyst in private practice in New York City. He received his Ph.D. in 1965 from the University of Chicago. He is a supervisor and training group analyst at the Postgraduate Center for Mental Health, where he graduated from the program in 1968. His paper, first published in this volume, was the winner of the Jack D. Krasner Memorial Award. It was chosen from the Postgraduate entries as the most outstanding paper in group therapy for 1988.

Kenneth Wald, C.S.W.

Board certified diplomate and a psychoanalyst in private practice in New York City. He has taught and supervised in the Postgraduate Center for Mental Health counseling training program. He is a graduate (1988) of the psychotherapy and psychoanalysis training program of the Postgraduate Center for Mental Health and, in 1985, of the New Hope Guild Center's child psychotherapy training program. He received his M.S. degree from the Columbia University School of Social Work in June 1982.

I

DYNAMICS OF THE SUBMERGED PERSONALITY

1

Historical and Theoretical Perspective

**Alexander Wolf, M.D.,
and Irwin L. Kutash, Ph.D.**

This above all: to thine own self be true.
—Shakespeare, *Hamlet*

There are certain patients, sometimes classified as borderline, who display specific dynamics, in which their own egos are submerged and replaced by an introjected parental self (Wolf 1957). These patients act as if they perceive the meaning of symbols and realities in their environment, but actually see them as their parents wanted them to. Needing their parents for security, these patients renounce their own egos for their parents' egos. They give up their own perceptions of reality and accept the reality and distortions imposed by their parents. They have their own positive egos in submergence and negative egos from their parents superimposed. The submerged patients have their parents inside themselves. The pathology of these patients is a consequence of how they were used and abused by their parents and their culture. Their perception is not their own; it was given to them by their parents, and it is an extension of their parents. Originally, these submerged individuals perceived reality accurately. Then their valid perceptions were repressed, and their parents' perceptions were superimposed. These patients reflect the struggle between their suppressed egos and the introjected parental ego, previously called "positive" and "negative" egos (Wolf 1957).

The concept of submergence was used in therapy by its originator and his supervisees and colleagues, but it did not emerge in print again until 1980, with the article "Di-egophrenia and Genius." The authors have since elaborated, reviewed, and refined these original reflections (Kutash 1984b, Wolf and Kutash 1984a, 1985).

The awareness of this concept, however, came in 1947 when one of us (Wolf) was stimulated to develop the idea of submergence when reading *The Ordeal of Mark Twain*, by Van Wyck Brooks (1920), in which the biographer made clear the impact that Twain's primary and secondary mothers had on his creativity (partly submerged), his sadomasochism, his ambivalence, his playful and depressed moods, and his passive-aggressivity. A biography subsequently appeared of Van Wyck Brooks himself (*Van Wyck Brooks: A Writer's Life*, by Raymond Nelson, 1974). The treatment he received from his mother was not unlike that of Mark Twain. Brooks developed many of the symptoms he ascribed to Clemens, so it is somewhat difficult to know to what extent Brooks projected his mental difficulties onto Twain. Or as Paul Murray Kendall so succinctly put it, "On the trail of another man, the biographer must put up with finding himself at every turn: any biography uneasily shelters an autobiography within it."

By 1949, Wolf's thinking on submergence was published in a report of a patient (Wolf 1949, 1950), although the term di-egophrenia was yet to be coined.

Perhaps the citation of a few examples of the transference process as it occurs in group therapy will serve to illustrate further the historical growth of the concept.

In previous individual treatment, H. P. evidenced erotic interest in me (Wolf) that was associated with some fear and anxiety, mixed unconscious feelings directed toward her father in childhood. These were never conscious or expressed. During an early group meeting, I complimented G. S. on his brilliant intuitive appraisal of her. She felt at once that I was favoring him and reacted with jealousy and feelings that he was being more highly regarded by me for his intellectual talent. Immediately anxious, she challenged his statement with marked hostility toward both of us throughout the duration of the meeting. Despite competing with him for my esteem, she felt that he would inevitably do better than she, and that I would just as certainly always promote him because he was a man. The compulsive nature of her conduct together with its interesting sequel came out at our next session. H. P. told us that upon leaving the previous meeting, she had gone automatically to a florist to order an elaborate bouquet for her mother. Suddenly confounded in the flower store, she stopped and tried to realize what she was doing. There was really no occasion for sending her mother a bouquet, for the latter was not ill, nor was it a holiday or an anniversary. Understanding followed directly. She knew then that in the group, I had changed from a father to a mother figure; G. S., the man I had complimented, had become a brother substitute with whom she had been in perpetual rivalry for her mother's attention. My praise of him elicited the projection of the mother onto me. The gift of flowers was to propitiate a mother who was annoyed by her conduct, to conceal her welling resentment, and to appease her mother for coming so close to fully expressing her anger toward her. Of striking interest was her abandonment of the father figure in me as soon as the group dynamics provided a situation in which I could reward a man who was at once invested with brother quality. Apparently she was able to recreate the father in me as long as I was alone with her. (Perhaps, alone with me, she could experience me as the good mother.) As soon as the original family was reanimated by the group setting and more particularly by my approval of a man, a particular familial constellation was revived that necessitated a revision of her earlier investment in me. A high estimate of a man unconsciously recalled greater admiration of her brother and disapprobation for herself. Her secondary mother was the prime agent in the construction of this historical configuration.

Later meetings brought out her (secondary) mother's actual preference for H. P.'s brother because he was a boy. H. P.'s compulsive penis envy (she would reconstitute the bad mother into a good one by being a tomboy for her), her disregard for her feelings (suppressing her own ego and self-regard), and excessive regard for excelling intellectuality, in the company of which she always felt doomed to come off second best, thus reproduced her relationship to mother and brother. By our attention to all aspects of her shifting transferences to me and to G. S., we were able at last to help H. P. relinquish familial claims on her and to react to us (with her own ego) in her own behalf (Wolf 1949).

In the course of our work with borderlines, it had become clear that our submerged patients were not borderlines, in whom the ego is split but not submerged. In our submerged patients, the ego was intact but suppressed, and these patients were functioning with pseudo-egos representing the incorporated mother. While these patients were compulsively compliant (the most apparent aspect of their problems) toward the incorporated bad mother often projected on others, they were just as much compulsively rebellious against her. This rebellion may have been overt or covert. When it was denied, it manifested itself in self-abuse, depression, masochism, hypochondria, or somatic or visceral symptoms. In any case, when we realized that in seeking in the word *submerged* a more descriptive label for the borderline, we were in fact not describing the borderline but another psychopathological constellation.

CURRENT THINKING

By age two the submerged character is established. The infant's mother is generally suffering from a narcissistic personality disorder. Her baby's ego is strengthened by her devoted preoccupation seemingly with his needs, but really with her own. This dedication is based upon his mother's making little distinction between him and herself. His thoughts, feelings, and activities, she unconsciously feels, should be merely an extension of her own. He will realize her own unrealized longings. In more traditional terms, he is her penis. We find this interpretation of her unconscious aims too limited a view. When the infant undertakes any autonomous movements, activities, or endeavors, his mother feels threatened, abandoned, anxious, rejected in her plans for him, and she tries to control and limit his autonomy—in traditional terms—to castrate him. We find this also too limiting a view of what is going on. Having up to this time experienced the mother as loving and devoted, that is, as the primary mother, the infant now senses that his mother no longer loves him, is controlling and denying, that is, as the secondary mother. In an attempt to recover the primary mother, he suppresses in degree his own ego and operates with two pseudo-egos, one representing the secondary mother and the other the rebellion against her, themselves contradictory, in conflict, and the basis of a troubling but persistent ambivalence. His hope is that if he renounces his own perceptions of reality, his own longings and aspirations, and tries always to please his mother, he will ingratiate himself with her and then she will resume her original primary love for him. Lurking quite alongside this obsession is an equally obsessive pseudo-ego, which is just as rebellious as the ingratiating pseudo-ego and is formed by the submerged ego as a defense against the latter's being totally swallowed. It is like an antibody, trying to repel the introjected complying pseudo-ego. Sometimes the ingratiation is manifest and the rebellion covert. At other times the rebellion is overt and the ingratiation is covert.

In addition to ambivalence, symptoms that characterize the submerged ego include sadomasochism, paranoidal and grandiose stances, homosexuality and bisexuality, and depressive and/or aggressive attitudes. With the emergence of the creative ego, the patient often displays extraordinary signs of creative activity. The sadism is a response to the internalized pseudo-ego of the secondary mother. The masochism is the compulsive response to the real and projected secondary mother in an attempt thereby to win her favor again, but is also always—as with all masochism—an indirect form of sadism. (It satisfies both pseudo-egos.) The paranoidal response is a protective reaction to the primitive secondary mother, especially in the assumption of a grandiose position of fragile invulnerability. The homosexual response is the identification with the mother as the aggressor, especially if there is a weak, passive, or absent father, or a father who never challenges the mother's domination. The bisexual response represents both basic and characteristic ambivalence. It is also prognostic of a better response to treatment in its possible indication of some identification with the father. Depressive symptoms are a response of disappointment to the overwhelming domination of the mother. The aggressive symptoms are the protesting reaction to the same domination. They frequently coexist, with one covert and the other manifest. The ambivalent response, however, is the most characteristic because it both protects the submerged ego by concealment and at the same time attempts to satisfy the demands of the two pseudo-egos.

Both the submission and rebellion are compelling and basically inappropriate, serving little constructive purpose in the service of the ego—and are so ambivalent that everyone who experiences this confusing adaptation is alienated by it. It should be pointed out, however, that the rebellious pseudo-ego is adaptive in one important service. It is created in part by the submerged ego as a defense against the complying pseudo-ego becoming the prevailing functioning surrogate ego. If the individual were to comply totally, the submerged ego would be lost and the person would become a carbon copy of the introjected parent. By rebelling, he wards off this loss of self by at least being at the antipode of the parental self at times. The ultimate adjustment, of course, comes when the submerged ego is able to emerge and take its rightful place. In this sense, the development of ambivalent pseudo-egos is adaptive in their defending and protecting the ego intact in a state of submergence.

We use the term *ego-submergence* to distinguish the development of such submergence from the idea of suppression and repression in coping with unacceptable, instinctual, and primary process material. In ego-submergence, there is submergence of the ego—in whole or in part. We prefer the word "submergence," for to use the words "suppression" or "repression" suggests superego imposition upon the id.

A distinction also needs to be made between the superego and the pseudo-ego as well as between the id and the suppressed ego. The superego is each person's conscience, the set of values he generally learns from his parents. The id represents the instinctual, biological, completely internal, impulsive demands of the untamed, untaught little savage each of us might have become without the superego. The ego balances and guards against the predominance of either the id or the superego. Its aims are reality oriented. Students of our view of the psychodynamics of submergence sometimes have the impression that in our support for the creative emergence of the suppressed ego, we engage in encouraging the id to express its needs, that where the ego is, we say, "Let the id be," that we encourage acting out. We make a distinction between id impulses and suppressed ego needs. The pseudo-ego is not the superego. It represents the internalized parent in toto and so projects itself. The suppressed ego is not the id. It represents all the individuating, growth-seeking, inventive, creative, and healthy self-assertive aspects of the autonomous individual seeking liberation from irrational restraints put upon the ego by the pseudo-egos. We say: "Where the pseudo-egos are, let the ego be."

It is worth noting that the ego-submerged child does not simply incorporate the parental ego. He incorporates at the same time the parental superego and even derivatives of the parental id. It is as if he incorporates the pathogenic parent in toto.

THE MOTHER OF THE SUBMERGED PATIENT

The narcissistic mother or mothering figure reacts to her infant's need to express his feelings, to pursue a path of his own, with disregard or by looking and feeling wounded or disconcerted. She indicates by word or gesture that he ought not to feel as he does but to feel as she feels. She then punishes him for his transgression by giving him the silent treatment for being, in her view, deviant. Her "love" for him is narcissistic self-love. In his natural curiosity he begins to explore his environment and make some autonomous moves. His mother experiences his attempts at independent activity as a rejection of her. In fact, his movement is toward a growing self-determination originally fostered by her when she was a good primary mother and ego-building with him. But now she becomes a "bad" secondary mother, fearful of losing him. So she tries to control him. This is the beginning of mother-induced submergence: as the child tries desperately to please his mother, to convert her into his loving primary mother, she resents this "demand" and tries to bind him to her. He is already suppressing his ego and responding ambivalently to her.

In the act of forbidding the infant or child from exploring the environment in his curiosity, inventiveness, and sexuality, the parent may induce in him a pervading and more intense pursuit of the very things he has been told to ignore. Thus his rebellious pseudo-ego becomes preoccupied, obsessed with the forbidden. And he may feel guilty that he has disobeyed authority, or he may become so fixed in opposition to what he experiences as an oppressive demand that he may take pleasure in his defiant pursuit, not of his own basic ego needs, but simply to upset the parental dictate, now internalized and projected. He functions with ambivalent pseudo-egos in order to save, protect, and preserve his submerged ego, in hiding, intact, using one to counteract the other.

The pathogenic mother is delighted with her infant at first. As one, they will realize all her unrealized dreams. He will fulfill her. He will always be there for her. He will support her one day, if she is in need. He will be the good parent. He will love her. In order to maintain this fantasy, she feels threatened by his slightest move away from her. She becomes possessive of him whenever he shows the slightest interest in anyone or anything in his environment. He must in her expectation be totally devoted to her. He will be her fully actualized self, instead of merely her. If her child removes himself from her pressing control, she may lose the sense that he belongs to her. He becomes a stranger, belonging to himself and not to her. She is hurt, disappointed by him. She tries to recapture him. If she fails, she neglects and abandons him or becomes embattled with him, becoming the tertiary mother (Kutash and Greenberg 1986).

The infant and child of a pathogenic mother is a child who is anxious, fearful, phobic, projecting on every stranger the primary or secondary mother. In this state of alarm he pacifies himself by sucking his thumb, trying to make of every unfamiliar-seeming apparition a more soothing image—more familiar, more comforting, the primary mother. If he bites his nails, he is expressing his resentment of her secondary character, now internalized.

The child of a submerging mother may undertake all sorts of danger-ous feats in counterphobic attempts to wipe out or master his underly-ing fear of the secondary mother and become a heroic figure in his mother's eyes—all to win back an experience of the admiring and smiling eye of the primary mother.

When the submerged personality ultimately fails and discovers that nothing succeeds, short of losing himself and being like the narcissis-tic parent in all ways important to the parent, the rebellious pseudo-ego comes to the fore to protect the suppressed ego in the form of a tantrum, rebellion, or withdrawal. This wards off the secondary mother and leaves the suppressed ego intact.

A central characteristic quality of submergence is the need to be alone. The submerged personality cannot really reveal himself fully to anyone. The persons he claims as "friends" are people who themselves, like him, have no close personal bonds. His friends have to subordi-nate themselves to his solitary need and ask for nothing in return. They must be more loyal servants than friends, providing only a listening silence for a man who has no interest in intimacy—the price is too high. His friends are required to make no comment or respond ac-tively to his behavior. He likes to be alone, and with his analyst he is. (With an effective analyst he need not be alone.) This pathological isolation is based on his inability to trust anyone. Isolated from any truly trusted friends who might give him useful advice or emotional support, he at times makes reckless judgments, removed from reality. He cannot take counsel from others, for he does not have enough of an available ego to make a reasonable decision. When not complaining, he polarizes others by converting every quiet exchange of ideas into a violent crisis in which he has to win by isolating and discrediting what he sees as his enemies. He does not believe anyone can be different from his betraying secondary mother.

THE MALE SUBMERGED PERSONALITY

In extreme cases of submergence, the patient is a distressed and constricted person who displays himself as quite the reverse: manly, composed, and commanding, for that is the image he believes others want him to have. He is often a creative person, or at least he has unrealized creative potential. Elsewhere (Wolf 1960), we have reported on the genius and submergence of Freud, Shakespeare, and Einstein. Secretly, the patient may be uneasy, panicky, pessimistic, unshrinking, brave, majestic, highflown, superior, for this image is what the submerged parent expected him to be. Covertly he may be homosexual. Manifestly, he is unhappily married and remarried and remarried. Unobserved, he is always hurting himself. In public he surpasses everyone in athletics. To his family he rarely tells the truth. With strangers he purports a reverence for sincerity. Most believe him. The more discerning see that he is bragging to sustain a veneer of bravado. His gusty performance suggests private doubt about his manliness. There may be clandestine homosexuality or self-shielding homophobia. He may be self-assaultive at the hands of the secondary mother introject or assaultive of others in the projection of the secondary mother introject. He strives to be the idealized love object of an adoring chorus of mother surrogates; then, unable to endure their responsive love, seen by him as demands for love and attention, he rejects them. He derides what he senses as delicacy in men who are tasteful, sensitive, poetic, homosexual. He may treat them contemptuously to suppress how much he is at one with them underneath. Covertly, he may endure fears, anxieties, feelings of inadequacy, terror. Manifestly, he is fearless, bold, impressive, or esteemed in a posture of humility, a masquerader to the more discerning. He embellishes stories of his experiences of which he is, in fact, frightened, and recitals of his dauntless action—all to be admired by multiple surrogate mothers. He is privately vulnerable and publicly invincible. He is a morbid boaster. There is a pressing resentment of the secondary mother, doubt about his prevailing over her, and fear of losing control over his rage against her or her internalized image projected now on all women.

He is covertly sensitive and manifestly brazen. He has a savage fantasy life and is basically artistic. He is uncertain about his virility. He depreciates the powers of other men in his need for approval. In his homosexuality he is castrating to men. He is demandingly dependent on a succession of women, irritating and irritable in his wish to be loved, and always in flight to the next protective but unfulfilling mother. His narcissistic mother, also often a person of confused and confusing sexual identity, imposes on her son the same inability to identify himself as clearly male or female. Betrayed by her secondary mothering, he projects betrayal everywhere. He continually seeks refuge in the hope of finding a primary surrogate, but always elicits from women, by his distrustful and tentative commitments, an anticipated yet disappointing rejection. He finds endless justification for his grievances against every woman, beginning with mother and ending with his last female seduction. He ambivalates between feeling hurt privately and pompously denying it publicly. Privately he is a sissy; publicly he is a superstud. Women are either cute little girls or hateful, spoiled monsters. In his submissiveness he feels unmanly. His image of himself is so offensive to him that he tries to renounce it by behaving boorishly and having to be right about everything. Privately he may be his true self and publicly the ambivalent submerged personality. Within him are multiple sets of opposites with different public and private selves.

The above is a description of a seriously ill submerged personality. When the mother is less pathogenic, her child is much less damaged and able in that degree to develop his own ego. This description suggests a severity of pathology that does not fairly characterize all of these patients. Later we shall describe patients who are less disturbed, more subject merely to ego-submerged maneuvers. Some submerged personalities introject such attractive pseudo-egos that it sometimes becomes difficult to see what is wrong with them. There are instances in which the mother had less of an axe to grind, so that her child was more able to pursue his own interests. In such cases, the severity of his disorder is a function of how freely the mother let him live on his own. It all depends on what the parent demanded or imposed. So there are black, white, and gray areas in submergence, with slight, moderate, or severe symptoms.

Patients whose mothers were only moderately narcissistic, for example, do not develop a full-blown submergence but are subject only to submergent maneuvers. In them, their ambivalence, paranoidal symptoms, sadomasochism, and bisexuality are not so prominent. They also have more ego functions available than the more seriously submerged personality. As a consequence, they are readier to accept insight and work with it from the onset of treatment.

Furthermore, it seems possible that this simultaneous duality at the hands of a pathogenic mother can occur with a controlling woman, not just with the narcissistic mother, although it probably occurs more often with narcissistic parents.

Finally, it is even conceivable that the beginnings of submergence take place in the womb. For nine months the mother provides for all the needs of the fetus. The child is then painfully and rudely thrust into the world to make his way. It is quite possible that, as in the submerged patient previously described, this prenatal experience corresponds to his blissful enjoyment of the security, safety, and care of the primary mother, and the expulsion from paradise corresponds to his experience of the secondary mother.

In short, the pathogenic mother may unconsciously or ruthlessly try to make her child into someone she wanted him to be, attaining goals she herself could never reach in her own life. At the same time, if his interest deviates from her choice for him, she tries to divert him from his aspirations. He has two alternatives: submit or rebel. Unfortunately, the untreated submerged personality does not have the freedom to choose, unless his suppressed ego finds an ally in some other member of the family or in a friend.

THE FEMALE SUBMERGED PERSONALITY

The submerged personality who is female is, like the male, always in search of the primary mother, but just as often disappointed in discovering her to be the frustrating secondary one. The apprehension of abandonment and separateness and the oppressive yearning for warm connectedness generally provoke and insure defeat. Having originally glimpsed the fulfillment of maternal "love" and the possibility of communion, the female submerged personality is set up for a crashing letdown. She is repeatedly stunned by failure to win the love of a mother surrogate, who may be a man or woman. Cherished illusions or beloved persons are lost to her in succession. She hungers for love, for love has the power to heal and redeem. Loved, in her eyes she can love back. Her love often resembles an obsession. Love may arrive unexpectedly, but it tends to skitter away just as precipitously, leaving her hurt, damaged, and often bitter. She may then withdraw, angry, isolated, and depressed. She lives a life of love and loss, redemption and damnation. She is a person who has to do things by herself. Others can claim someone else. She cannot.

She is a child pretending to be an adult, a child imprisoned by her pseudo-egos, a child who has no power because she does not understand what has happened to her: that she is her mother's prisoner. With someone's help, she needs to experience that she has been taken advantage of, that she can resist and defy domination, that she can discover and oppose her keepers, that she can be an ally of her suppressed self, that she need not be overcome by scruples in dealing with her parents. Through the manifest parental devotion, she needs to see the denial of her growth and recover her identity. She need not be the disenfranchised, remote child, but discover the outrage beneath the acquiescence. A therapist needs to be an ally of the defiance, until the patient's own ego asserts itself. A therapist can help keep her ego alive. When a daughter becomes just like her mother, her pseudo-egos have prevailed over her own ego.

As with men, the pathogenic parent of ego-submerged females is usually the mother. Occasionally or exceptionally, the father is the source of illness in the female child, particularly if he aggressively dominates the household. Even though the female submerged personality has nightmares in which the menacing character is the father or a surrogate, the patient may have been persuaded by her mother's distorted view of the father to see the threat as paternal rather than maternal. The patient feels nothing at the death of either parent. She is often a manifest caretaker of her mother with underlying resentment of her, one of the roles she assumes and resents, all in the wish to be loved and taken care of herself. In marriage she is manifestly faithful and covertly given to affairs. She lies and hides her real feelings. It is only apart from her husband, who is a projected mother, that she can experience her feelings. She needs to maintain a relationship with her husband that is full of friction. She is often sexually and/or romantically involved with an older man, enjoying the power of a younger woman over an aging man. Knowing that her husband suspects her of adultery, she can go on with extramarital adventures or let them go. She is thus enabled to set herself apart from him, his needs and inclinations, keeping herself safe from all forms of harm. She is a phallic woman who keeps emerging to victimize others. She lives a very private, isolated, and paranoid life. She stands outside events, observing. Just as, as a child, she stood outside the pathogenic parent's reach, sensing danger real or symbolic, so as an adult she removes herself from her own life, watching the play both as actor and as audience.

The female submerged personality may sacrifice self-assertion to win love. In this endeavor she tries always to please but is covertly angry. She attempts manifestly to please men, to meet their expectations and needs, never challenging male authority. She is often a tomboy in childhood and bisexual as an adult. As a phallic tomboy she felt happier in a sense of mastery, which she had to relinquish in a patriarchal society. She may bear illegitimate children in defiance of convention and unleash on her children the resentment she is obliged to subdue. She is manifestly a conformist but with vast stores of anger, which she may suddenly express, terrifying men who at first were interested. She is in conflict between being charming and cruel. The brutality she inflicts on her children often induces homosexual difficulties in them. She is always trying to get her way under a cover of submission. Her primary aim is to acquire power, control over others, all of whom she mistrusts. Her distrust renders her incapable of any genuine devotion to another. She is too seemingly powerful to form a wholesome relationship with a man.

The pathogenic mother first "loves" and then "hates" her daughter, producing in the daughter a great unmet need for a loving mother as well as loathing of her. The child becomes obsessed in her pursuit of a good mother, whether her own or any possible surrogate, who always betrays her, for her need is so demanding that it provokes rejection. Every maternal surrogate betrays the child, and the child betrays every maternal surrogate in her overwhelming expectation and wish to be loved. Some pathogenic mothers reject their infants if they are repelled by their baby's illness or some mild physical deformity. The pathogenic mother dominates her husband and tortures him and her infant by her aloofness and need to control them. Her child tries to coax tenderness out of her without success. The mother cries that she would prefer her daughter dead to be spared the shame of her rebelliousness. In her sadism she lays the groundwork for her child's sadomasochism.

The pathogenic mother in her secondary role abandons, suppresses, misunderstands, and tries to control her rebellious child. Such a mother induces her child to identify with her in the hope of having such power. This striving for eminence as well as the longing for maternal love often produces in the child a homosexual adaptation. The disturbed mother elicits conformity and rebellion. She deprives

her child of individuality. She wants her child either to be an extension of herself, a replica, or to fulfill her unmet needs. She is dismayed
by her child's defiance, or her flight to bohemia or drugs. Occasionally
the adult who has had a pathogenic mother will, in her determination to lead her own life, abandon or neglect her own children. In
leading her own life she becomes too busy to listen to her child, urging
her to decide for herself just what she wants to do: a subtle, rational-
ized way of dismissing the child with only casual attention; a manifest
way of suggesting that she does not wish to impose herself on the
child.

The daughter of a pathogenic mother is usually envious of and
competitive with other women, angry with them because she was let
down or deserted by her own mother. Such attitudes may be unconscious and disavowed, only to burst forth in distrust of women. Struggles to manage withdrawal and independence are full of self-blame,
upheaval, and turmoil. Even while absorbed in the wished-for warmth
from women, she struggles for liberation from them. The lost comrade-
ship with women interferes with self-determination. She needs to
develop disentangling friendships and mutual freedom.

THE FATHER OF THE SUBMERGED PATIENT

The father, who also elicits responses from the infant and child, may
also be pathogenic; probably not as much as the mother, because the
mother has primary contact with the infant in the early years. If the
father is comparatively healthy, to that extent he is more supportive
than the mother in affirming the child's experience of reality. In the
degree to which he endorses the child's creative exploration of his
environment, he helps the child and in some measure neutralizes the
mother's pathogenic pressure. If the father is withdrawn, depressed,
unavailable, absent, or allies himself with the mother, the child becomes the victim of the mother's dominance with little if any support
from the father.

In some cases it is the father who is the demanding pathogenic parent. When the child reaches two and is less in the orbit of the primary mother, the father begins to impose his will, driving the ego into submergence. The complying pseudo-ego takes over to please the introjected authoritative father. The rebellious pseudo-ego emerges from the suppressed ego as a defense against the introject, an antibody against the invading transplant.

The father who molests his child sexually is frequently impotent with his wife because he felt powerless with his own mother, whom his wife represents. When he forces himself on his child, he feels powerful, in command. He is a submerged personality, expressing his sadomasochism via pseudo-egos. His abused child grows into an adult who then betrays and abuses her own children. She is operating with pseudo-egos in ambivalence. Her pseudo-egos are paternally derived. Both the father and his daughter do and do not want to be abusive to their children.

There is more than a single source of ambivalence. In submergence, there is the incorporation of the primary and secondary mothers as dual and mutually oppositional pseudo-egos. Another source of ambivalence is the ingratiating pseudo-ego that is repeatedly tempted to comply with the internalized and projected secondary mother in the exciting hope that she will become primary, only to find itself disillusioned and rebellious again. There is the ambivalence in response to the primary mother. Is it safe to respond to her caring and love? For may she not at any moment turn into the secondary mother? The most manifest ambivalence in submergence is the submission and rebellion. Either one may be more manifest and the other more covert. It needs to be kept in mind that both are always there. The resistance to the analyst is usually a most obvious indicator of whether the patient is openly defiant or openly "in love" with everything he has to say. Quite apart from these is the ambivalence that is a part of transference. There is still another source of ambivalence: the emergence of the suppressed ego in the course of treatment creates a conflict between the recovering ego and the compliant and rebellious pseudo-egos.

MANIFESTATIONS OF SUBMERGENCE
IN RELATIONSHIPS

The submerged personality, to the extent he ambivalates, seldom gets what he wants and more often than not seldom knows what he wants. He is usually interested in another person and may glance at her or him with the initial hope of finding in that person the caring primary mother. But he very quickly turns off and away from the other, convinced that the other will surely or very shortly become the controlling and hurtful secondary mother. The other may have been stirred by this initial display of interest but protects him- or herself by turning away as well.

A good many submerged personalities are easily seduced by another person's responsive warmth, and very quickly invest the friendliness with an idealized quality and promise of fulfillment by the projected primary mother. As long as the other can genuinely maintain a dedication to him, or if not genuine, a pretended devotion, the submerged personality can for a while experience a childlike bliss. Before long, this self-indulgent ecstasy becomes so evident and infantile, it quickly turns off the maternal other unless he is masochistic. Even then, the relationship is doomed, for the self-abuse in the masochistic person is covertly or overtly sadistic and the ego-submerged one once more feels betrayed by the secondary mother.

When two submerged personalities marry each other, they at first transferentially project on each other the idealized primary mother, both convinced that they will now at last be beloved. With exaggerated expectation they discover to their dismay that the other is in fact the secondary mother, denying them the love, care, affection, devotion, and attention they long for. They are disappointed, hurt, betrayed, angry, and separate, only to renew the search and betrayal in successive commitments and divorces.

An article in the *New York Times* (August 11, 1987, p. C1) reports "the old belief that married couples eventually begin to look alike . . .

after 25 years of marriage. . . . All the couples. . . . were between 50 and 60 years old at the time of the second picture. . . . A Dr. Robert Zajouc proposes that people often unconsciously mimic the facial expressions of their spouses in a silent empathy and that over the years, sharing the same expressions shapes the face similarly. . . . Evidence for mirroring of expressions has come from research by Olaf Dinsberg, a psychologist in Sweden, who measured the tension levels in the facial muscles of volunteers while they were shown photographs of various facial expressions. When the volunteers saw an angry face, for instance, their facial muscles mimicked the anger. . . . Dr. Zajouc suggested that shared facial expressions bring on identical emotions. . . . When people mimic their spouses' facial expressions, they also evoke the same emotions, thus empathizing all the better. . . . Dr. Paul Eksman says, 'There is no question that we unwittingly use our facial muscles in the same way as the person we are looking at.' . . . Dr. Zajouc contends that this mimicry is sustained in married couples because experiencing the same emotional state is reinforced by its effects in strengthening feelings of closeness. . . ."

Rather than being evidence of empathy or closeness, this report suggests a mutually pathological process with one spouse probably more so inclined than the other. It is worth noting how difficult it is not to yawn if one observes another person yawning. Also, mimics and impersonators use their skills both to idealize and to ridicule the persons they are exalting or caricaturing. And after twenty-five years of marriage couples may well at times be doing the same thing sadomasochistically and with submerged personality.

The submerged personality can become a compulsive caretaker of other people's problems. His obsessive dedication is not helpful because its aim is intended to suppress in others and in himself the emergence of mutually destructive feelings. This can be a serious problem when it occurs in the therapist who fears the patient's or his own affect, whether caring or hostile.

We have also encountered in the course of supervision of student analysts in training that some of their patients are submerged personalities, and at the same time the student analysts themselves are submerged personalities.

The comic is often trying to please the projected mother in his audience and tends to become antagonistic if his listeners do not respond warmly. The comic may respond to the heckler, possibly also submerged, with ingratiation, making himself more masochistically entertaining or sadistic in counterattack. There are really two types of comics: the one who masochistically makes fun of himself, and a second who sadistically ridicules his wife, mother, mother-in-law, or a member of the audience.

Mimicry can be creative if the mimic not only duplicates the original, but imaginatively interprets the person he seems to be impersonating. Mimicry is uncreative if the mime simply mirrors the original without adding any inventive illumination to his performance.

MANIFESTATIONS OF SUBMERGENCE IN OTHER BEHAVIORS

Actors are especially subject to submerged ego responses. Their wish to be loved by the primary mother, projected on the audience, is great. And equally strong is the dread that the audience will not only be disappointed with a performance but will become, like the secondary mother, hostile and ridiculing. The wish to please the observer is often accompanied by a desire to express the feeling: The audience be damned. In this conflict, the actor may forget his lines, strut and stamp, overact, become unrelated to the role he is supposed to be playing, try to upstage his fellow actors, step out of character, and otherwise behave inappropriately. Invited to a party without the dramatist's script, he may become anxious, unable to participate, and unable to find ideas and words of his own without his playbook.

Not far removed from this dynamic among actors is the anxiety, sometimes mounting to panic, at the prospect of recitation in a class, or the dreadful anticipation of being expected to make a public address—both possibilities often handled by avoidance.

Procrastination is also an expression of the ambivalence of submergence. The procrastinator submits to the demands of the secondary mother introject that he continue and complete the work he has undertaken at her behest, and at the same time resists its completion because her expectation of him has become a towering demand on him.

The common problem of losing a thought, forgetting what one was about to say, of not recalling a fantasy, of forgetting what just a moment before seemed to be an original or creative idea is in all likelihood a submergence problem. In such situations, it is of little avail to try stubbornly to recall what one has been about to think or say, for the incorporated parent just as stubbornly resists our effort. It is much more useful to let the ambivalent struggle rest and turn to other matters. Then, without one's trying, the lost thought tends to revive, to appear suddenly on its own when we are making no effort to retrieve it.

Stuttering may well have a similar basis. It is as if the speech problem manifests itself when the stutterer is most conscious of making an effort not to stutter, or when he most strongly senses in his audience a disapproving or controlling parent. The same might be said of the actor who forgets his lines or develops stage fright as he projects on the audience the pathogenic parent he wants to please and displease. Some dynamicists may view these problems as inhibitions by the superego. We see them rather as submergence maneuvers.

Difficulty in concentrating, like stuttering, has a submergence quality. The stutterer knows what he wants to say but is stuck in his ambivalence about saying it. The artist may have a vague notion about what he wants to write, paint, or compose, but the image may fade or fail, as in writer's block, and get lost under the invading and compulsive pressure of vacillation and irresolution.

Gambling is a symptom of submergence. There is the ambivalent drive to gamble, and at the same time there exists the wish to be free of the compulsion. There is masochism in the self-destructive imposition on oneself to pursue the squandering necessity to bankruptcy versus the sadistic impact on one's family and on the unfortunate loser who is defeated. There is the paranoidal fantasy of omnipotence and the reality of ruination. There is the homosexual fantasy of unmanning an opponent and the terror of being emasculated oneself.

Despite increasing evidence of genetic links between alcoholic parents and alcoholic children, it may well be that such forebears pathogenically induce the same self-destructive process in their offspring.

Our clinical experience in fact does not confirm Freud's view of death wishes as instinctively derived. We see them rather as derivatives of the incorporation of the secondary mother and the unconscious wish of the suicidal person to destroy her in himself. If he projects the secondary mother on another individual, he may exhibit aggressive intentions toward his victim and become physically assaultive, even homicidal. Or he may become alternately masochistically suicidal and sadistic.

Other disorders may also stem from submergence. The attention-deficit hyperactivity disorder may be a consequence of having a pathogenic parent. The child's subjective feeling of restlessness and his fidgeting and squirming may be his expressions of compliance and rebellion. His easy distraction by external stimuli may represent the readiness to suppress his own thought, feeling, or activity and yield place to the demand of the secondary mother. His difficulty in waiting for his turn may make him a problem in group therapy and in social interaction. He has problems in following instructions, which he hears and does not hear. His attention is hard to sustain. He cannot listen to lectures. He cannot complete an activity, bring it to a conclusion. He talks a lot or cannot talk at all. He interrupts and intrudes on others or isolates himself. He undertakes dangerous activities or avoids such risks. He wants to be a hero to recover the mother's adulation, and at the same time he wants to disappoint her.

The patient with asthma, incontinence, or thumb sucking and nail biting is searching for the primary mother and rejecting the secondary one. Each may be a submerged personality with oral longings for the primary mother and suppressed rage at the disappointing one. The rage may be denied, only to become manifest in psychosomatic or visceral symptoms. Making appointments but coming late for them has similar origins. So does owing money and not paying a debt on time. All of these symptoms represent in part fear of assuming independence, autonomy, and responsibility.

Is not the anorexic patient possibly someone who rejects her secondary mother in starving herself at the same time that she longs for food (the primary mother)? Is not the bulimic patient who overeats and vomits expressing in her great appetite a longing for the primary mother at the same time as symbolically and angrily she eats her up? When she vomits, is she not rejecting the secondary mother? Perhaps she is also at the same time rejecting the primary mother in the conviction that at any moment she will become secondary. Is not the refusal of food in both the anorexic and the bulimic saying to the mother in effect, "I will not please you"? Is not the bulimic expressing in overeating a yielding to the mother's demand that she eat at the same time as she is telling the mother to get lost?

In bulimia, the patient incorporates the mother surrogate and disincorporates her. The patient does this with some insight provided by the analyst: he lets the idea enter one pseudo-ego and rejects it with the other, hearing and understanding it and then vomiting it back at the analyst.

Multiple personality disorder is in all probability a submergence illness in which the patient has incorporated his familial figures as well as other significant extrafamilial figures of his childhood. A patient with multiple personality disorder probably does not stop with merely incorporating the mother. He incorporates father and older siblings and other significant figures of his early life, all of whom were experienced ambivalently. He has learned from his experience of his mother that this is the fundamental adaptation with every other person. So in adult life, depending on how much he unconsciously reexperiences from others the impression that this person is like his mother, and the next person not unlike his father, and so forth, he suddenly shifts from one pseudo-self to another, only occasionally displaying his genuine self with an immature ego.

It seems possible that in some cases of catatonia the underlying dynamic may be submergence. We recall a hospitalized catatonic, who, before he became ill, was a gifted tennis player. When he was escorted to the tennis court on the hospital grounds, a tennis racket placed in his hand, and a ball hit in his direction, his catatonia disappeared and he played skillfully with all his former grace and execution. When the tennis racket was removed, he once again subsided into catatonia, a state of passive immobility demanded by his secondary mother.

We believe submergence is most related to passive–aggressive personality disorder, the consequence of a pathogenic upbringing. The passivity is a manifest form of compliance, concealing the underlying aggressivity. There is a seeming yielding to the expectations of others, but a basic oppositionalism is present, characterized by forgetfulness and procrastination. These patients are dependent on the mother figure and lack self-confidence. They are ineffective socially and occupationally. They put off things that need to be done and do not meet deadlines. They refuse to do what they were expected to do and do not know what they want to do. They resent suggestions from others, because they feel put upon, "demanded."

THE REINFORCEMENT OF SUBMERGENCE BY SOCIAL INFLUENCES

Just as the primary mother seduced her infant by professions of love and security, there are various social influences that similarly assure the more mature submerged personality with promise of fulfillment. Just as the secondary mother disappoints the growing infant by trying to control his subsequent attempts to achieve selfhood, so, too, do subsequent environmental pressures attempt to limit his freedom to choose, grow, and create.

Let us first consider the individual's struggle to achieve monetary security. No one ever does, no matter how much wealth he accumulates. Even if he is a member of a huge corporation, all his life savings can be gobbled up in one arbitrage. To begin with, all sorts of inviting assurances are made to tempt students to study law, medicine, dentistry, or to get an M.B.A. in order to achieve freedom from anxiety and financial invulnerability. But lives dedicated to fulfillment of such solicitations always end in frustration because of the shallow existence that such a pursuit entails.

Another source of power and control is sought in the dedication to attain high political office. No matter how idealistic such persons are, after years in public office they tend to lose their early dedication, to become bureaucrats, purchasable by the highest bidder. In political office attained through giving rosy promises, they irresponsibly misuse their high station.

A third category of pledge and betrayal is the clergyman or the religious fundamentalist who promises his devotees one or another nonsensical happiness in an afterlife, or every fulfillment in this life, if only the faithful dedicate themselves to the devotions of one faith and not another. One unfortunate consequence of such a commitment is a nationalistic investment each group makes, even to the point of war-like undertakings against one another.

Still another primary and secondary social influence lies in the search for status in the cultural, artistic, scientific, and psychological fields. In the arts, there are various schools of poetry, painting, dance, music, and literature, each of which lays claim to being the highest form of art, attracting followers and forming virtually exclusive clubs. The same may be said of psychiatry and psychology. There is some attempt, usually unsuccessful, to bridge the gaps between these various schools, but in the main they remain absolutist, each claiming the highest status and deceiving its adherents by creating an illusory sense of grandiosity, leading to ultimate disappointment.

Most people, particularly Americans, tend to be optimistic, having been raised by relatively normal mothers. But submerged personalities, always searching for the good primary mother, tend to have faith in every zealous promoter, to gamble on his goodwill, and to be fleeced again and again. It requires considerable experience of painful disappointments before cynicism and despair take place.

In conclusion, we have some evidence that submergence existed from at least the eleventh or tenth century B.C. in the text known among Sumarian scholars as *The Dialogue of Pessimism*, translated by Joseph Brodsky as "Slave, Come to My Service" (*The New York Review of Books*, November 11, 1987, 34:23). This dialogue between a master and his slave not only illustrates the existence of submergence in ancient times, but suggests also that the pathogenic parent may well, in his or her masterful position, impose upon the child a slavelike submission and rebellion. It also suggests that the perfect parent (an impossibility) may create the perfect child (another impossibility).

Submergence is not the neurosis of our time. It is the neurosis of all time. Every one of us has had parents. As long as we have had parents, we have also had transferences, with their accompanying ambivalences and all the qualities that constitute the nature of transference. So, too, we have always had with us submergence and creative individuals denied the freedom to liberate their talent and genius.

2

Place in the Diagnostic Spectrum

Irwin L. Kutash, Ph.D.,
and Jeffrey C. Greenberg, Ph.D.

*One of the unpardonable sins, in the eyes of most people, is for a man to
go about unlabelled. The world regards such a person as the police do
an unmuzzled dog, not under proper control.*

—T. H. Huxley

DIFFERENTIATION OF SUBMERGENCE
FROM BORDERLINE DIAGNOSIS

Submergence has been confused with borderline disorders. This is
not surprising, since confusion exists as to what constitutes borderline
pathology. Much is written about these patients who fit into this
"borderline" range of emotional functioning (LeBoit and Capponi
1979, Meissner 1984). Giovacchini (1979b) describes the borderline
person as having a lack of ego organization, characterized by an ability
to decompensate fairly easily into a psychotic state, and a lack of
adaptive techniques in dealing with reality. Kernberg (1975) views
borderline pathology as a personality organization that is stable but
pathologic. Searles (1965) views the borderline individual as ambivalating between symbiosis and object relatedness. The Blancks (1979)
view borderline pathology as comprising deficits in the organizing
ability of the ego, varying so widely in degree of severity that they do
not consider it as a diagnostic entity. Masterson (1976, 1981) views the
borderline personality as one that has introjected both accepting

"good" parental objects and rejecting "bad" parental objects, with the ego "split" between these introjects. While much disagreement exists as to what constitutes borderline pathology, theorists generally agree that (1) splitting, projective identification, and denial are major defenses of the borderline, (2) borderline pathology is well entrenched into the personality structure, and (3) borderline symptoms are varied and can involve depression, rage, fear, anxiety, somatic concerns, impulsivity, helplessness, and feeling void, with primary problems centered on unstable interpersonal relationships.

One reason for all this confusion regarding borderline pathology appears centered on numerous developmental issues that contribute to this disorder. What is grouped under the borderline rhetoric is probably a multitude of disorders with different etiologies. Although agreement prevails that borderline conditions have their origins in the early preoedipal years of life, with symptoms first manifesting themselves in adolescence (Leboit 1979, Meissner 1984, Rinsley 1980), confusion arises beyond this point.

In order to differentiate better the various types of pathology labeled "borderline," we feel it is imperative to look at specific developmental interactions that occur between the child and his or her environment. It appears that the nature of the problematic interaction as well as when the problematic interaction starts to occur will affect the type of pathology produced. This is in terms of whether the ego (1) has begun development, (2) has structural damage, or (3) has been thwarted with regard to its progression or continued development. These developmental factors appear to determine and differentiate the type of "borderline" pathology inherent within an individual, or whether it is indeed "borderline" at all. While some theorists have focused on developmental issues and their relationship to borderline pathology, usually their focus has been on one particular developmental issue with little regard for differential diagnostic concerns in terms of the different types of pathology within patients who are diagnosed as borderline.

Giovacchini (1979b) sees borderline pathology developing in the symbiotic phase of life (through the third month). Whereas the psychotic had traumatic assaults, the borderline's symbiotic phase was characterized by a lack of available libidinal energy. Winnicott (1965a) terms this as "privation," in that the person does not know gratification. As such, he has "only limited ability to form introjects" (Giovacchini 1979b, pp. 148–149). His self-image is imperfectly formed and he has few adaptive defenses. Unlike the psychotic who withdraws from contact due to trauma, the borderline in his symbiotic state clings to others except when rejection occurs. Kernberg (1972) sees borderline pathology as a fixation occurring during the fourth through twelfth months, when the self and object representations within an "all-good" and "all-bad" self-object representation split. "This is the stage where ego boundaries become more firm and effective in providing the capacity to differentiate the self from the outer world" (Capponi 1979, p. 130). Kernberg sees disturbances in this phase caused by excessive frustration and aggression due to constitutional factors or problematic parenting interactions, with splitting serving to separate the good and bad parental images. This splitting reduces integration and synthesis of self and of objects, resulting in a weakened ego with poor anxiety tolerance, impulse control, and sublimatory defenses.

Masterson (1979, 1981), in line with Mahler's (1979) works, views borderline pathology developing in the rapprochement subphase (18–25 months old) when difficulties in individuation and separation occur. Masterson views parental figures as providing adequate parenting skills except when individuation is attempted by the child, which is met by rejection and libidinal energy withdrawal. Thus regressive behaviors become reinforced, and the child's ego becomes split with one part introjecting the parents' rewarding part-unit and the other introjecting the parents' withdrawing part-unit. The person ambivalates between feeling good and fostering dependency relationships and feeling angry, frustrated, abandoned, depressed, and helpless when involved with others. In essence, these theorists appear to be focusing on patients who have a commonality with regard to (1) the presence of a preoedipal condition, and (2) relational difficulties being present, but showing marked difference in ego development. It appears that what Giovacchini describes as borderline is what Knight (1953a, 1953b) had in mind when he coined that term for those patients who had very early emotional damage and who hover close to the edge of psychosis. With regard to ego development, these patients in essence have a lack of it. While inappropriate interpersonal experience has produced relational difficulties, problems in drive and instinctual control are readily apparent, due to a lack of ego development. Kernberg describes patients whose pathology occurred at a time when ego organization and structure is more developed and when a modest amount of interaction with the environment has occurred. Since interpersonal problems occurred at a time when the regulation of drives and differentiation of self and objects were developing, ego damage has resulted. These individuals have difficulty in regulating instinctual drives and boundaries effectively. Relational difficulties are present in that the ego has structural impairment with a resultant distortion in the view of the world and self.

Masterson describes his patients as having damaged and "split" egos. With a development or history that involves a consistent object, particularly a consistent accepting object before two years of age when ego formation is occurring, it is questionable whether their egos are as truly damaged as he indicates. Giovacchini (1979b) describes Masterson's borderline patients as character neurotics in that they are more stable, have developed adequate boundaries, possess psychic cohesion, and have developed well-entrenched defenses. In fact Horner (1979) states outright that rapprochement crisis is not where borderline pathology develops.

Many of the patients Masterson (1976) describes appear to have a developmental history and resultant pathology better understood in terms of a ego-submergence diagnosis (Wolf and Kutash 1984a, 1985). This point of view holds that many "higher-level" borderline individuals are not truly borderline in that their egos are split, but rather that these patients have submerged their own egos to protect them and have introjected a parental ego that they alternately comply with and rebel against. Their egos are not weakened but suppressed. This submergence causes an arrest in further ego development or progression, yet their egos, per se, are not damaged. With two years of appropriate parenting when instinctual drive regulation was developing, the pathology of these patients appears centered less on drive and instinctual concerns and more on relational difficulties. The submerged patient's conflict is centered on loss of self versus loss of object. Developmentally, these individuals experienced consistent, "good-enough" mothering until the rapprochement subphase occurred, when separation and autonomy were threatening and unacceptable to parental figures. As such, strides for autonomy were met with disapproval and rejection.

> The toddler looking for maternal approval, if not love, and fearful if he (or she) does not submit to mother's will, denies his own perceptions and abides by her judgments. To the extent that the (toddler) submits to mother's persistence, he suppresses his own ego and incorporates her views as a negative pseudo-ego against which he repeatedly and compulsively rebels with an equally protesting pseudo-ego. Thereafter, the child, and later the adult with these superimposed pseudo-egos, separate from his own real self and oppositional to each other, is ambivalent about any suggestion of another person, projecting on him or her the original mother or parenting figure. [Wolf and Kutash 1984a, p. 12]

While the submerged patient protects the primary accepting mother from the secondary rejecting mother through defensive compliance, complying is at a cost to the self. Rebelling behaviors not only indicate the underlying anger created in the loss of self from complying, but create a greater loss because ambivalating between complying and rebelling leaves little energy for expression of self. This loss of self is not only apparent in the patient's affect but in a lack of creativity, flexibility, or ability to use internal resources. When one's ego is allowed to emerge and strengthen, and as complying and rebelling behaviors are diminished, more constructive, appropriate, and organized behaviors emerge that express one's own genuine ego, judgment, appreciation of reality, and contentment with self. These behaviors, as well as others, including more appropriate daily functioning, better interpersonal skills, and an intact observing ego help to differentiate the submerged patient from the borderline, whose own ego is split and damaged. The above material is applied to a case in Kutash and Greenberg (1986).

Symptom and Treatment Differences between Submergence and Borderline Diagnosis

Submergence is distinct from the borderline in that the former has not encountered psychotic breaks, whereas the borderline is more vulnerable in this respect. The borderline clings in dependency to the analyst at the same time that he devalues him. The submerged patient loves and hates his therapist. The borderline tries to manipulate the analyst. The submerged patient tries to manipulate the therapist but also feels manipulated by him. The borderline needs structuring from the analyst. The submerged patient needs nonresponsiveness toward the expression of his pseudo-egos and empathy whenever his cautious ego shows itself. If the analyst is too warmly responsive, the patient may become depressed in the assumption that the therapist is orchestrating whatever expression be communicated. The borderline is intensely emotional, unstable, and unpredictable in his response to the analyst. The submerged patient is usually predictable, especially with regard to ambivalence and to paranoidal and sadomasochistic reactions. While ambivalence is also seen in the borderline, it is usually less focused or "centered." This is due to their etiologies being different, that is, the borderline has a damaged, split ego, the submerged patient has a submerged ego with two controlling pseudo-egos. Medication and hospitalization are often indicated in the treatment of the borderline. This is not true of the submerged patient. Borderlines are subject to suicidal gestures and occasionally, actual serious attempts. In spite of the submerged patient's masochism, a healthier ego apparently inhibits these severe acting-out behaviors.

When in the course of treatment the submerged patient begins to express his unambivalent rage against parental objects projected onto the analyst, the latter may feel wounded and angry, and may want to retaliate through the use of a sedative medication or other means of reducing the expressed anger. Such intervention is contraindicated. The borderline and submerged seek professional help for different reasons. The submerged patient, while hoping to find in the analyst the primary mother, before long discovers, in paranoidal proclivity, his secondary one. On the other hand, the borderline, looking for a parental figure in his dependent, helpless caution, soon becomes afraid of engulfment, rage, and boundary concerns with the therapist. The patient has experienced all of these emotions in unpredictable ways with other parental figures. Substance abuse in the borderline may be a reaction to the internal storms or an expression of his masochism. In the submerged personality, it can represent a rebellion against complying and/or experiencing the bliss of lying in the tender arms of the primary mother. The belligerent substance abuser, in particular, is battling the secondary mother. In either case, substance abuse is an assault against oneself.

With regard to treatment difference, in summary, the borderline needs structure, realistic guidance, focused orientation, and at times a supportive stance. The submerged personality would simply comply and rebel (ambivalate) with this approach. He cannot accept input until his own ego is strengthened. The therapist seeks an alliance with the patient's true (submerged) ego.

Differentiation of Submergence
from Other Personality Disorders

We will now differentiate submergence further from established personality disorders according to a schema derived by Kutash (1985). By age two or earlier, the ego begins to emerge as the child's mental and nervous systems develop. The climate in which this emergence occurs will determine the personality traits or enduring patterns of perceiving, engaging with, and contemplating the environment and the self. In some individuals, these personality traits are rigid or maladaptive and result in unhealthy social or occupational adjustment or in psychological disorders. Such disorders have been labeled personality disorders. We put forth the position that these disorders have as their etiology the environment prior to ego emergence, the psychological climate at ego emergence, and the psychological climate as the ego further develops, and that these conditions are the behavioral results of various ego conditions that come about due to these ongoing psychological climates.

In *DSM-III* the personality disorders have been grouped into three clusters. The first cluster is that which includes those disorders that appear "odd or eccentric," including paranoic, schizoid, and schizotypal. The second cluster includes those disorders that appear dramatic, emotional, or erratic, which include histrionic, narcissistic, antisocial, and borderline. The third cluster includes those disorders that appear anxious or fearful: avoidant, dependent, compulsive, and passive-aggressive. These are all based on descriptions of symptoms or behavior.

DSM-III describes the essential features of borderline personality disorder as "instability in a variety of areas, including interpersonal behavior, mood and self image." *DSM-III* describes the essential feature of a narcissistic personality disorder as "a grandiose sense of self-importance or uniqueness; preoccupation with fantasies of unlimited success; exhibitionistic need for constant attention and admiration; characteristic responses to blows to self esteem; and characteristic disturbances in interpersonal relationships, such as feelings of entitlement, interpersonal exploitativeness, relationships that alternate between the extremes of overidealization and devaluation, and lack of empathy." *DSM-III* describes the essential feature of a passive–aggressive personality disorder as a "resistance to demands for adequate performance in both occupational and social functioning; the resistance is expressed indirectly rather than directly." Finally, *DSM-III* describes the essential feature of a dependent personality disorder as "passively allowing others to assume responsibility for major areas of his or her life because of a lack of self-confidence and any inability to function independently; the individual subordinates his or her own needs to those of others on whom he or she is dependent in order to avoid any possibility of having to be self-reliant." For the borderline personality and the narcissistic personality, *DSM-III* lists "no information" for predisposing factors and familial pattern. For the passive-aggressive, they describe as the predisposing factors "oppositional disorder in childhood or adolescence," and for the dependent personality, "chronic physical illness," and that "some believe that separation anxiety disorder and avoidant disorder of childhood or adolescence predispose to the development of dependent personality disorder." No information on familial pattern is provided for either.

We believe that relying solely on symptomatology to differentiate diagnoses, such as using the *DSM-III* approach, can at best be confusing and at worst may lead to an inappropriate diagnosis. Many disorders present common symptoms, or symptoms that may fluctuate in their presence or intensity from one point of observation to the next. For example, not only do dependent personalities allow others to assume responsibility for major areas of their lives, but this can be seen in disorders such as narcissism, where the individual feels a sense of entitlement, or in the borderline, where one feels helpless. Also, borderlines and narcissists both have instability in self-image and mood, for example, when the narcissist is not gratified or when the borderline is tuned into internal thoughts or feelings that activate an external response of depression or aloneness. To avoid ambiguities in symptoms such as those just mentioned, and to achieve a more precise, lucid, and differentiated understanding of diagnoses, which it is hoped will lead to more effective and articulated treatment approaches, we feel it is more useful to divide the diagnostic spectrum into categories based on the type of environmental interaction that one has experienced. Specifically, we propose that these disorders be classified based on developmental predisposing factors. We would divide the personality disorders into four clusters based on the ego-development conditions: those with heavily armored egos (the paranoid and compulsive), those with split egos (schizotypal and borderline disorders), those with weak egos (schizoid, histrionic, and narcissistic), and those with submerged egos (dependent, avoidant, passive–aggressive, antisocial, and dual pseudo-ego disorders). We would label the first cluster as armored ego disorders, the second as split ego disorders, the third as weak ego disorders, and the last as submerged ego disorders.

The various types of personality disorders described above may be understood better in terms of concepts we are exploring, such as ego emergence climate, and the resultant ego condition. For example, those whose ego emergence is met by inconsistent reactions from parental figures experience ego emergence trauma, and upon the ongoing experiencing of this inconsistency develop damaged or split egos. Those whose ego emergence and ongoing growth are met by apathy or neglect or a lack of affirmation develop weak egos, egos that have a feeling of making little impact. Those whose egos' emergence and ongoing growth are met by affirmation when the resultant behavior conforms to parentally endorsed patterns and a lack of affirmation or rejection when it does not, develop submerged egos with an introjection of a parental pseudo-ego, which the individual repeatedly and compulsively submits to and rebels against with an equally protesting pseudo-ego, derived from the submerged ego, a kind of antibody response to the parentally introjected pseudo-ego. Those with split egos we would label borderline personalities; those with weak egos we would label as schizoid personalities or narcissistic personalities, depending on their symptoms. Those with submerged egos we would label as dependent personalities if they primarily comply; as avoidant personalities if they avoid relationships to avoid complying; as passive–aggressive personalities if they outwardly comply and inwardly rebel; as antisocial personalities if they compulsively rebel; and as dual pseudo-egoed personalities if they alternate between complying and rebelling.

We will now describe the ego-emergence conditions and ongoing climate that lead to each of the personality disorder clusters we have proposed except for the submerged described in Chapter 4. Those whose ego-emergence is met with parenting that engenders a lack of basic trust in others, either because they could not trust their parents or their parents could not trust the world at large, begin to develop pervasive and unwarranted suspiciousness and distrust of others. Their attitude of suspiciousness becomes their armor in a world that seems unsafe (paranoid personality). Others whose emerging ego is met with regimented parenting lacking warmth and tenderness, but fraught with rules and hierarchies of family power, develop restricted ability to express their own warm feelings, become perfectionistic, insist others submit to their way of doing things, and can be compulsively productive. Their driven, cold perfectionism is their armor in a world where one's only safety and rights seem to come from rules and not from others' warm regard, and where one is only in a superior position if the rules are one's own (compulsive personality). These are the armored ego disorders.

Those whose egos' emergence is met with very inconsistent reactions from parental figures develop a split in the ego itself. A prime example of this would be the borderline. These individuals had parents whose behavior was guided by internal stimuli rather than external events. The child of such parents can receive unpredictable reactions for the same behavior, based on the internal state of the parent on the day or moment of the action. The ego cannot deal intactly with mediation between these individuals and an external world where the ego's mediation seems only intermittently to have an effect. The ego becomes split into two parts, one of which functions according to the pleasure principle, the other according to the reality principle. An intact ego cannot develop to deal with reality, since reality is not fixed or integrated, and in such an environment following id impulses is not less effective than ego control. Furthermore, impulses are unchecked, as a damaged ego, lacking integration, cannot effectively contain drives. These are the split ego disorders.

Those whose emergence and ongoing development is met with apathy or neglect will develop a weak ego disorder and be deficient in their sense of self or of others. The child assumes that others like the parenting figures will not find him or her worthy of notice. Not having experienced a warm, satisfying relationship as the ego emerged, the child may become schizoid, lacking the capacity to form social relationships, or tending toward histrionic overreactions to get some external response from a world he unconsciously expects to be apathetic like mother, or narcissistic. With narcissism, however, we have observed at least two forms of the disorder. Both of these types we would describe as being weak ego disorders. The first type are those who had too little nurturance before and after ego-emergence.

Unlike the schizoid, who is not aware that gratification exists, these types of individuals may have seen others being responded to as important, so they in turn employ reaction formation as a defense against feelings of inadequacy and worthlessness. They present a weak, fragile facade of grandiosity or self-importance with any situation that goes against this facade, experienced as a confirmation or blow to their own underlying weak view of themselves. Related to this type of narcissism are the persons whose available and gratifying parental figures became largely unavailable to them. These individuals are constantly trying to compensate for their loss. This condition is differentiated from submergence in that individuals with the latter are able to recapture the primary or accepting parent through complying, whereas the former lost this type of parent due to conditions outside their control.

The second type of narcissism appears to result from too much nurturance and approval before and after ego-emergence. With this type of narcissism, the child can do no wrong. The home literally becomes the child's oyster, with this expectation being transformed onto the world at large. The ego structure is distorted and weakened as first the child and then the adult has not learned to modulate himself, to tolerate frustration as well as develop a realistic perception of his own boundaries. Therefore, any experience that does not conform to earlier life experiences is tolerated poorly.

Although the model presented dichotomizes the intrapsychic structures into four separate diagnostic categories, these categories are not mutually exclusive. A patient's psychopathology can be accounted for by more than one type of ego structure, depending on parental–child issues dating from the time of ego-emergence and development. Such is the case when one has had to comply to insure parental love and approval, but if compliance was not elicited, the parental response was extremely harsh or very abusive. One would expect to see a personality structure that was both submergent and armored. Another example would be a patient with one inconsistent parent who reacts to the child in a way that would lead to a splitting of the child's ego, and a second parent who is submergent, and when this parent turns from the primary to the secondary mother when the child is about two, the child submerges an already split ego to defend it from further damage. This may also occur in the case in which a submerging parent has a temporary decompensation due to trauma in his/her own life, and the child receives a dose of inconsistent parenting interspersed with consistent but submerging parenting, which creates the introjected complying pseudo-ego.

Our focus here has been primarily on the development and nature of the intrapsychic structure, particularly with regard to ego development. Another aspect that must be considered with regard to personality formation is the development of object-relatedness, which we feel is related to, but separate from, the development and formation of the formal intrapsychic structure. Kohut and his associates have contributed greatly to the understanding of this aspect of the interaction between parent and child. Specifically, it appears that "transmitting internalization" (Kohut 1971), internalizations derived from the interaction between parent and child in the form of admiration, warmth, empathy, and general emotional availability, become the foundation for the development of the self. While the structure of the ego is related to an individual's ability to reality-test and negotiate with the world, the development of the self colors how a person emotionally perceives and experiences oneself, the objects, and the interaction between them. Technically, we view the self, the object, or the interaction between them as one entity because they are internalized as self-objects, that is, experience of the self is derived through objects and vice versa. They cannot be experienced separately. It appears that the development of the self-object is derived from the affective states that initially comprised the interaction that the self and the object had with the child. In summary, the development of the self, based on the emotional availability of the parent(s), is transmitted to the child in the form of affective states and determines the child's perceptions of himself, the objects, and the interaction between them in the intro-jected form of self-object. One's perception and experience within the self-object unit correspond to the object relatedness of the individual with others and can be assessed by the noted affect between the person and others. The experience of self-object can be assessed along a continuum from schizoid through degrees of object-relatedness, and can vary somewhat within each of the four types of intrapsychic structures previously discussed.

For example, a submerged intrapsychic structure can be used to highlight the variability within this schizoid-object-related framework. An individual who as a child got much consistent love, warmth, concern, and emotional availability from parents as long as the child complied with their wishes should develop an intrapsychic structure that is submergent, and should also possess object-relatedness. In this situation, even some empathy may have been present outside of areas in which parental figures demand compliance. But withdrawal of these positive affects would be forthcoming if the child made any autono-mous strides. With regard to the self-object experience, it is the object that is affirmed and experienced as strong and important. The self part of the dyad is experienced as weak and unacceptable. In fact, the self in essence is experienced as a part of the object through a compliant pseudo-ego. Yet, while the pseudo-self is able to experience strength and gratification from the object, a true sense of self still exists within the self-object experience, creating ambivalence with regard to feelings toward self and others. Feelings of anger toward the object are experienced by the individual through a rebelling pseudo-self, in that the person alternately feels negative emotions toward others as a way of feeling individuated from the object in the self-object dyad. Due to the unacceptability of those feelings by original objects in the self-object experience, feelings of anger toward objects may become manifest toward less significant objects in the self-object experience.

This type of submergent personality that possesses object related-ness can be readily contrasted with a submergent personality that has minimal relatedness to others. While in terms of the self-object dyad, in the former case the object part is perceived as affirmed by the self part, with noted relatedness present, and in the latter, neither the self nor the object is experienced as affirmed. In this situation, the object has never been able to relate to the individual under any condition. The development of a submerged-ego intrapsychic structure without object-relatedness may develop as follows: in infancy the child is provided with all the basic physical needs such as food and physical comfort, but due to either a lack of parenting ability or life circum-stance, the child is unable to receive much positive emotional stimula-tion or gratification. This scenario may be the result of a parent who is depressed or schizoid, or it may be due to a long-term illness in which the young child needs to be hospitalized. As the child enters separa-tion–individuation subphases (ego-emergence) such as practicing and rapprochement, independent strides are met with a negative conse-quence, such as punishment or anger. This may be the result of having a parent who needs the child to remain a child in order to feel less threatened, or who needs the child to engage in activities that the parents themselves cannot fulfill. As a result of the basic needs being met in a consistent way, structurally, ego development has begun to occur but is thwarted at rapprochement, as a complying pseudo-ego develops with submergence of the individual's own ego, in order to stay out of harm's way. While these individuals have minimal self-object experience, resulting in little if any object relatedness as they do not know how it feels to be gratified by another individual, they do engage in much complying and some rebelling behavior as these pseudo-egos have developed. While structurally there is an intact ego submerged, a lack of emotional availability from significant others appears to prevent any true ego strength from developing, even in the ego's submerged state. It appears that emotional availability received by the child as the ego is developing not only fosters a sense of self and others, but acts as an energy source within the ego. Therefore, a very weak submerged ego results in the development of a weak rebelling ego. In this situation, rebellious behaviors take a more insidious form, with complying behaviors appearing dominant. This may result in a submergent personality with schizoid and possibly dependent features noted.

Although a submergent intrapsychic structure with two diverse types of self-object experiences has been presented, it is warranted that the self-object aspect of the personality be considered with patients whose intrapsychic structures fit into any of the diagnostic categories discussed earlier in this chapter. From a schematic point of view, we feel that the ego becomes the framework of the person, with the self-object experience being the substance that is enclosed within the framework. Thus, while these components of the psyche are different, it is apparent that the type of ego structure formed will affect the substance that is held within its parameters, and the amount and type of substance (self-object) will have an effect on the structure that contains it. A wet-cell battery is analogous to this. Not only does one have to look at the size of the battery (ego) and its encasement (ego structure), but also at the amount and type of battery fluid (self-object) that is within the battery encasement. Variability in battery size and the condition of the encasement, as well as amount and type of fluid, will affect its operation (the personality).

3

Treatment Approaches

Irwin L. Kutash, Ph.D.,
and Alexander Wolf, M.D.

The young always have the same problem—how to rebel and conform at the same time. They have now solved this by defying their parents and copying one another.

—Quentin Crisp

In this chapter, treatment for the submerged patient will be described through a form of psychoanalytic psychotherapy, "The Drive/Relational Model" (Kutash and Greenberg 1986). This model draws on instinctual drive, interpersonal, and object relations theories. For the submerged personality, it is used to effect introject dispersion. This approach will be described as a treatment of choice for submerged patients, to be supplemented with psychoanalysis in groups when the patient is ready. First, this approach will be differentiated from psychoanalysis and other newer psychoanalytic approaches.

DIFFERENTIATION OF PSYCHOANALYTIC PSYCHOTHERAPY AND PSYCHOANALYSIS

Psychoanalytic psychotherapy has been differentiated from psychoanalysis in two ways. Some therapies see psychoanalytic psychotherapy as a modification of psychoanalysis, designed to treat specific disorders that are less amenable to psychoanalysis, for example, recon-

structive therapy for disorders not previously approached by psychoanalysts. Kernberg (1982), for example, feeling that "the structural
characteristics of borderline patients defy applying the model of psychoanalysis to psychoanalytic psychotherapy, unless the model is
modified," devised psychoanalytic psychotherapy modified to take
into account "the defenses and resistances, the transferences and drive
derivatives of patients with severe character pathology and borderline
personality organization" (p. 21). Second, psychoanalytic psychotherapy has been differentiated from psychoanalysis based on their
respective goals and aims; for example, in ego psychology theory,
psychoanalytic psychotherapy is designed to resolve only partially
unconscious conflicts and resistances, and for a partial integration of
repressed impulses into the ego with reinforcement of some defenses
attempted. To these we would add a third goal: psychoanalytic psychotherapy has added to psychoanalysis psychoanalytic approaches designed to help liberate as opposed to reconstruct the ego, to facilitate
the progression of the ego as opposed to its repair. Freud talked about
"regression in the service of the ego"; to this we caution progression
not be overlooked as a service to the ego, the primary need of the
submerged patient with his submerged ego.

NEWER PSYCHOANALYTIC APPROACHES

Psychoanalytic psychotherapy has evolved from psychoanalysis in the
development of new techniques, applicable to the more restricted goals
of psychoanalytic psychotherapy or derived as more applicable to
specific types of patients. These would include ego psychology, object
relations theory, self-psychology, and the drive/relational model. Some
of these were designed to repair damaged egos as in psychoanalysis,
which was conceived for neurotic patients, but also extended these
formulations to the understanding and treatment of narcissists or
borderlines, for example, self psychology and object relations theory.
Other techniques such as self psychology and the drive/relational

model were meant to enhance ego progression for submerged, arrested, or not fully developed egos, a group ignored by orthodox analysts. The former focuses on affirming weak egos by supporting the self, and the latter, facilitated by a neutral therapist, is designed to help the patient affirm his own ego.

Greenberg and Mitchell (1983) have described two trends in psychoanalytic theory. The drive/structure model, in which relationships are entered and shaped by the need for drive satisfaction, for example, Freud and the relational/structure models in which relationships in and of themselves are taken as a primary motivating force, for example, Sullivan. These authors feel there is an intrinsic incompatibility between the drive/structure and relational structure models and presented mixed models such as Kohut (1971), Modell (1975), or Sandler and Sandler (1978) as failures for that reason.

Modell (1975) posited a two-factor theory, accepting both instinct theory and a psychology of object relations and self with each viewpoint seen as fitting different disorders, but he suggested two types of instincts in attempting this: libido and aggression from the id, and object-relational instincts from the ego.

Kohut (1977) himself replaced his two-factor theory, which was meant to complement Freudian theory, with his self-psychology, which was intended to replace the id-ego model altogether. His main difference was his belief in a narcissistic developmental line separate and earlier than psychosexual or ego development.

Within psychoanalytic theory, the traditional idea that all behavior and psychic functions originate from, and are secondary to, instinct was first challenged by those who saw ego functions as primary (Hartmann 1958, 1964). This modification is at the core of ego psychology. That these theories are not incompatible and in fact complement one another is the position we take after having worked within such a model for many years. Drive gratification and relational needs are existent within each individual and developmentally play different roles at different times. One or the other, or both can be thwarted or subverted and lead to different emotional problems.

An individual goes through two stages of relationship development, a primary stage and a secondary stage. The primary relationship stage occurs before the development of the individual's secondary drives, such as curiosity or exploration or other characteristics equated with independence. In the primary relational stage, all relationships are based on drive gratification. In the secondary relational stage, some primary drives have been sublimated, and some relationships are entered not only for primary drive satisfaction but also for gratification of relational needs. In short, it is postulated that the ego emerges to mediate between the id and the external world to help achieve drive gratification, but that the more developed ego, perhaps as early as within the second year of life, seeks gratification in contacting other separate and unique egos. Such relationships can lead to the discovery of new drive gratification strategies from another person, but can also satisfy the desire of the individual to establish relations that can be pleasurable in and of themselves. Relationships later in life may involve attempts to reestablish these early relationships for various reasons.

What can go wrong in these stages comprises the work of psychoanalytic psychotherapy. Freud believed that a basic goal of psychoanalysis was to help the patient's ego to appropriate to itself part of what was formerly functioning as id or instinctual drives. He put this succinctly when he said, "Where id was, there shall ego be." We would add to that what we see as the second basic goal of psychoanalysis: psychoanalysis must help the patient to distinguish his own ego from introjected parental pseudo-egos. We must ask if "Where id was, there shall ego be," whose ego? We need to help the patient to differentiate his own ego from introjected parents. Hence, in therapy a patient may gain greater control and delay over instinctual drives implicated in intrapsychic conflict. But if this has been accomplished by a loss of self or lack of separation/individuation from parents, there are well-functioning pseudo-egos rather than a patient with increased ego development and control. In 1976, Schafer reinterpreted Freud's original quote into English with the id as an impersonal "it" and the ego as personal "I." He felt that the ego is helped to appropriate to itself that which is impersonal or disowned, so it can be owned and experienced as part of oneself. In fact, "Wo es war, soll ich werden" can be literally translated "where it was, there shall I become," wherein the ego alien drive becomes a sublimated personal desire. This comes closer to the goal of psychoanalytic psychotherapy in the drive/relational model but still excludes the effects of the parental hands that first "helped" the child turn instinctual drives into controlled aims of parenting figures. A therapist can help the child to learn to satisfy the child's own wishes, or the parents', or even society's wishes for the child. If the former is the case, the child can grow to be an autonomous adult. If the latter, the individual will become a socialized automaton with great ambivalence about any aim, since *his* aims actually belong to someone else. Analysis then can be used to help one replace id with ego if one was never helped originally to do so, and/or to replace pseudo-egos with ego, the goal with the submerged personality. The former is the case in more primitive patients with a building form of therapy, the latter is the case in patients with less primary process but socialized pseudo-selves. It is observed, therefore, that instinctual drive theory is adequate to describe the process in the former patients, and that drive qualification and interpersonal theory must be combined to explain the latter more adequately. Even after the patient can satisfy his instinctual drives, his sense of self and well-being can be shaped by early parental relationships, determining whether he is self-affirmed, selfless, or pseudo-selved.

In the drive/relational model, we go on to relate unconscious internal object relations to current interpersonal relationships. As therapists who practice within a drive/relational model, we often analyze the relationship between unconscious internal object relationships in our patient and the patient's distortion of present day interpersonal relationships based on these internal objects. We never ignore instinctual drives, however. So far we have related drive to interpersonal theory, and now we will examine object relations theory.

Object relations are intrapsychic structures consisting of the mental representation of self and the object or other. This intrapsychic constellation has an overriding bearing on a person's interpersonal relationships. This constellation is formed during the early years of life, based on the individual's relationship with parental figures who helped to fulfill his or her early needs. This definition is in line with Freud's statement in *The Ego and the Id* (1923), when he referred to the ego as "the repository of abandoned objects."

The relation of drive theory or instinct theory to object relations theory has been a central difference among object relations therapists in the emphasis given to drives. Some see instinctual drive as no more important than any other aspect of experience. They see instinctual drives as requiring the same integration within the self as any other characteristic, and believe that ego controls are an outcome of this overall integration (Horner 1984). Others, such as Kernberg (1984), emphasize constitutional factors and propose "that the units of internalized object relations constitute subsystems on the basis of which both drives and the overall psychic structure of ego, superego, and id are organized as integrating systems" (p. 85). To Kernberg, instincts represented by psychologically organized drive systems along with the overall psychic structures make up the systems of the personality constituting the suprasystem. In his view, the units of internalized object relations constitute an integrating system for subsystems, including inborn perceptive and behavior patterns and affect dispositions. He stresses that libido and aggression represent the two overall psychic drives that integrate instinctive components and the other units of internalized object relations. Theorists from both extremes in the object relations school would agree with drive theorists that failure to control instinctual drives represents inadequate development of organizing processes that structure the ego or self, and that drive and affect must be integrated within a cohesive object-related self-representation.

We are now left with three distinct categories of disorder: (1) disorders in those who could not integrate instinctual needs and drives with reality, having undeveloped or poorly developed egos, or enduring mental configurations of self, for example, autistic children; (2) those who cannot meet relational needs based on poor early relationships with parents, for example, schizoid personalities; and (3) those who could not form internalized self-representations because the self was not affirmed, for example, narcissists. To this we would add a fourth group: those who appear to integrate instinctual needs and drives with reality, form interpersonal relationships, and seem to have intrapsychic structures that continue throughout life to be modified by experience. In reality, their own egos are submerged, due to a particular type of maternal failure or parenting figure; they are submerged personalities (Kutash 1984b, Wolf 1957, 1980, Wolf and Kutash 1984a, 1985). Such a person complies and rebels around parental needs. His relations are built around meeting or thwarting those needs. His own sense of self has been submerged by the introjection of a parental pseudo-ego. For him or her there is a submerged internalized self, introjected pseudo-selves, and the other.

TREATMENT

Treatment for the submerged personality was first outlined by Wolf (1957). The goal of treatment was described as "the freeing of the patient from the tyranny of the negative parental ego."

In therapy with the . . . di-egophrenic we do not try to achieve synthesis of various conflicting ambivalent attitudes, but we try to accent the positive ego and to de-emphasize the negative ego. We try to build the original ego and diminish the importance of the parental ego. By allowing the repressed ego to emerge, the patient can play a part in ejecting the superimposed pseudo-ego. Knowing that the di-egophrenic patient's aggression is the aggressive energy of the parental pseudo-ego, the therapist encourages the patient's repressed ego to new assertion. The therapist does not start by attacking the negative ego, because the patient's security system depends too much on this incorporation. The therapist supports the personal ego first. He does not set about depriving the patient of his present adaptation until he has a more secure new one. The therapist is not initially concerned with interpreting the patient's hostility. It is important to free the patient's own thoughts, feeling, perceptions, cognition, functioning and activity. This process strengthens his own ego enough to enable him to be angry with the parent or parents for having castrated him. . . . With the di-egophrenic patient, the therapist can reduce the patient's hostility by first encouraging the positive ego until it is strong enough to withstand interpretation of the incorporated negative pseudo-ego which it can eject. In the beginning, no insights should be proffered. [p. 139]

Other key ingredients Wolf presented in 1957 in regard to the treatment of the submerged personality included the idea that the submerged patient "always has ambivalent transferences, until his own ego develops. Then he forms positive transferences too; . . . with the di-egophrenic, you do not treat the parent and the child as separate figures. You treat parent and child in the patient" (p. 139).

In regard to the submerged patient and group psychotherapy, Wolf (1957) writes that the "group provides him with essential face-to-face relationships, which give him day-to-day contact with others. The group helps him to overcome his isolation. The group provides him in the main with good auxiliary egos to support his weakened positive ego. The group gives him a testing ground for strengthening his own original ego" (p. 139).

Before we go on to present our latest thinking on ego-submergence and its treatment, we will differentiate this concept further from that of the borderline in terms of dynamics, developmental history, and treatment strategies that will clarify what follows. A more global differentiation of the disorders appears in Chapter 2. Here we highlight some important specifics. Submergence is a broader entity than borderline, extending to both those more severely ill and those less so. In fact, submergence maneuvers exist in all of us, since we all introject our parents' attitudes to a degree.

To differentiate this view from the borderline: in borderline personalities the ego is split, whereas in the submergent, the ego has been partially arrested in its emergence. The borderline has an ego that is damaged, one that during its emergence was confronted with an environment that included inconsistent or bad mothering from birth, with an ego that, in coping with this inconsistency, has split in an attempt to deal with an unpredictable world. The submergent received good consistent mothering until he began to differentiate and become more independent, and then consistently bad mothering any time his being himself differed from the beliefs of the parent. He therefore, in an attempt to save himself from loss of mother's love or from punishment, and in a defense of his submerged ego, introjected the parental unconscious demands as a pseudo-ego that coincides with the parent's wishes, leaving him safe within the maternal orbit. Subsequently, his own ego defends against this alien intrusion by setting up a defensive second pseudo-ego that battles the introject by adopting a stance opposite to it. It could be likened to the antibodies formed by the individual who has received a heart transplant—his own body tries to exorcise it. The energy drained from the submerged ego in forming the second pseudo-ego, and in the subsequent complying and rebelling, leaves the ego itself in a state of partial arrest. In opposing the parental introjects, energy is less available for the child to find his own ways of being separate from the conflict.

If a mother is schizophrenic, she is borderlinogenic to her child. If, at the same time, the father is submerging, the child is subjected to two different kinds of traumatic experiences. He has a suppressed split ego. Treatment at first should be directed toward the liberation of his suppressed split ego; after his split ego has emerged, he should be treated as a borderline. If the mother is submergent and the father is borderlinogenic, their child should first be treated as a submerged personality who has a less damaged borderlineness because he has some intact ego, and because the father's borderlinogenic influence comes later in the child's life than the mother's pathogenic influence. If both parents are borderlinogenic, then the patient should be treated as a borderline. If both parents are submerging, the patient should be treated as a submerged personality. If the mother is submergent and the father relatively normal, the patient is more treatable as a less disturbed submerged personality. If the mother is relatively normal and the father is submerging, again, the patient is more readily responsive to therapy as a less disturbed submergent, since he had good mothering.

We will not attempt to relate submergence to all the borderline literature (see Chapter 2), but we will use the work of Masterson as representative of the differences we hope to establish in treatment.

According to Masterson (1976), "The ego is split into two parts, one of which functions according to the pleasure principle, the other according to the reality principle" (p. 65). In submergence, the ego is suppressed rather than split. The dual pseudo-egos give the appearance of a split. Masterson suggests that in the treatment of the borderline, "Good and bad self-representations coalesce, as do good and bad object representation" (p. 65). In the treatment of the submergent, the aim is not to seek a coalescence of the split pseudo-egos, but rather their disincorporation by promoting the liberation of the suppressed ego. Masterson (1976) "supports moves toward individuation (in the borderline) in order to provide the patient with an appropriate external object (the therapist) that he can internalize" (p. 90). We suggest that this is inappropriate for the submergent as well as the borderline because such a procedure would substitute for the introjected parental pseudo-ego the therapist's self, which becomes the patient's pseudo-ego. Masterson would transform "the split ego into a whole ego" (p. 94). He regards "confrontation [as] needed throughout the therapy" of the borderline (p. 102). The submerged personality reacts to confrontation in the earlier phases of treatment with characteristic ambivalence: submission and rebellion. It is only when his own ego has been sufficiently liberated that he becomes able to work constructively with insight proffered by the therapist. Masterson asserts that with the borderline the therapist cannot "relax his vigilance at any time; if he does, the pathologic ego will again reassert itself" (p. 186). In submerged personalities, we do not regard the ego as pathologic, only the introjected pseudo-ego, which when disincorporated by the liberated ego, permits the ego to pursue its wholesome creative course. Masterson says, "The evidence . . . suggests that the mother (of the borderline) is (also) borderline" (p. 346). Our experience is that the mother of the submerged is more generally narcissistic, depressed, or schizoid, or may become depressed as her infant tries to individuate, and the mother of the seriously ill submerged is also submerged. The submerged personality gets a message from the parent: "Do it my way or else—after all you are an extension of me."

In terms of therapy, therefore, the borderline needs reconstructive therapy to help repair a damaged ego; the submerged needs constructive therapy in an environment conducive to the emergence of an intact but partially developed ego. The borderline, therefore, may require more direction, interpretation, a more active confrontive therapy experience. The submerged needs a therapist with a strictly neutral stance and little interpretation or confrontation for the patient to comply or rebel against, but a clear goal: "Let's find out what you really want, separate from parental messages, and separate from my point of view as well. It is safe to be you here; let's find out what that is through dreams, fantasy, and free association." The therapist is a nonjudgmental facilitator who makes it safe to exorcise the introjected and defensive pseudo-egos. Be consistent with a borderline, and he can accept interpretations and direction toward health; a submerged needs to find his own way and has an intact ego that can potentially do it. He needs a safe, nonjudgmental environment designed to separate his own ego from his pseudo-egos and to let him feel the differences between "I and thou."

The intent of therapy with the borderline may be to help him integrate the sides of his ego; with the submerged, the intent is to help him exorcise the introjected pseudo-ego that would leave him without the need to maintain the rebellious pseudo-ego formed as a defense by the formerly submerged ego. With either condition, it is antitherapeutic to work toward integrating external values with internal values to form a homogenized group value (as, for example, in some forms of group therapy), but the goal is to promote individuality. A person who appreciates his uniqueness can appreciate that of others. He can then derive cohesion with others from being able to appreciate differences as well as similarities, and he does not then have to create a compliant pseudo-self or a rebellious one to feel safe; nor does he have to seek the refuge of a group mood to feel whole.

To summarize, the infant looks to its mother for love and nurturance. When they are given freely, he develops normally. When he is severely denied, as by maternal psychosis with its inconsistencies, her postpartum depression, or her death in childbirth, his ego is split, even shattered. Then he operates, if his mother survives, with the distorted and irrational misperceptions of his mother. Her hallucinations and delusions become reality for him. His views and judgments are as misperceived as hers. He is a borderline.

If his mother suffered from a narcissistic personality disorder, he experienced his mother as "loving," because she saw him primarily as an extension of herself. He would, she expected, realize all the unfulfilled wishes she had been unable to realize for herself. In traditional terms, she envisions him unconsciously as her penis. This is too limited a view. Her expectations of him are all-encompassing. She controls him absolutely, if she can, to follow her plans for him. For the first year or two of his life he experiences her "love" as genuinely caring and nurturant, only to discover that any curiosity of his own, any attempts at distancing himself from her, any moves toward autonomy, toward independence are met with anxiety on her part and denial of his wishes. She feels abandoned by her child, anxious, lost, and therefore annoyed or angry with him. Her unrealistic demands of him for control he experiences as frightening, hurtful, and limiting. In his fear that if he follows his need for any independence he will lose his mother's love and support, he suppresses his curiosity, his own exploration of his environment, his creative ego. Instead he incorporates her choices, her preferences, her aims, her ambitions, her views, her perceptions of what is best for him in a pseudo-ego. He does this in the hope that he will regain the good, loving, caring primary mother and not be threatened by this bad, angry, uncaring secondary mother.

He operates then with two pseudo-egos: one, the incorporated second-ary mother, and the other, his rebellious pseudo-ego, derived from his own ego in opposition to the demands of the introjected mother. Now he has an internal struggle that can be characterized by ambivalence, sadomasochism, grandiosity and feelings of inferiority, paranoidal symptoms, depression and elation, and overt or covert homosexuality.

He projects his pseudo-egos onto others in transference. He is am-bivalent about everything. He ambivalates between being good and bad. He submits and rebels. He says yes and no. He is heterosexual and homosexual. He is clear and unclear. He is reasonable and unreason-able. He is charming and unbearable, rational and irrational. He is submergent. As soon as his narcissistic mother feels threatened at the prospect of his pursuing his own autonomous way and consequently becomes persecuting to rein him in, he is rendered submergent by age 2. So associated with the ambivalence imposed by his pseudo-egos, we find oral, anal, sadomasochistic, homosexual, depressive, and paranoidal psychopathology. If the mother dies about this time, the father, an older sibling, an uncle, aunt, or any other who assumes the caretaking role becomes the surrogate for the mother and plays whole-some, ego-supportive, or pathogenic roles. When the mother is less narcissistic, her distortions of reality are less imposing, the infant is less victimized, does not become so submergently disturbed, and exhibits muted, ambivalent maneuvers rather than becoming seriously submergent.

Initial Phase of Treatment

We have found it to be useful, therefore, to begin treatment without dealing with the patient's ambivalence or other expressions of his dual pseudo-egos. Any attempt to analyze his psychopathology is met with ambivalence: compliance and opposition. If the therapist expresses enthusiasm, there is associated overt and covert opposition. If the patient is ingratiating, it is associated with overt or covert opposition.

In the treatment of the submerged personality, the patient needs to rebel or diverge from the parental general conceptions of his time, and even those of his analyst in order to recover his submerged ego.

Since it is necessary in the treatment of submergence to encourage the emergence and growth of the submerged ego, this purpose is difficult to achieve by traditional psychoanalysis. This is especially true in the case of the severely ill submergent patient who functions primarily with his two pseudo-egos and cannot, therefore, benefit from externally offered attempts to give him insight since he has so little available ego to accept and integrate externally provided understanding. Instead, he continues manifestly to accept insight but at the same time to reject it in the submission and rebellion so characteristic of the dual pseudo-egos. The patient who is subject only to submergence maneuvers with only moderate suppression of creative ego functions and a more available ego can more readily accept offers of insight. Nevertheless, it is our clinical practice with both types to withhold offers of understanding until the patient stops ambivalating around any attempts on the part of the therapist to provide it, and until after the patient becomes unambivalently hostile to the therapist as the surrogate for the ego-submerged parent. In fact, it seems likely that transference responses derive their ambivalence from the dual images of the primary and secondary submerged mother. This view of the origin of transference provides the student of psychoanalysis with a more vivid and dynamic conception of transferential etiology than was heretofore available. This aggressive attitude does not last long because the patient feels free at last to protest against a lifetime of sadomasochism, paranoid and bisexual submission, and rebellion at the hands of a stand-in in the therapist for the pathogenic parent. His hostility is also short-lived because he deeply appreciates the freedom he has gained with the therapeutic help of the analyst and fellow patients, as well as the recovery and growth of his own ego. With his creative ego available, he can now appreciate and constructively utilize offers of insight.

The treatment of submergence is to try to attend to the suppressed aspirations of the ego and not to respond to the demands of pseudo-egos. Some therapists have viewed this approach as indulging the id needs and thereby encouraging acting out. This is far from the case. The continued attention by the therapist to the voice of the suppressed ego, whether in fantasy, free association, dreams, or interaction, will gradually lead to the emergence and growth of an autonomous and creative ego, while pseudo-egos will die from an atrophy of disuse. Before this happens, the patient will gradually cease to ambivalate and begin to be very angry with the therapist, on whom he projects the secondary mother, for all the years of his enslavement to the mother he used to endure. This hostility is relatively short, a matter of a few weeks or a few months at most. However, there is a danger during this period that the patient may flee from treatment in anger rather than remain and express it. The therapist must use all his powers to keep the patient in treatment and get him to ventilate his rage. The therapist does not show himself as wounded. As a result, the patient recovers his suppressed ego and is now able to work actively with the therapist in his own interest. This is in sharp contrast to the period of ambivalence, when he responded either with manifest delight to an offer of insight, only to "forget" it by the next session, or to react with irritability and a subsequent apology for having been so rude as to reject the therapist's interpretation of his associations.

In treating the submerged ego it is important for the therapist not to respond to patient communications that are expressions of pseudo-ego activity. This includes not only the patient's ambivalence, but his paranoidal, sadomasochistic, confused gender identity, and depressive manifestations. The therapist needs only very gently to respond to expressions of the suppressed ego, whether in dream, free association, fantasy, or imaginative and creative communication. By so functioning, the pseudo-egos wither from inattention. The therapist should respond positively to the patient's indications of grandiosity until his suppressed ego emerges, when his pretensions can be analyzed and worked through. If the patient turns out to be very talented or a genius, we are content to see him retain his self-image, which is a realistic view of himself.

The submerged may be afraid of any intimacy with another because of his compulsive need to comply and rebel around the proffers of the other's ego. He feels that to be close means to comply and lose the self, not yet aware that he can be close and independent with non-submerged others. Through his relationship with the analyst, he comes to learn that he need not comply in order to be accepted or rebel to protect the submerged ego. Through his experience with the neutral analyst, he learns that people exist who are different from the secondary mother. When, in the course of treatment, he develops an adequate ego, the analyst no longer needs to fear as much failing to be neutral, and the patient and the analyst may disagree without the patient feeling threatened.

Occasionally, the dread of again encountering the secondary mother in later years is so terrorizing that a patient may defend against experiencing his own counterattacking pseudo-self and compulsively ingratiate himself with a mother-surrogate. Or he may project onto him or her an idealized mother transference who can do him no wrong no matter how deceptive or sadistic she or he may in fact be. (This is what the German people did with Hitler and the Russians with Stalin.) In psychoanalytic therapy, we frequently encounter patients who exalt their ego-submerging parent in the person of the therapist, and deny their own victimization.

We also encounter patients who experience only the projected secondary mother in every other, and never seem to encounter in any parental surrogate the primary, caring, and tender mother. Of course, more commonly the analyst meets with patients who ambivalate in their transference to him as both the good and bad mother. Less frequently, patients seem to experience him as more one than the other.

The atrophy of the pseudo-egos is a function of the gradual emergence and growth of the creative ego. The pseudo-egos cannot be disincorporated by an effort of will. They dissolve because each time the ego asserts its strength, the pseudo-egos, unresponded to by the analyst, die a little more from the therapist's disregard. In the initial phases of therapy, it is important, as explained above, for the therapist not to try to provide insight. The patient will always respond to this kind of help with ambivalence. The therapist needs to remain empathically responsive only to glimmers of the suppressed ego's showing itself. And he must not make his pleasure in detecting such a development too evident, for the patient will then feel that his delight in recovering his ego is being taken away from him, and he does not want this creative act to be appropriated by the analyst. He is too full of unexpressed hatred for his mother in the analyst to give her any satisfaction. If the analyst displays his reactive delight, the patient becomes depressed and angry. For some time, the therapist needs to conceal his pleasure in the patient's progress. Some patients do well; then the analyst displays his pleasure. When the patient develops enough recovery of his own ego, he displays great hostility for all the years he has felt enslaved by his pseudo-egos. This may be a time when the patient may try to escape further treatment rather than remaining and experiencing and expressing his rage toward his parents as well as the analyst. If his therapist is hurt or fearful of being the object of this aggression, the patient may well leave treatment. It is most important for the therapist at this time to encourage the patient to remain and to express his rage. This lasts only a few weeks or a few months. Then the patient is not ambivalent, he is purely angry. His anger passes, he can more readily experience his own ego. Then he can accept insight and work with it constructively. A therapeutic alliance is emerging, and the middle stage of therapy has begun. At this point, work with dreams can be particularly useful.

Middle Phase of Treatment

The dream is a useful product to explore, because it contains evidence of the creative ego. It needs to be listened to for evidence of creative ego expressions, and to help the patient use the dream to differentiate true ego presentations contained therein from working state pseudo-ego manifestations. It can be used further to help the patient unearth his true wishes from those of a pseudo-ego. The analyst should help the patient resist responding to pseudo-ego manifestations. If he doesn't, he may entrench the pseudo-egos. He should respond to indications of creative ego functions, whether realistic, imaginative, or inventive. If he does this, the pseudo-egos further atrophy from disuse. The dream is not the only communication which should so be responded to. Equal attention needs to be given in the same way to patients' fantasies and free association. With some patients, the therapist may become too enthusiastically responsive to evidences of creative ego expression. The patient then, as explained above, may immediately become depressed, feeling that the secondary mother in the analyst has appropriated, taken away, his creation. The patient may also feel that he does not want the mother to get any gratification from his self-discovery. On the other hand, other patients may appreciate the therapist's enjoyment of this creative advance and feel nourished by it. The analyst should tentatively test out with the patient which response the patient needs in order to recover his creative ego.

A patient's dreams can be the tool to the patient's feeling the accomplishment of progress. They contain the true wishes of the dreamer, and in a creative format. For this reason, dream analysis is perhaps even more vital with a submerged ego. With it the patient can tune in on his own uncensored self and get to know this self through his own associations. Dreams are utilized in group therapy as well, to bring out the creative associations of all group members.

The analysis of transference also becomes very significant at this point in helping the patient differentiate the therapist and others from the parents. Transference must be differentiated from the introjection of the parent as a pseudo-ego.

In transference, the patient misperceives present-day figures as if they were persons in his past. In submergent introjection, the patient acts as if he were a figure from the past or present, functioning with the introjected pseudo-ego derived from the pathogenic parent.

Transference differs from submergent reactions, in which there is an introjection of the parent as a pseudo-ego in the child. In transference, the patient experiences a present-day figure as if he or she were a member of his original family. In submergent introjection, the patient acts with a pseudo-ego (that represents the pathogenic parent), rather than with his own ego, which is in suppression and not available to him.

In an earlier paper (Wolf and Kutash 1985), Kutash coined the term *introjective transference*. In this chapter, we expand upon this concept and utilize the terms *projective transference*, which is the projection of parental figures onto present-day others, and *introjective transference*, which is the introjection of the parental figure into the self. We feel this latter concept is as important as projective transference but has never been really utilized until its identification in the submerged personality. Projective transference is transferring the early parent outward. Introjective transference is transferring the early parent inward.

Submergence is not merely the persistence of transference, that is, the compulsive pursuit and resistance to the mother surrogate in repetition compulsion, a rigidity leading to inevitable frustration if acted out, and so forth. While submergence has some of the qualities of transference, its resolution is more than the working through of transference. The resolution of submergence is the liberation of the creative ego from suppression. As this gradually takes place, the pseudo-egos recede from inactivity, while transference may also, at the same time, diminish in intensity. If the mother does not have a narcissistic personality disorder, her child will develop projectence but not primarily introjectence. The symptoms of submergence are specific constellations that differentiate it from disorders with primarily projectence.

Transference traditionally has been the projection onto others of the patient's familial figures. Introjective transference as another form of transference adds introjection of the mother or parent. The patient may act like the mother to the extent that he functions with his submissive pseudo-ego, the parental introject. A rebellious pseudo-ego derived from the suppressed ego develops as a defense against the submissive pseudo-ego and defends the true self.

The addition of introjection to transference provides analysts with the most specific way of understanding the ambivalence in transference. Since everyone introjects some parental aspects, everyone must in some degree be subject to some ambivalent symptoms. The incorporation of the mother in the submissive pseudo-ego and the infant's self-generated rebellious pseudo-ego provide the arena for ambivalating. The introjection of mother as a pseudo-ego (introjective transference) and then its projection onto surrogate mothers (projective transference), both in and out of the treatment room, is the most logical way of accounting for the ambivalent quality of transference, the love and hatred of the surrogate parent.

In understanding the introjection of parental figures as pseudo-egos, we can more clearly and dynamically group the origin and projection of transference and divide it into two significant components: projective and introjective. Since introjection is universal, either very minimal, or maximal, as in psychosis, everyone must in some degree, whether lesser or greater, suffer from some submerged personality symptoms. Because both types of transference are never totally worked through, everyone must have some residual symptoms.

Since a submerged personality contains an introjected parental ego and a rebelling pseudo-ego, there may be some creative aspects of transference, for example, in rebelling against what is, the individual may create what isn't—something new. This, however, is limited when compared with the liberation of the creative ego. In terms of creative endeavor, the negative of acting with projection or with pseudo-ego with introjection is its ambivalence, its compulsivity, its repetitiousness, its inappropriateness, its faulty perception, and its unreality. The creativity in transference is more limited by its compulsivity, its repetition, and its predictability, while the creativity of liberated ego is freer, welcomed by others and the creator, more original and more diversified.

Submergence is the persistence of these two kinds of transferences, that is, the compulsive pursuit of and resistance to the mother surrogate by means of repetition, compulsion, and rigidity, leading to inevitable frustration and disappointment if acted out. While submergence must have all the qualities of transference, its resolution is more than the working through of transference. The resolution of submergence is the liberation of the creative ego from suppression. As this gradually takes place, transferences and introjected pseudo-egos die from disuse. If the mother does not have a narcissistic personality disorder leading to the secondary mother, her child will develop transferences but not submergence. If the mother is only very slightly narcissistic, her child will be subject only to submergent maneuvers rather than the invasive depths of a submergent personality. Therefore, while everyone is subject to the demands of transference and some introjection in varying degrees, not everyone is of necessity ego-submergent.

Perhaps the best example of introjective transference in submergence is the multiple personality. A person with multiple personality disorder incorporates not only the father, mother, and siblings but more remote familial and nonfamilial persons significant in early life. Such a person will often also include some alter egos that are the diametric opposite of early figures as a defense for his submerged ego. These internalized others are not projected in transference but introjected as alter egos.

A study of multiple personality disorder illustrates as well the defensive function of the various incorporated multiple others. They protect the submerged ego. If, for example, a patient with multiple personality disorder feels that any one particular personality facade is threatened by an observing individual, the patient may suddenly transform his facade by assuming another personality. This is an extreme example of how the pseudo-ego can protect the submerged ego from external threat. It is a function of the submerged ego's erecting multiple barricades against its invasion.

Countertransference of the Pathogenic Therapist

In all phases of treatment, the therapist must be careful not to fulfill the patient's projection of him as the primary and secondary parent. This can be elicited by the transference of the patient. If it is responded to in countertransference, the therapist himself may have been seduced into being the pathogenic parent.

The analyst, seeing in his patient a psychodynamic process, may in conceit offer the patient an interpretation more in self-appreciation than in terms of what the patient needs. The submerged patient may respond with manifest appreciation but private rejection of the proffer of insight. Or he may openly reject what he is told and then apologize for his impoliteness. The analyst in such a case may be as narcissistic as the patient's mother, and equally damaging. Besides, insight should not be provided until the patient has an ego of his own, which he can achieve better by discovering his suppressed ego more on his own than with any premature interpretation by his therapist. The patient has been given too many directives and cues that were supposed to be in his interest in the past. He has already spent most of his life either looking for directives, which he hates, or tuning them out like a rebellious marionette. The patient pretends to listen, and he is so busy doing this that he loses his own thoughts and feelings. In his deception he is self-deceptive.

The Later Phase of Treatment

By the working through of the initial transference to the therapist as the primary and secondary mother, a therapeutic alliance can emerge. This allows dream interpretation and analysis of later transferences in a partnership with an emerging observing patient's ego, previously submerged. Psychoanalysis in groups becomes the treatment of choice, once this occurs.

It is important not to place the submerged patient in a therapeutic group before he has gained some accessibility to ego functions. Otherwise, the prevalence of his pseudo-ego functions leads to repeated and frustrating ambivalence. The submerged patient may sit in silence in the face of a group propelled by the therapist who chooses to emphasize overpowering group-as-a-whole interpretations, a silence that is manifestly submissive and latently rebellious and hostile, in which he endures his own solitude as the group must endure it. We need to encourage his newly emerged ego again and again to say his piece, no matter what. We need to support his courage, his right to say what is on his mind, to tell his dream, his fantasy, to experiment, to differ with the group, to be original, to be independent, not to be trampled by the others' moods or determined insistence. The severely ill submerged patient needs to be treated individually until such time as his own ego emerges sufficiently that he can enter a group with less subjection to his compulsive ambivalence. In individual treatment preparatory to group entry, the therapist neither attempts to offer insight nor responds to the patient's efforts to manipulate him into taking a stand around which he can continue to ambivalate. Rather, the emphasis needs to be placed on what the patient thinks, feels, fantasizes, and dreams, on his perceptions, judgments, creative impulses, and ideas. This is not to imply that we promote id functions, but rather the wholesome evolution and growth of creative ego resources. Furthermore, we caution the therapist to not support too vigorously all these possibilities, but with only mild or moderated affirmation of them. For with too emphatic or enthusiastic encouragement or signs that the patient is daring to recover his suppressed ego, the patient feels the therapist is appropriating him and that the surrogate parent in the therapist is getting too much pleasure out of the treatment process. The patient then becomes too eager to frustrate the stand-in parent, tries to deny him the satisfaction of any accomplishment, and suppresses once more the glimmer of his creative ego function.

A milestone for the submerged patient comes when he is able to accept insight. He has spent so much of his life utilizing most of his energy for either conforming or rebelling around introjected parental constructs and values, and has never truly found himself. At this point the submerged needs psychoanalysis in groups to discover further his complying and rebelling, so he can ultimately resist functioning with his pseudo-ego and be himself. The patient's transference to the therapist can become sufficiently diluted in the group to allow the acceptance of interpretations around his ambivalating within the group and affirming his emerging ego.

In general, the patient in individual analysis is under constant scrutiny in his therapeutic hours, whereas in the group, attention shifts from him from time to time, giving him freedom from such "oppressive" examination, a time to explore his own responses, time to evaluate what he thinks and feels, time to be "alone," to be creatively active in secondary rather than in primary process. Peers in the group help to free the patient from the projected parent in the analyst and the introjected parent in himself.

To achieve recovery, group members help the submerged patient to achieve freedom. The submerged is bound to unfreedom by his ambivalently compulsive pseudo-egos. He is limited by his lack of a freed ego, which would enable him to choose, to be selective. A liberated ego would help him to examine what he has been told, appraise it, and then create a new perception. He would have the autonomy, the strength, to go beyond the given and propose an independent view. In the analytic group, he is encouraged to free associate, to fantasize, to dream, to have regard for his own intuition, to be open to his thoughts, feelings, perceptions, and not to resist saying what is on his mind. He is supported in his right to have access to his suppressed self and to allow himself and the other members similar privilege. To this end he is encouraged to take the risk, despite his anxiety, to explore the unknown in himself and in the other patients, and to get ego-promoting confirmation in the process from group members.

The core of unfreedom in submergence is the persistence of ambivalence, a result of the incorporated pseudo-egos. This persistent transference with its characteristic ambivalence and unfreedom here again suggests a pathogenic origin. The submerged patient's responses to fellow members are less intense, because the others are less the controlling mother figure than is the analyst, due to his position in the vertical vector. Comparing each patient's differing perception of co-patients and the analyst offers a striking study in contrasts and allows all the participants the freedom to choose where and when to resolve any distortions. The regular meeting with the therapist, but more especially the alternate sessions (meeting in the absence of the therapist), support the right to be free of the projected parent in the group leader. The absence of the analyst gives all the members that distance from the suppressing parent invested in the leader that liberates them to question his authority as well as the imposing internalized authority of their own pseudo-egos. The group member is free to consider what the therapist offers, and yet take room discriminatively to dismiss it from his own perception or those of his fellow patients. This can be furthered by the use of the alternate meeting.

Alternate Sessions

Psychoanalysis in groups with and without the analyst helps the patient to work through his maternal transference as well as liberating his creative ego from his internalized, maternally derived pseudo-ego. However, the alternate session has some particular advantages for promoting ego autonomy, independence, and reciprocal interdependence based on reality. The presence of other patients at alternate sessions displaces control from the external and internal authority to the members and to the emerging self, so that each patient directs his own life and encourages every other to do the same in complementary, creative difference.

In promoting the alternate session, the therapist says to his patients in effect: "I trust and respect you. I have confidence you will not act out in my absence, but rather interact with each other reasonably within limits." The analyst's conviction that group members can, independently of him, exercise their creative, resourceful egos impels them to do so. His belief that he can rely on their mutual responsibility to one another supports their growing, creative autonomy. Every submerged patient has had some positive, nurturant experience with the primary, ego-promoting mother. It is the analyst's conviction that this treasure can be liberated by the therapist's regard for the patient's unused potential that helps the wholesome ego to blossom. Group members, supported by the analyst's stance, develop increasing regard for themselves and for each other.

THE PATHOGENIC POTENTIAL OF AN EMPHASIS ON GROUP-AS-A-WHOLE PROCESS IN GROUP PSYCHOTHERAPY

In every group there will be a patient or a therapist who will subtly or manifestly try to establish a tyrannical presence, and group members will follow and/or rebel against him, establishing a characteristic submerged presence in varying degrees of intensity in each member.

All recovery in psychotherapy is based on nonconformity. Each patient needs to win a victory over his submerged ego servitude. To begin with, the patient with a suppressed ego thinks little of himself; as a result, he feels he matters little to others. If he tries to be someone for everybody, he is nobody to anyone. Years ago, one of us had the following experience teaching a class at the Postgraduate Center for Mental Health. A dozen students or so pressured him regarding his teaching the importance of individual, differentiated needs in group therapy. The students insisted there was an important place for the understanding of group-as-a-whole therapy. Their exhortation was so imposing that the leader yielded (quite in opposition to his real conviction) to their coercion and admitted that perhaps they were right, to their great delight, and to the teacher's internal, private embarrassment at his falseness to himself. A group-as-a-whole emphasis would make robots of the individuals subject to it. The mechanical robot cannot rebel against and displace his living architect. Fortunately, living individuals can and do rebel against their programmers, unlike machines, which are incapable of hearsay and self-fulfillment (an example of this is occurring throughout Eastern Europe today). The patient subjected to an oppressive group process needs to be encouraged to opt for a life of shared responsibility and mutual respect in the group, an atmosphere in which each participant can express not only kinship, but also mutual concern and personal accountability. The devotee of group-as-a-whole treatment at some level knows that such an accommodation is not really helping him, for before long, the individual members begin to protest against their submission to the demands of this abuse of group process. They begin to protest against their unfreedom, the appropriation of their creative egos. As they do so, the emphasis on group-as-a-whole treatment gradually fades. Therapists who endorse this type of group process are promoting an inappropriate convention by means of a structure too distant from the growth-enhancing and genuine needs of individual patients. Locked in a closet by group-as-a-whole emphasis, the healthier members plead for release. The patients in a group will no longer be seen as individuals if they are parts of a group-as-a-whole. They are not encouraged to describe inner experience, dreams, or fantasies. They not only suppress themselves, they lose every significant other. They have become cogs in the machine of group process. They are handled in the group like persons living in a totalitarian country. Personal problems become intensified by a frustrating bureaucratic group-as-a-whole, which maximizes vulnerability and minimizes individuality and causation. To the degree we do not accept responsibility for the evolution of a creative ego in patients, we mistreat them.

In the current emphasis on group-as-a-whole treatment, there is a danger of contempt for the individual mind and, therefore, for individual freedom. To those who prefer a homogenized di-egophreno-genic (submerging) group, the individual patient in it is an eternal thorn in the side. His opposition, however, is a very precious human commodity. His uniqueness is a vital antidote to all would-be group tyranny. We need to hear his lonesome voice, not keep him as an outsider, in exile, or as a prisoner caged by group process.

Group-as-a-whole phenomena and group process certainly exist. Our concern for the present and future of analytic group psychotherapy is the extent to which such an emphasis distracts the participants from uncovering and working through individual psychopathology. In the prevailing climate of group-as-a-whole treatment, beleaguered rationality needs skilled analysts and sweet reason to resist the overwhelming autocratic pressure to stifle the creative ego of individual members. The tendency to believe in the magic of group process is a search for an easy way out of the hard work required to attend each member. Our will to believe, to belong, is unbounded, and dogmatic disciples are easily found even in multiple analytic societies, each of which has its own convictions and its own cult.

Some group psychotherapists are trying in an emphasis on the group-as-a-whole to reduce anxiety in therapist and patient alike, for by making every personal crisis part of a group process, we minimize each member's personal anxiety. In so doing, we maintain a malequilibrium or pseudo-equilibrium by denial, repression, suppression, and reaction formation, rather than by exploring the unconscious resistance to discovering the underlying cause of the anxiety.

Our roles are assigned to us by the nuclear family and later by society, by an employer, by a spouse, and by our incorporated parents. Group-as-a-whole treatment tends largely to repeat this process, keeping patients in pseudo-adulthood. Many parents try to get their children to follow in their footsteps for the survival of a business with too little regard for their children's potentials and preferences. It is as if, like a business, the group process survives but the child languishes, and individual identity, integrity, and authenticity suffer.

Among both therapists and patients, there are those who are profoundly anti-intellectual and others who worship reason. The devotee of one view or the other may try to impose an enforced conformity to his position. The result is to thrust upon the group a further drift toward a previously existing identity crisis, a pathogenic position. The individual ego is thereby further suppressed. The patient may seek security from criticism in the group by compulsively submitting and/or rebelling against the group-as-a-whole dynamic. In our view, it is not the group-as-a-whole position that has therapeutic value, but each individual's ideas, feeling, and perceptions. It is the promotion of the liberation of the ego of each member, previously in submerged thrall, that leads to healthier interaction in the group and more constructive social function.

Psychotherapy is not the art of letting a patient have your way or the group's way. Allegiance to the group-as-a-whole is usually determined by the most controlling or dominant member of a group, whether therapist or patient. The other patients, particularly the submerged personalities, simply surrender to the will of this prevailing person and suppress their own egos to the person in charge. He triumphs, and the others retreat, defeated but relieved. Though patients submit to the group process initiated by one authority or a homogenized group, and though they dislike the oppressive discipline, they are too timorous to be without it. If the imposing authority of the group-as-a-whole is not maintained, the patients break through the authoritarian restraint into a delightful but terrifying climate of freedom and anxiety. When they have attained the liberty they hoped for, they become frightened, because there are few, if any, controls or little leadership available to contain their aggression. So they again seek the restraining authority, whether in another patient, the group-as-a-whole, or the therapist. It is only when each member is repeatedly encouraged to function with the emerging resources of his suppressed ego, that his submerged compulsion dies. Then the catering to and rebelling against the actual or projected authority of the group fades away.

A manifestly harmonious group, whether in society or in group psychotherapy, may achieve this pseudo-harmony by pathogenic means. Each member may be in submission to the group-as-a-whole, covertly rebellious but apparently agreeable, finding it politic to be acceptable in order to belong. When a group is in psychotherapy, it is important for the therapist, first, to make himself the ally of each subdued ego in the group, second, to be aware of the group process, and third, to expose and analyze it. He may be attacked by group members who are fearful of having their accustomed ambivalent response and its associated secondary gratifications exposed. Others may join him in equally submissive attachment, as they were just before, to the group majority. Still others may join him in the more realistic search for personal ego growth. An awareness of this group process is especially useful when the group members scapegoat any individual patient. While what the members are concertedly doing may in fact be provoked by the scapegoat, the therapist needs to support the victim, analyze what is going on in the group members individually, and subsequently analyze what the victim is doing in his sadomasochism. In a well-functioning therapeutic group, the members may well do this work on their own. In fact, this is preferable.

As to our views on group-as-a-whole emphasis in treatment, Emily Dickinson (1924) put it better than ever we could when she wrote:

> Much Madness is Divinest Sense
> To a discerning eye—
> Much Sense—the starkest Madness—
> 'Tis the Majority
> In this, as All, prevail—
> Assent—and you are sane—
> Demur—you're straightway dangerous—
> And handled with a Chain—

The submerged personality needs to hear his own internal messages and, for the therapist (rather than a dogmatic and despotic other), to hear them empathically alongside him. He needs to heed his own imaginings and dreams, and we need to listen to him in attunement. It is only when his own ego is liberated that he can heed others and then freely choose the useful, creative, growth-promoting, realistic, and imaginative from what is offered to him, and reject what is stifling. The freeing of the suppressed ego is experienced by the submerged as a personal and liberating revolution. Whereas before, he was carrying his troubles as a compulsive, private burden, the defensive and useless core of parentally invested pseudo-egos, he can now operate with his genuine self.

One of the most exciting aspects of this approach to the treatment of submerged personalities is that it does not result in an "every man for himself" climate, but rather one in which, as each creative ego emerges with its characteristic self-regard, there develops mutual complementary support for every other's differentiated ego growth.

The submerged was imprisoned by his conformity and/or his compulsive rebelliousness. He is blind to his submission and/or sadism, to his humiliation and his tormenting of others, his helplessness and his abuse of power. It is only by the release of his own ego that candor, tenderness, plain-speaking, integrity, stability, the reality of mutual regard, generosity, autonomy, emancipation, and material and immaterial satisfaction can be retrieved.

Once the ego is liberated in the course of treatment, the patient can go on shaping his life on his own, continuing the refinement and self-development with no need to subvert himself, always refurbishing, refreshing, cultivating, and refining his ego, no longer uncertain or ashamed of revealing himself. He has a confident and very personal urge to experience himself in depth and both to welcome disagreement with himself as well as to resist compulsive imposition without succumbing in submission or rebellion.

Since much of the case material to follow in Part II of this volume focuses on treatment in individual psychotherapy, we will conclude this chapter by briefly describing a group one of us (Kutash) has been working with, composed solely of individuals with submerged personalities, including Mr. M. from Chapter 10.

The group was composed so as not to include overpowering mother, father, or sibling figures and only at a later date were less ambivalent potential transferential mothers or fathers added. At this point, members' egos were more secure from their previous experience with the leader as a "neutral parent." The patients gradually developed respect for their own participation and the regard of siblings who were not perceived as overpowering or parental favorites. Initially, all having submerged personalities, members could count on resistance to whatever they interpreted to others but it soon became apparent to them that all they needed to do was to switch sides to bring out the opposite point of view in their antagonist. They found a pro person for every con person, or vice versa, and again felt safe in the absence of scapegoating and in the evenly divided numbers the rebellious pseudo-egos created. This allowed many patients to get past their initial fear of being overpowered by a parent or the therapist and encouraged members to let their own submerged egos emerge safely. A milestone for this group came when one member, when offered a new job in another state, asked the group what to do. Each in his own way told him to trust himself, not to listen to parents, bosses, or even them, but to discover what he wanted to do. He did, moving forward on the road to recovery, and this encouraged the others. He heeded his own internal messages.

4

Identifying the Defensive Pseudo-ego Maneuvers in Therapy

Michael Lindenman, Ph.D.

To do just the opposite is also a form of imitation.
—Georg Lichtenburg

INTRODUCTION

Alexander Wolf (1957, 1980), later Kutash (1984b) and Wolf and Kutash (1984a, 1985) described and defined the condition of the submerged personality (di-egophrenia) and the related concepts of the authentic ego and the pseudo-ego. A close examination of these concepts as they are described by the authors reveals implications valuable for further understanding the dynamics involved in certain defense formations.

Wolf and Kutash suggest that, for certain individuals, defenses are organized into at least two identifiable formations: the submissive and the rebellious pseudo-egos. They say that these pseudo-ego defense formations serve conflicting purposes and leave the submerged person in a state of irreconcilable ambivalence. The concepts of the authentic ego and the pseudo-ego, when further elaborated by a study of their implications, become useful additions to current theories of defense formation.

Submergence

According to the concept of submergence, one pseudo-ego formation, the submissive pseudo-ego, protects against the loss of connection with the mothering object and against the loss of supplies that the object may provide. The submissive pseudo-ego develops at a conspicuous cost, however. The cost is free expression of the essential, creative part of the self: the authentic ego. The other pseudo-ego formation, the rebellious pseudo-ego, arises in protest against the demands of the mothering object and as a defense against the depletion, by the submissive pseudo-ego, of the authentic and creative part of the self. It is the authentic ego's defense against the threat of self-annihilation.

The condition of submergence includes the possibility that there can exist within the same personality more than one ego or one kind of ego. In their original use of the term, Wolf and Kutash imply that ego, whether "pseudo" or otherwise, can refer to various formations of organized psychic activities that, as is generally assumed for ego activities, employ conscious, preconscious, and unconscious operations.

The concept of pseudo-ego appears to refer to a phenomenon of ego distortion similar to that described by Winnicott (1965a) as the *false self*. Unlike Winnicott, however, who saw submissiveness as the distinctive feature of the false self, Wolf and Kutash emphasize the role of rage and rebellion, as well as submission, in the development of defensive inauthenticity.

As implied in the notion of submergence, ego formations are categorized as either authentic, proactive, and autonomous (i.e., the authentic ego), or as inauthentic, reactive, and defensive (i.e., the rebellious pseudo-ego and the submissive pseudo-ego). Beneath the two defense formations, the essence of the person is the authentic ego—a formation that may have to be relinquished to some degree, forced into repression, and contained by disavowal. The necessity and the means for uncovering and retrieving the repressed portions of the authentic ego will be central to the discussion in this chapter.

Equally important within the concept of submergence are developmental inferences that can be drawn from studying the pseudo-ego formations. These inferences reflect on both the intrapsychic and interpersonal conflicts that can impede the authentic ego's emergence and development. On the intrapsychic level, the concept illuminates the child's dilemma when his innate quest for autonomy and unencumbered self-expression is pitted against his early narcissistic needs and object-seeking motives. In the interpersonal field, the concept addresses the conflicts that develop when the intrapsychic, narcissistic needs of the child and those of the mothering object are disjunctive or at odds.

Purpose

This chapter will examine the concepts of the authentic ego and the pseudo-ego in an attempt to identify some previously unexplored implications. An effort will be made (1) to detail some of the dynamics inherent in the adaptive origins of each of the pseudo-egos, (2) to explore and to emphasize the narcissistic investment in the pseudo-egos, and, most vitally, (3) to emphasize the critical need to establish the presence of the authentic ego before the real work of analysis can go forward. What is expected to emerge from this examination is a clinical perspective on the relative strengths of the pseudo-egos and on the means for encouraging the authentic ego.

SUBMERGENCE: IMPLICATIONS
OF THE ORIGINAL CONCEPT

The Authentic Ego

There exists at birth a nascent authentic ego that has, out of its biological and developmental uniqueness, the potential for viewing the world from its own subjective and original perspective, and for synthesizing original and, by definition, creative conclusions about itself, the world, and itself in relation to the world.

The concept of submergence suggests that as this uniqueness and these potentials increasingly seek expression, which is manifested in limit-challenging actions as well as in the communication efforts of the child, the pathogenic mother experiences the child as growing intolerably unresponsive to her rules for proper conduct—rules that are, in part, derived from and fueled by her own unconscious narcissistic requirements. Consequently, she responds to the child's efforts by expressing disapproval and demanding compliance. In this process, the mothering object abandons her primary mothering role, characterized by attentive and empathic responsiveness, and replaces it with a secondary role. In this role she withdraws some, much, most, or all of her empathic interest, communicates disapproval, and demands compliance. It is this mothering action that sets the stage for and necessitates the child's self-protective reactions.

Origins of the Submissive Pseudo-ego

The child's response to the experience of maternal dissatisfaction and empathic withdrawal is three-fold. First, it reacts with open expressions of unambivalent rage toward the mothering object for her failure to comply with its narcissistic demands. Second, with the failure of this tactic to provide the required empathic response to its narcissistic demands, the child, aided by the mechanism of repression, shuts down its grandiose self-actualizing strivings along with its overt attempts at rageful protest. And third, to the degree that it has experienced an intolerable loss of narcissistic supplies from the mothering object, the child attempts to retrieve the lost supplies by making reparation. (See Winnicott's discussion of reparation [1963] for comparison.) The child enacts its attempt at reparation and at reestablishing connection with the attentive and empathic mother-that-was by assuming a submissive, accommodating, and self-denying stance vis-à-vis the perceived requirements of the mothering object.

This is a three-part strategy for defending against the loss of unconditional empathic attunement and positive mirroring—the child's early narcissistic requirements for the unrestricted emergence of the authentic, if grandiose, ego. The three elements: reactive rage, repression of the grandiose strivings of the authentic ego, and accommodation to external requirements, form the basis for an unconsciously organized mode of transaction. This mode of transaction, thoroughly reactive and defensive in its character, may be assumed whenever there is a perceived threat, in fact or fantasy, to the strivings of the authentic ego or to its demanded narcissistic supplies. With enough reinforcement over time, this will become the habitual mode of relating for some individuals, irrespective of circumstances.

Based on the original outline for the concept of submergence and elaborated by what can be learned from studying some of the implications inherent in the concept, this would appear to be the origin and the essential organization of one of the two major defense formations: the submissive pseudo-ego.

Origins of the Rebellious Pseudo-ego

At this point in the natural history of the submerged personality, the authentic ego has been driven into some degree of repression and frustration. It has been thwarted in its attempts to express clear signs of its unique and creative presence by its failure to find an atmosphere that is unconditionally accepting, affirming, and encouraging. To the degree that its presence has been experienced as unwelcome or intolerably conditional, the needs of the grandiose authentic ego (acknowledgment, affirmation, positive mirroring, and unconditional acceptance by the mothering object [Kohut 1984b]) remain unstated and unmet.

With the repressed and frustrated authentic ego having set into motion a self-denying defense formation (the submissive pseudo-ego), there arises a reactive effort to oppose the experience of maternal demand by attempting to deliver the message, "No! I don't want to have to abandon myself to be *your* way." This defiant reaction is a paradoxical attempt on the part of the authentic ego to defend itself against the mothering object, as well as against its own submissive impulses. It is, at bottom, the authentic ego's attempt to ward off the threat of complete self-denial and self-abandonment—an implicit potential of the submissive pseudo-ego formation. It is the authentic ego's attempt to prevent its own existential death.

This, in keeping with the original ideas of submergence, forms the basis for a second reactive and defensive formation: the rebellious pseudo-ego.

"Ambivalating"

Wolf and Kutash (1985) state:

> The ambivalence that is so central in the di-egophrenic is all consuming and compulsive in the seriously ill di-egophrenic. He alternates between neurosis and psychosis. Such a patient often had a narcissistic parent, more commonly the mother, whose distortions of reality were incorporated by the child. When the di-egophrenogenic parent is only mildly neurotic, the child is subject only to di-egophrenic maneuvers, and his ambivalence is between normal–neurotic and neurotic with no evidence of psychotic decompensation. [p. 523]

The degree to which "ambivalating" [*sic*] ultimately dominates the personality is related to the degree and persistence of the narcissistic demands of the mothering object and the resulting requirements for the child's reactive pseudo-ego formations. The requirements for, and presumably the continued reinforcement of, the two pseudo-egos leaves the child in recurring states of ambivalating—wishing to comply and required to rebel.

On the compliant side of ambivalating, there exists an unconscious certainty that the reappearance of the empathic mothering object is a prerequisite to the free emergence and continued development of the authentic ego. Accordingly, hope for the eventual emergence of the authentic ego is based on yielding to convincing pressure that the child is unacceptable as is, and that it can, through submission and accommodation, become more or better vis-à-vis the requirements of the mothering object. In other words, the child's hope for the survival and ultimate free expression of the authentic ego is predicated on the belief that reappearance of the primary mother is necessary and that it can be made possible through the bribery of self-denial and accommodation to external requirements.

On the rebellious side, the authentic ego's hope for survival and eventual emergence is based on (1) successfully warding off the mothering object's demand for change by reasserting (in a sublimated way) its initial rageful opposition, and (2) successfully warding off its own secondary impulse to submit and comply. After all, to the degree it gives in to its own impulse to comply and change, the authentic ego necessarily abandons the very thing it craves to have nurtured: itself.

Both the rebellious stance and the submissive stance contain the unconscious wish for the eventual reappearance of the primary mother. In rebelliousness, however, her reappearance will be accomplished by opposing her demands—an insistence that she cease and desist—and by expressing rageful cries (now sublimated into rebelliousness) to "Notice *me!*" Within this stance is the authentic ego's implicit hope that the mothering object can be convinced to return to her earlier attentive and empathic role.

To review, the submissive pseudo-ego keeps alive the unconscious hope that the primary empathic mother, with enough accommodation on the part of the child, can be bribed to reappear so the process of emergence and development of the authentic ego can go forward. The rebellious pseudo-ego, on the other hand, is predicated on the grim

belief that the secondary mothering object is contemptuous of the
authentic ego's narcissistic needs and that eventual authentic self-
expression is contingent upon being successfully oppositional to her.
Both pseudo-ego defenses will be activated, of course, by the mothering object's transferential counterparts.

Ironically, neither defense formation directly serves the developmental needs of the child's autonomous ego-in-waiting, except in
unconscious wish, hope, belief, and fantasy. In fact, both defense
formations, the submissive pseudo-ego and the rebellious pseudo-ego,
have the real effect of keeping the child inextricably involved with, and
intensely attentive to, the wishes of the mothering object. It should be
emphasized, however, that both defense formations have an unassail-
able motivation—seemingly an innate mission—that the authentic ego
should survive and be protected at all costs. Both pseudo-ego formations defend against the existential annihilation of the authentic ego
and keep alive the wish for its eventual emergence. With submission
and rebellion in operation, with trying to change and resisting the
pressure to change, according to Wolf and Kutash (1985), it is "the
ambivalence that is so central in the di-egophrenic" (p. 523).

THE TWO PSEUDO-EGOS: A CLINICAL PICTURE

Considering the formulation for submergence, characterological ambivalating should indicate the presence of the two antagonistic pseudo-egos,
and, by inference, the submerged formation. In many individuals, of
course, ambivalating is not so clearly present as the primary or characteristic mode of being. Yet there is little doubt that, in many of these same
individuals who are not so ambivalent in their presentations, there are
clear indications of repression of the one-of-a-kind autonomous ego—
that portion of the self that would dare to have original, independent
views and that would dare to voice autonomous and creative positions.

This failure to find clear signs of ambivalating, and by inference the
two pseudo-egos, appeared to point to a needed expansion in the

original conceptualization of submergence. The original concept did not provide an adequate developmental explanation for the individual whose authentic ego lies in repression, at least to some significant degree, but who does not show clear indications of the presence of *two* pseudo-egos. This led Kutash (1985), Kutash and Greenberg (1989) to describe the submerged ego disorders (see Chapter 2). Clinical observations suggest that, submergence ambivalating aside, the pseudo-ego defense formations may be more ubiquitous and sometimes less obvious than may appear at first glance.

With many individuals in whom the authentic ego lies, more or less, in a state of repression, the two pseudo-egos are not always equally developed or equally manifest. In such individuals, the personality is not dominated or characterized by ambivalence, but rather by a steadfastly compliant, accommodating, generally self-sacrificing pseudo-ego, the formation that first arises in response to the secondary mothering object (Kutash 1989). The alternate case, the personality dominated by hostile and rageful attitudes, will not be dealt with in detail in this chapter. It is possible, however, that those individuals will be found to have experienced empathic neglect beginning and persisting from a very early point in authentic ego development—so early that the authentic ego was developmentally unprepared to mobilize a submissive and accommodating response sufficient to satisfy the narcissistic requirements of the mothering object. In such cases, the authentic ego would be arrested in an extremely primitive state of development and would exist only in germinal forms. Such an individual would be defensively suspended in the earliest reactive stage of protest and, as has been suggested by Kernberg, Kohut, and others, would be capable, reactively speaking, of little more than rageful and splitting defenses.

When it is the compulsively compliant feature of the personality that is presented as the individual's public stance—what may loosely be referred to as masochistic—such individuals function publicly, including with the analyst in the initial stages of treatment, as if they do not have an adequate capacity for anger or aggressive self-protection and as if there is no rageful sadism lurking beneath the self-concealing masochism. The self-protective maneuvers of these individuals usually look like passivity and compliance, a compelling need to be "nice" or helpful to others, submission and accommodation to the perceived needs of others, an abnegation of healthy self-interests, extreme or thoughtless obedience to rules, or a sort of anything-to-pacify-the-gods stance. As an example:

> Ms. A. described herself as spending much of her life in near total subservience to the desires of her parents. She tried to fulfill all their wishes. She practiced piano as they wished, joined the clubs they recommended, chose the kind of friends she felt they would approve. This extended, even, to her avoiding rock and roll music, which her parents had judged to be subversive. She never, as she reported it, rebelled in any way so long as she lived at home. Not surprisingly, it was only when she was safely away at college, hidden behind the anonymity of voting-booth curtains, that she voted Democratic: her first self-acknowledged stand against her conservative arch-Republican parents.

The rebellious pseudo-ego in such an individual may seem completely nonexistent or, at best, bereft of aggressive capacity. Where it exists at all, it is often barely evolved and poorly organized. Along with its confrontational messages to the secondary mother of, "I don't want to have to be *your* way!" and, "Notice me and *my* needs!" the rebellious protest is kept in check and in hiding by attitudes of fearful caution and self-doubt. These self-limiting attitudes derive from feelings of shame for the imagined unacceptability of one's authentic ego yearnings, guilt for one's defiant impulses, and fear of potential retaliation and abandonment by the mothering object.

Certainly, associated feelings of helplessness, hatred, and rage hide beneath the submissive surface. They may even exist in extreme degree precisely because they have not previously found opportunities for acceptable and productive expression. Nevertheless, to the degree that the rebellious pseudo-ego has functioned at all, in these individuals it has operated covertly. It has been kept hidden from the feared retalia-tory or abandoning mothering object as though its protest were a dirty and dangerous secret. In the initial phases of the treatment this will be the same with the analyst as he or she is transferentially cast into the role of the secondary mothering object. As Kernberg (1979b) has phrased it:

> In obsessive characterological submissiveness, a chronically submissive self-image, relating to a powerful and protective parental image, may defend the patient against the repressed, violently rebellious self relating to a sadistic and castrating parental image. [p. 210]

Such individuals, therefore, unlike the purer submerged personality, do not readily show two pseudo-ego formations having equal strength, operating side by side, producing irresolute ambivalence. What such individuals do present are pseudo-ego formations that are stratified. The one seals over the presence of the other. The compliance and accommodation conceal the reactive opposition and rage. The mas-ochism masks the sadism. It is not the irresoluteness of ambivalence that characterizes such individuals, but the excessive self-denying accommodation to others.

THE AUTHENTIC EGO

In Repression

The authentic ego, then, is in a state of repression, more or less. The individual is protectively and predominantly operating out of the defensive submissive pseudo-ego. The authentic ego is not assertively revealed either in its frustrated protest or in its creative originality. The proactive capacities of the authentic ego to perceive, experience, integrate, or react authentically, as well as to remember, will have been impeded. Certain individuals in this state may, in fact, appear to have surprisingly poor memory. For example, they may not remember discussions or issues from session to session or they may appear to have forgotten significant moments from their own history. In many instances they may act as though they had not been on hand when momentous events occurred. And indeed, to the degree that the authentic ego has been buried in repression, they may not have been.

As a consequence, these individuals may act as though they do not know how to really *be* in life. They may express the wish to be "a fly on the wall" in the life of others; manifestly, to learn how others *do* life, but more profoundly, out of a yearning for attention to and validation of their own repressed authenticity.

There will be difficulties with assertiveness, confrontation, or the ability to express such feelings as anger or criticism. There will be difficulties with competitiveness, decision-making, or other activities requiring a degree of access to, and comfort with, healthy aggression. Identifying personal needs and wants or coming to clear understandings of their own emotional reactions may seem like totally alien enterprises to these individuals. For after all, in repressing the authentic ego and accommodating to the mothering object, these individuals have become quite accustomed to setting their own emotional reactions aside and dissociating from their own authentic needs.

Over a lifetime, the affectively capable authentic ego will have gotten little attention—its presence will not have been encouraged, its absence will not have been noticed. Throughout their lives, *these individuals will have been most consistently rewarded for what they know and for what they can do*; for thinking and acting, but not much for feeling. They will have learned to rely most on their ability to reach intellectual or active solutions to their life problems with little consideration given to emotional needs or subjective reactions. Out of a profound fear of loss of connection with the mothering object, much attentive energy will have been focused on the wishes and reactions of others and away from oneself. As one patient metaphorically put it,

I'm so tired. Sometimes I hear a whispering voice inside which wants me just to stop and rest awhile. But it scares me. I'm afraid if I do, I'll lose everything that I ever believed was important.

One result of this is that experiences of rewarding self-fulfillment may come only rarely, and then in the form of stolen moments. In the analytic work, it is essential that both the absence and the presence of the authentic ego be noticed. For in its significant absence, these individuals will make little or no long-term affective use of interpretation and demonstrate little or no capacity for lasting insight. In this state of affairs, experience-distant interpretations by the analyst may be compliantly accepted by the patient as yet another submissive pseudo-ego maneuver intended to satisfy the narcissistic requirements of the analyst in his transferential surrogacy.

In Protest

With the authentic ego repressed, developmentally stymied, and un-available for rich and authentic experience, these individuals will often report feeling cheated by life. In response to such feelings, there may be attempts at rebellious, if feeble, protest by the authentic ego. To the degree that there are such attempts, whenever and however they may be enacted, such individuals will be comforted by the thought that they are justifiably, if shamefully, challenging the tyrannical power of authority. In their external lives, they may act out their attempts at transferential protest and defiance with an infinite variety and degree of secret rebelliousness, often with an appearance of testing the limits. A few examples are procrastination, duplicity, and other passive forms of aggressiveness. Some may engage in such marginally antisocial behaviors as petty "white collar" thievery, income tax cheating, and the like. Some may involve themselves in secret love affairs, or possibly

"shameful" sex practices. Some may live as though they are forever
testing the limits of the law, even in such minor areas as accumulating
an unmanageable level of debt or driving cars at excessive speeds or
other dangerously aggressive ways. The forms of enactment of the
rebellious message are virtually limitless. One brief illustration:

> Mr. B., a middle-level executive with a degree of public recognition, felt
> stymied in his job. He complained that he could not present himself well
> enough to his superiors to gain the recognition and advancement his
> "unrecognized talent" deserved. He also revealed that he regularly shop-
> lifted small items, usually valued under five dollars. He was aware that
> getting caught could place his career in jeopardy. Nevertheless, he justified
> his obsession, one that had persisted since early adolescence, saying that
> the stores could charge whatever they wished and of course would over-
> charge. Stealing, he came to understand, became his only way of "fighting
> back" and "holding his ground against those in authority." He came to see
> that this attitude of "fighting back" applied to his experience with the first
> authorities of his life, his parents, an experience in which he keenly
> desired to fight back, but never did. He felt prevented from doing so with
> his parents by an overwhelming wish to comply with their standards and
> aspirations for him and, in that way, win their acceptance of him. In that
> situation, too, he felt unable to gain appreciation for his unrecognized
> talent.

Whatever the *form* of rebellious protest, as with Mr. B., it is always
indirect and usually poorly defined, enfeebled, and cloaked in secrecy.
And whatever the *degree* of rebellious protest, these individuals, like
Mr. B., will inevitably experience themselves as unfulfilled in life. The
blame for this lack of fulfillment will often projectively be placed onto
"stupid" or "unfair" others. More deeply, however, they will explain
their plight with an unconscious depressive belief that it is they
themselves who are flawed and inadequate and, as a result, incompetent and unacceptable. During the course of analysis, the individual
will come to understand that these instances of rebelliousness are the

hostile acting out of rageful feelings. He will learn further that these feelings are comprehensible reactions to the self-denying experience of compulsively accommodating to the needs of others; that this, in turn, derives from an archaic fear of not having the uniqueness of his authentic ego, even in its most naive grandiosity, adequately acknowledged, understood, and valued. (As a concept, *grandiosity*, like *narcissism* in the past, has taken on a pejorative tone for many who use it. A full discussion of clinical grandiosity would be useful and may produce conclusions in which grandiosity has to do with the expression of original and creative thoughts, ideas, and wishes that are as yet unfettered by real-world data—data normally generated by real-world testing.)

THE ANALYTIC WORK

In the analysis of an individual whose authentic ego lies in repression to a significant degree, and who presents the submissive pseudo-ego as the dominant defense formation, the analyst has a three-fold task. The first is to be aware of the exact nature of the transferential transaction that the patient is attempting to conduct with the analyst. The second is to identify the particular defensive maneuvers the patient utilizes to enact the transferential connection. And the third task, the ultimate task, is to encourage, to identify, and to welcome assertive expressions of the unique authentic ego, no matter how grandiose their proportions.

Transference

As a means of identifying the particular transferential transaction operating at the moment, the analyst can wonder if (1) the patient is attempting to bribe the analyst with submission and accommodation, (2) the patient is reactively being oppositional, duplicitous, or covert,

or, (3) the patient is attempting communication from the authentic ego
to the wished-for primary mothering object. Of course, awareness of
the transferential mode is greatly aided by attending to the countertransferential pulls toward or away from the patient. Still, it is of no
avail to offer transference explanations to the patient unless and until it
can be determined that the authentic ego is sufficiently emerged and
safely present in the analytic space so that its capacities for affective
learning can be engaged.

Wolf and Kutash (1984a) specifically recommend that there are to
be no "offers of understanding . . . until after the patient becomes
unambivalently hostile to the analyst as the surrogate for the di-
egophrenogenic [pathogenic] parent" (p. 525). It is their idea that
unless and until that has occurred, transferential ambivalence toward
the analyst will prevent the patient from utilizing insight. Their position is that the authentic ego will not dare show itself until after
sustained expressions of the repressed hostility have been well received. There is reason to believe, however, that, at least for the sort of
individuals described in this account, the authentic ego does attempt
to reveal itself and can, indeed, be enlisted into the work of understanding unconscious motives prior to a full-blown expression of
hostility toward the parent surrogate. More of this will be discussed
later.

Defense Analysis

The second of the analyst's tasks is to identify the specific defensive
pseudo-ego maneuvers as they occur outside, as well as inside, the
analytic space, to define them as such for the patient, and to explain
the self-protective and self-actualizing motives behind them.

The defensive pseudo-ego maneuvers occurring outside the analytic
space will be revealed by the patient as he discusses facts about his life
and life-style. In the process he will be describing behaviors about
which he may feel shame and embarrassment. Often, in revealing this

information, the patient will unknowingly be describing his best unconscious efforts to deal, submissively or rebelliously, but adaptively, with what he perceives to be an unempathic world. These adaptations will be the unconsciously organized efforts to do what seems necessary and possible to guarantee the survival of the unevolved authentic ego.

The shame and embarrassment often attached to these behaviors are a reflection of the patient's grim unconscious belief (Weiss and Sampson 1986) in the contemptuousness of the secondary mothering object for the needs and views of the authentic ego. The fear and trepidation with which these facts are revealed are a reflection of the patient's unconscious belief in the empathic abandonment he will experience as the secondary mother reacts to his best—at least until now—efforts. The patient assumes at the outset that the analyst, in the transferential role of unempathic mothering object, will judge the conduct of his (the patient's) life with the same contempt and disregard that typified his childhood experiences. The effects of shame and fear are illustrated in the following vignette.

Ms. C., an intelligent, mature woman in her late thirties, for more than a decade living in a large city hundreds of miles from her birthplace, spoke with a deep sense of self-rebuke for not having returned to her family home to attend the funeral of her father five years earlier. This behavior was especially incomprehensible to her since she had, over the course of several years of therapy, come to know her father as by far the favorite parent of her childhood years. In describing her attitudes about herself for what she called her "moral failure," she used such adjectives as "inappropriate," "selfish and uncaring," "ghastly." Although, in the past, she had spoken of others whom she had mourned deeply when those relationships could not continue for a variety of reasons, she saw her behavior surrounding her father's death and funeral as a clear sign that she "was incapable of having connections with others." Based on his assessment of her previously demonstrated capacity for deep involvement and mournful loss, the analyst's intervention at this point was to simply comment, "You know very well who to miss." After a considerable pause, Ms. C. reacted by confirming that that was, after all, probably true. She was then able to remember that, although her father had been a valued object in her early childhood, he had, in fact, ceased to show any active interest in her from her teen years onward. "Sadly, that was his limitation," she added. They had had little or no relationship for more than twenty years, by the time of his death. She concluded, "There was little to mourn by the time he died."

The analyst's comment, Ms. C. later reported, had made her feel trusted and not judged. It also made her feel that her behavior could make sense. She had felt sure that the analyst's judgment of her behavior would be harshly negative—the judgment she placed upon herself in defensive anticipation. This was exactly in line with the harshly judging, demanding, and untrusting way she had experienced her mother. Subsequently, it was possible to examine the self-judging stance she had initially assumed. The exploration centered on the submissive and self-denying nature of that and similar positions she would take and how, in assuming such positions, she was able to hold secure to an unconscious fantasy of eventually winning over her unempathic and intractable mother.

Reacting to revelations of "shameful" conduct by commenting on their adaptive, self-protective functions and, still further, by specifically acknowledging the resourcefulness involved in generating such maneuvers, the analyst can help the patient make the facts of his life intelligible and acceptable to him. By assuming a stance of nonjudgmental inquiry and explanation, and even by encouraging appreciation for the unconscious creativity involved in the adaptive pseudo-ego maneuvers, the analyst can eventually be experienced as different from the archaic secondary mother. Such experiences of the analyst's attunement prepare for the disconfirmation of the patient's grim unconscious beliefs related to the invariability of the unempathic other. This allows the patient to begin (1) relinquishing his fear of object-judgment and object-reprisal and (2) releasing the self-protective, but punishing, self-judgments that stand in the way of feelings of positive self-worth.

The following exchange illustrates how an empathically conducted defense analysis can be effectively augmented by asking to hear from the authentic ego and, by implication, indicating to the patient the fact of its absence. In this example, the analyst's invitation to hear from the authentic ego results in clear statements from the patient of authentic needs, wishes, and feelings.

Ms. D. described a recent visit to her mother's home: She was watching a "trashy" TV show, one that she enjoys. Witnessing this activity, her mother reacted by saying, "Do you have to watch *that*?" This left the patient in a state of unexpressed frustration. She wanted to watch the show, but believed she couldn't. She described spending the rest of the weekend visit being very deferential toward her mother but, underneath, being secretly angry. She could not speak any of her angry feelings to her mother. "I had no voice for it."

ANALYST: If you had been able to speak, what would your voice have said?
Ms. D.: I know I wanted to get a message across to my mom. Appreciate *me*! I only wanted her to appreciate that I just need to hang out.
ANALYST: Your secret wish was to watch a trashy show and hang out. What if you chose not to be silent, but to say your wishes?
Ms. D.: I'm afraid of letting her down. If I'm not in sync with her, I will lose her. I want to say, to hell with her! . . . but I'm afraid.
ANALYST: Afraid of what?
Ms. D.: I need her approval. I don't like saying that, but as long as I have her approval, things are in control.
ANALYST: You keep yourself closely tied to your mother.
Ms. D.: Yes. I picture her up there and me here (indicates low) . . . far away and yet . . . (her voice trails off and then, after a pause, she describes a fantasy). I would just love to go on the road with a band for a year and say to her, "So long!" I'd drop her a postcard saying, "Doing fine. Glad you're not here!"

In describing the show she enjoys as "trashy," Ms. D. presents a strong self-critical judgment of her own preference. This functions as an anticipatory defense against her grim certainty of finding the unempathic, critical other. And, as she expected, her mother's comment fails to find value in Ms. D.'s personal (authentic ego) preference, instead implying contempt for it. Ms. D. is left in a state of frustration. She wants to have her mother's appreciation, but gets her contempt instead. She would like to express her reactive rage and angry protest. But fearing the retaliatory abandonment of the mother-that-is (the secondary mothering object) ("If I'm not in sync with her, I will lose her"), she keeps it hidden. She assumes, instead, a defensive stance of deference (the submissive pseudo-ego) in the hope of negotiating for the return of the mother-that-was (the primary mothering object). It is when the analyst asks to hear directly from the authentic ego, "If you had been able to speak . . . etc.," that the patient learns that her authentic reactions can and should count for something. With her grim certainty of empathic absence weakened, the authentic ego's protest risks being heard, in Ms. D.'s fantasy of going on the road and, more directly, as described to the analyst: "I want to say, to hell with her!"

As the patient, with the help of the analyst, comes to make intelligible his unconscious self-protective and self-actualizing motives, three things occur: First, there is created an ambience of trust in the benign motives of the analyst. Second, as the patient develops confidence in the validity and the acceptability of his own reactions, he is able to risk bringing the now affirmed and welcomed protestations of the authentic ego (work previously carried on covertly and ineffectually) into the safety of the analytic space. It is clear that this is occurring when, in response to the inevitable experience of empathic failure (Atwood and Stolorow 1984), direct and unambivalent expressions of disappointment and hostility can be safely expressed toward the analyst. Third, and finally, as the analyst meets this reactive hostility with nondefensive equanimity, there is established a climate of trust in the resilience of the analytic relationship.

This necessary foundation of trust in the analyst and in the analytic relationship will develop after a period of testing by the patient of his grim belief. The patient will test his belief (really an unconscious certainty) that the analyst, in the transference and in fact, will replicate the early empathic failures of the secondary mothering object. Consistently experiencing the analyst in ways that disconfirm this belief allows the patient to shift gradually away from his defensive pseudo-ego maneuvering and to risk disclosure of heretofore repressed portions of the original ego. The significance of these disclosures can be measured by their potential for creating vulnerability to the dreaded empathic failure (Ornstein 1974).

Recognizing the Authentic Ego

During the process of denouement, of unraveling by analysis the pseudo-ego defensive maneuvers, something new (or, as in these cases, something previously hidden and callow) will begin to emerge. What will appear, of course, are aspects of the authentic ego previously buried in repression, now daring to find voice.

Interspersed among the defensive pseudo-ego maneuvers will be attempts to announce the presence of the authentic ego. The authentic ego's presence may appear only in the form of the faintest shadow, or it may be presented as a full-blown product of creative self-expression. In areas where the authentic ego has previously found room for some degree of expression and development, its creative efforts will take their most concrete and fully elaborated forms. The patient may make only the vaguest reference to them or may bring them directly into the analytic space to exhibit them for the transferential mothering object with an admixture of pride and trepidation, looking for the "admiring gleam," and dreading devastating indifference. Examples of concrete self-expressions are such creations as drawings, paintings, photographs, musical creations, and literature, including poems, diaries, stories, letters, essays, and to be sure, all manner of handcraft. As one analysand has put it, "all things which speak for me."

In areas where the authentic ego has lived largely in repression and where there has been little or no room for free expression, as with affects, for example, experience and development will have been limited. This will have resulted in great difficulties with unabashed, assertive expressions of authentic inner experiences and reactions such as feelings, wishes, fantasies, dreams, associations, elaborations, beliefs, opinions, and original ideas. Attitudes of self-doubt, buttressed by shame, guilt, and fear will have kept authentic self-expression in check. Sometimes the signs of authentic self-expression will appear as less, even, than a shadow. Sometimes, as in the vignette below, authenticity is only foreshadowed as a *wish* for self-expression and, as here, in disguised form.

Ms. A., whom we previously learned could express her defiance only by secretly voting Democratic, had great difficulty giving free voice to her authentic opinions or reactions, much less feelings. Nevertheless, she wondered aloud, one day, about her analyst's geographic origins. Encouraged by the analyst to offer her own speculations about it, Ms. A. was thrown into a protracted inner struggle and outer silence on the matter. Finally, in a later session, she blurted out, "Connecticut!" When asked what her thoughts were about someone who would come from Connecticut she was able to say only, "Learned . . . without affectations." She was visibly disturbed, however, apparently panic-stricken during and immediately after her brief foray into self-expression.

ANALYST: You seem to be having some reaction as you tell me that.
Ms. A.: (With hesitation.) This makes me feel silly.
ANALYST: Silly?
Ms. A.: Telling you what I think. I feel so exposed—like naked on a stage.
ANALYST: And that made you feel silly.
Ms. A.: Nervous and scared. Silly, too. It's because it's about you. If it were about me then you wouldn't know if I'm right or wrong. But since it's

about you, when you hear my opinion you'll know the right answer and laugh at me.

ANALYST: And then?

Ms. A.: I won't be accepted here anymore.

Exposure of inner authenticity, even if, as in this case, it involves only the exposure of some innocuous stereotyped associations, can be fraught with fantasies of great danger. Here, Ms. A. operates as though she has a grim certainty that to voice her own ideas is to risk devastating disparagement and humiliating dismissal from the transferential mothering object. Nevertheless, and although this was not specifically addressed by the analyst, it can be assumed that her very speculations about the analyst's origins constituted a disguised wish to be able to say some of her own authentic thoughts, a kind of door to the outside that the patient unconsciously constructed for herself and through which she would inevitably have to step. This is entirely in keeping with the view of the authentic ego as tenacious in its struggle for survival and as resourceful and opportunistic in its wish for self-expression.

In addition to the work of providing coherent and clarifying explanations of the pseudo-ego maneuvers, the analyst must be attentive to the faintest glimmerings and the most shining examples of the authentic ego in operation. Whichever the case, each expression of the unique authentic ego calls out to be acknowledged and specifically identified for what it is: authentic and original, therefore valid and valuable.

The two tasks of identifying the defensive pseudo-ego maneuvers and inviting the authentic ego to emerge and express itself are parallel efforts to be conducted in tandem, each augmenting the other. The more safely present the authentic ego, the greater the capacity for dreams, fantasies, associations, insights, and affective remembering.

As the analyst is experienced as welcoming all the patient's authentic expressions with interest and respect, the patient's grim unconscious certainty of an uninterested mothering object begins to be disconfirmed. The process of disconfirmation allows the patient to relinquish some of his defensive pseudo-ego posturing and to retrieve some amount of psychic involvement previously committed to archaic protective maneuvering. As a result, the potentials of the authentic ego, previously buried in repression, are permitted to surface. These unique and creative potentials can then be better employed for such activities as perceiving, experiencing, processing, integrating, remembering, associating, dreaming, wishing, creating, thinking, and learning—all the mental activities necessary to the freer expression, analysis, experimentation, and growth of the self.

II

TREATMENT OF THE SUBMERGED PERSONALITY

5

A Homosexual Patient

Irwin L. Kutash, Ph.D.,
and Alexander Wolf, M.D.

Nothing has a stronger influence psychologically on their environment and especially on their children, than the unlived life of the parents.
—C. G. Jung

Hate is often used to describe manifestations of the aggressive drive. It should be distinguished from rage, however. Rage can best describe a primitive reaction that occurs before the formation of stable object representations, and hate describes a type of object-directed representation of aggression.

The submerged personality is the epitome when it comes to this distinction. The submerged received good nurturant mothering up until about the age of two and therefore has little need for rage, but he has a strong component of hate when the nurturant "primary mother" becomes the "secondary mother" as he or she reaches an age when he/she is ready to strive for individuation.

He operates with a pseudo-ego on the surface and a submerged and arrested true ego. The real ego develops hate, hate over the oppression of the introjected pseudo-ego. As a response to protect the submerged ego and to combat the introjected pseudo-ego, a second pseudo-ego forms, which is in opposition to the first. He now has two pseudo-egos and his predominant symptom is ambivalence. He is ambivalent about every superimposed parental belief. He ambivalates between compliance and rebellion, between being good and bad, between saying yes and no. He can be heterosexual and homosexual. He is ego-submerged. Because the pathogenic mother can be persecutory after the emergence of the child's ego, the most serious damage is done at about age two and thereafter.

The following case will illustrate how the working through of the hatred for mother in a female homosexual submerged personality led to the emerging of her submerged ego and a heterosexual resolution. This patient was seen by one of us (Kutash) from 1972 to 1976, and her case was presented at the Postgraduate Center for Mental Health, but never previously published. It was frequently discussed during that period and subsequently by the two authors.

IDENTIFICATION OF CASE

The patient, Ms. P., entered therapy in September 1972. She was 32 years old when she began treatment. She was single and a buyer for a large department store chain with several branches in New York. Her salary had gone from $27,000 to $40,000 annually as she was promoted to a chief buyer position in the central office of the company. She had two years of college education, having dropped out of college in her junior year.

Ms. P. was a very attractive, well-groomed blonde, who was always immaculately dressed in the most fashionably tailored businesswoman's attire. She wore her hair drawn back in a bun, man-tailored shirts, and blazers or suits. She always appeared poised, with very straight posture, and rarely smiled. She was articulate, highly intelligent, and showed intellectual awareness. She was always very serious and businesslike about therapy and arrived for sessions precisely on time. She almost seemed to have prepared for the sessions, perhaps to comply with her expectation of the therapist's wishes in an initial mother transference to the therapist with her parental pseudo-ego. Initially, she proceeded in a monologue, seemingly overlooking the presence of another human being in the room, perhaps with her rebellious pseudo-ego in action.

Ms. P. began therapy on a once-a-week basis. She increased to two weekly sessions in October 1973, and from February 1974 through June 1976 was seen three times a week. She left treatment in June 1976 to accept a promotion, moving to another city where she transferred to a leading therapist.

Ms. P. entered therapy initially under the following circumstances. For the six years prior to therapy, she had lived with another woman in a homosexual relationship. She was dissatisfied for several years with her lover but could never quite break up. When she finally did break up and found that she had established a similar relationship with another woman, she felt her interpersonal life was "a mess" and sought therapy. She was the compliant partner to mother surrogates, and, while hating the subjugation, needed it too much to feel safe to express her hatred and anger. During all this time, she had advanced steadily as an executive in business. While this circumstance precipitated her seeking treatment, she entered therapy with some more general aims and goals in mind. She recognized her inability to feel and express her feelings in personal relationships, particularly anger. She consistently believed that she would not be able to hold up her end of any prolonged relationship. She felt this was related to her homosexual life-style, which she described having "fallen into as the path of least resistance." With women she felt more capable of maintaining her end of the relationship, but felt her affairs were simply a second-rate imitation of heterosexual married life. She hoped that with the ability to experience her feelings would come the strength to establish the kind of personal life she wanted.

The Patient's Central Problem

Ms. P.'s central problem was her inability to experience her feelings, particularly her hatred and anger. To do so would mean feeling the pain of not having the type of relationships she wanted, the conscious guilt over having homosexual relationships, the unconscious guilt of wanting heterosexual relationships, the deep hatred toward her mother, and ambivalent feelings toward her father, including erotic feelings generalized to women and men. Not to experience her feelings, however, had left her in a malaise, stalemated in a nonfeeling state as her anxiety rose over life passing her by.

Her homosexuality was a significantly burdensome and conscious source of anxiety and symbolized to her her inability to have a satisfactory personal life. She could not admit to herself any enjoyment in it, but clung to it, as it did satisfy many unconscious needs and was more fulfilling than no relationship at all. Her unconscious compromise of living homosexually while acting the feminine role in her relationships in an imitation of heterosexual life was no longer allaying guilt and anxiety, as she was passing childbearing age. Her unconscious fears of a retaliating mother or mother figure, and of becoming domineering in a relationship with a man as her mother had, were being outbalanced by a feeling of urgency in coming to terms with all these conflicts while choices still lay before her in life.

History of Current Problems

Upon reaching adolescence, Ms. P. became a threat to both parents. This beautiful girl aroused intense unconscious jealousy in a lame, ugly mother who had an attractive sister whom the patient closely resembled. She also brought out erotic feelings in her father, who, up to then, had been very close to her. The repressed feelings drove him from her. Ms. P. began to develop a "tomboy" life-style. She avoided relationships with boys, only going out on occasions when it would have been conspicuous not to, and devoted her efforts to scholastic achievement and sports. She played ball with her younger brother and would play golf and ride horseback with her father, something her lame mother could not do. Her mother encouraged her to buy very masculine clothing and found any boyfriend to be inferior; in general, both parents were most comfortable with her boyish style.

Ms. P. chose a college far from her Midwest home, and there, while geographically far away (rebellion), still followed the unconscious wishes of the family (compliance). She felt she could not satisfy men, accepted dates with men who were backward in some way, and then rejected them while developing a passionate relationship with an older female student in her dormitory. When this woman graduated from college, Ms. P. moved to New York with her, leaving college. Ms. P. left this woman to become involved with what she described as a weak man, to whom she became engaged.

When she introduced him to her family and announced her engagement, the parents found fault with him and finally, in some argument over which church to marry in, they split Ms. P. from him. Ms. P. went back to a relationship with a domineering woman and vacillated between domineering women and weak men, including a second engagement that was sabotaged by her mother. This went on until the six-year-long relationship with the woman she broke up with just prior to therapy. The anxiety already mentioned, which propelled her into therapy, came about after their breakup, when Ms. P. found another such relationship developing.

Family History

The patient was raised in a small midwestern town by very socially conscious, alcoholic parents. The patient's mother was the daughter of one of the town's leading families, who owned an estate and were considered socially prominent, going back many generations. The family was very wealthy by the standards of the community. The patient's father, while also from a long-time local family, was the son of people of far less prominence in the community and of moderate means. Both parents were college graduates. There was one brother, twelve years younger than the patient. When Ms. P. began treatment, he was a college student, doted on by the mother and ignored by the father. The brother was described as immature, self-centered, and lazy, who, despite his parents' present poor financial state, did nothing to support himself. Ms. P., however, helped support him, sending him money that she pretended came from her father. She in some ways took the father's role in teaching her brother to play ball, as the father had little time for him. While Ms. P. often derided him, she described a real attachment to him when he was young and she would have liked to be close with him again.

Ever since Ms. P.'s childhood, each of her parents alternately went on alcoholic binges while the other protected their front in the community. However, the father was recognized by all as an alcoholic, while the mother's secret remained intact much longer. The parents needed each other, yet fought constantly in an interlocking symbiotic, hostile, co-dependent relationship.

The mother was the stronger controlling partner, and the father was weak and retreating. The mother ran the family and controlled the others down to the smallest detail, as in selecting all the patient's clothing, ruling on her friendships, and making decisions for her. The father inherited his father-in-law's business and mismanaged it until he lost the property and held a nominal (no-voice) executive position in the new owner's estate. He never heard the end of it from the mother. He retreated from the mother's onslaughts, using alcohol as an outlet, and relegated the patient's upbringing to his wife. Father and daughter were close in her prepubescence. The patient's younger brother, on the other hand, was strictly the "mother's son" and under her wing, having little contact with his father.

Patient's Life History

Ms. P. was born shortly after the death of her mother's father and was a keen disappointment to the mother who wanted a son to name after her father. She had planned to name the son after her father, rather than "junior" after the husband. Ms. P.'s mother always bragged about how early Ms. P. did things, such as becoming toilet trained, talking, and walking. But as the patient described this in therapy, she reached an insight when she realized that her mother never said, "Ms. P. was toilet trained early," but "I toilet trained her very early," or "I taught her to talk and eat with a spoon." Ms. P. was apparently a showpiece for the mother to establish to the community what "a model mother" she was. Ms. P. remembers from a very early age always being dressed and groomed perfectly, "like a little doll," until her "tomboy" adolescence was necessitated by the family dynamics. An early memory involves her being entered in a department store fashion show and crying not to have to do it because she was scared, but her mother insisted. She says she remembers hearing, "I'll not abide such nonsense," in similar situations later on. Kissing and hugging were not in her mother's nature. Praise came when she was pushed to some new success that satisfied her mother's goals for her. Ms. P. was always terrified to defy her mother, was a "good girl," did what she was told, but never felt close or loving toward the mother. A kindly grandmother provided her only warm experiences with a mothering figure in childhood after her mother became the domineering secondary mother whenever she tried to assert herself.

The patient had two distinct types of early memories of her father. She remembers him as being warm and affectionate toward her, and she remembers her mother's constant tearing down of her father as weak and maladaptive. In this light, she has early memories of sitting on her father's lap when he came home from work and telling him all about the day, and at the same time of her parents fighting late at night, the father sometimes drunk and always derided about money or the business. Ms. P. felt close to her father in a warm relationship until she was 13.

Ms. P.'s earliest memory is significant and crystallizes this early period. This screen memory seems to represent a pattern in her life. Ms. P. was playing in the kitchen and spilled honey on her dress while climbing up on a chair. She was wearing a new pink dress and waiting for her father to come home from work. Her mother must have been upstairs, she related. She went out the back kitchen door alone, something she was not allowed to do, to hide, although no one had heard the honey jar drop. When her father came up the back walk, he thought she was greeting him and picked her up and carried her in. Suddenly, the mother was on the scene, aware of the mess on the kitchen floor. She proceeded to berate the father for "hugging such a dirty little girl," and the parents began to argue over other traditional matters concerning the father's inability to handle problems at work and at home.

Ms. P. grew up in this small town as the parents gradually lost their money and prestige, and it became known that the father drank. Ms. P. was increasingly pressured to maintain a family facade of still being well-to-do, and to dress in an exemplary fashion. When she was 12, a change took place when to everyone's surprise, her mother became pregnant and had her long-desired boy. Her mother doted on the little baby boy, giving Ms. P. a little more "breathing room" as Ms. P. described it. This also meant, however, that she lost whatever attention her mother gave her. It was "John, John, John" from then on. Her mother continued to be ultra-critical of her, however. Her closer relationship with her father remained until around the age of 13.

When the patient reached puberty, the mother became threatened by Ms. P.'s closeness to her father and told him not to kiss or hug her. The father, also threatened, withdrew emotionally from her because of his wife, but also because he was probably controlling his own repressed eroticized feelings toward her in these years. Ms. P., from 13 to 18, in an unconscious effort to recapture her relationship with her father and also to neutralize her mother's feelings, was a tomboy. The mother covertly encouraged this, for instance, buying her masculine clothes, and the father encouraged it too, if only by the failure to object to this and by continuing to be involved with her in athletics. At the same time, her brother was getting warmth from the mother, something she had never gotten as a girl child, fostering her tomboy solution.

During adolescence, Ms. P. only recognized positive feelings for her brother and in some ways, played a fatherly role with him. Her jealous or angry feelings were suppressed, and she never openly competed with him for the mother's affection. She did compete in school as she did later in business, perhaps to achieve the business success her mother so admired in her own father and wanted in her son. In this regard, Ms. P. recalls most male students as being "two steps behind her." She did not openly feel, however, that she was competing with women, not seeing her female classmates as sharing her interest in academic success.

Sexually, she avoided relationships with either sex, and only after over two years in therapy did memories of sexual fantasies in that time return to her, including sexual fantasies about her father. Despite her lack of social life, her mother still consistently grilled her on sexual morality and warned her to distrust men's intentions.

At 18, Ms. P. went away to a distant Southern university as far as she could get from home. She left college two years later to follow a female lover to New York. She had had a series of transient relationships, either with women whom she allowed to control her, or with weak men whom she would quickly discard. In two somewhat better relationships with men, she was prevented from reaching genital primacy by her mother's interfering in possible marriages. For the six years prior to therapy, she lived with another woman, was dissatisfied for several years with the relationship, but could never quite break up. When she finally did break up and found she was establishing a similar relationship with another woman, she felt her interpersonal life was "a mess" and she sought therapy. During all this time, she remained with the same company and advanced to an executive position.

While far from home in New York, she communicated with her parents by telephone several times weekly and visited home on holidays. Her parents rarely visited New York except for some business trips by her father. Her relationship with her family when she entered therapy was superficially friendly. The patient was unaware of her anger toward her mother or ambivalent feelings toward her father and would always say, "My folks are okay but. . . ." She did blame them for discouraging her relationships with men who were never considered good enough for her. Her parents and brother were unaware of her homosexuality and of her being in therapy, and would have been overtly critical of both.

Along with her success in a demanding job, she had established superficial friendships at work. She had kept these friends and her "gay friends" completely separated, but as a consequence had a very compartmentalized existence prior to treatment.

Evaluation of Patient's Personality Development

Ms. P.'s personality development was seen largely due to the following environmental influences:

1. A domineering, demanding, unaffectionate mother, who (a) wanted a boy to replace her symbiotic relationship with her father, (b) rewarded Ms. P. only for performance and success in doing things the mother's way, (c) rejected femininity in her daughter, and (d) derided the father as weak and inept.
2. A weak but affectionate father who (a) could only be affectionate to a prepubescent female, (b) created in her mind the image of men as possibly affectionate but weak and backward, and (c) was more comfortable after pubescence with a masculinized daughter who helped him repress his erotic feelings, which his wife could not satisfy.
3. Ms. P.'s brother was born just as she reached pubescence, and she was further separated from her mother and father.

4. She had to help maintain a declining family facade in the community, so image was more important than substance, and she must not show how she felt inside. She had further to submerge her ego to comply with what she perceived as the community's expectation.
5. Her success in school and later in business were allowed by her mother, who felt she was following mother's wishes: Mother could thus enjoy these as a vicarious extension of herself. The mother surreptitiously enjoyed her rise and her competition with men.

Psychodynamics

The patient's developmental history and resultant pathology are best understood in terms of a submerged personality diagnosis. The patient submerged her own ego to protect herself and has introjected a parent as a pseudo-ego, which she alternately complied with and rebelled against. The pathology is centered less on drive and instinctual concerns, and more on relational difficulties. Her conflict is centered on loss of self versus loss of object. Her strides for autonomy were met with disapproval and rejection. She projects on present figures the original "secondary" mother whom she hated, yet felt a need for. She protected the "primary" accepting mother from the "secondary" rejecting mother through defensive compliance, at a cost to herself. Her rebelling behaviors were not only an indication of the underlying hatred created in the loss of self because of complying, but they created a greater loss, as ambivalating between complying and rebelling left her little energy for expression of herself. This loss was not only apparent in the patient's affect but in a lack of flexibility or ability to use internal resources.

Ms. P.'s life-style and transient relationships were conceptualized in the following manner. The patient had not been able successfully to resolve her oedipal relationship and identify with either parent. To be a woman would mean competing with mother and suffering retaliation for success with men, and also fear of incest. Becoming a lesbian, while affording her the opportunity not to compete with her mother, left her controlled by mother. Being successful in business at least allowed her to identify with the mother's idealized image of her own father, while she could be the boy her mother wanted (and finally got in her brother). To form a relationship with a partner of either sex could only mean loss of autonomy. She alternated between strong women and weak men. She alternated between being controlled by women she hated, who represented submission to mother, and her incestuous object relationships to weak, ineffectual men, neither being satisfying. She would desist most rapidly from her grasps at father surrogates, while being involved longer in passivity with mother figures, where she seemed more secure. Such involvements allowed her to gratify her dependency needs. Being close to women might allow her to get what she didn't get from mother. With women, she could at least satisfy needs by submitting to them while, in exchange, fantasizing being loved by a man.

Ernest Jones, in 1925, while analyzing five homosexual women, came to some conclusions that seem applicable in this case as well. He found homosexual women to be unconsciously extremely ambivalent toward parents of both sexes. These women first had an unusually strong mother fixation in the oral stage, followed by a strong father fixation. Jones felt that to them, castration anxiety is only a part of what he called "aphanisis," the threat of total extinction, particularly of sexual capacity and enjoyment; to this we would add fear of extinction of the ego, which is therefore submerged. Jones's women felt a tremendous unconscious deprivation, since they couldn't share the father's penis in coitus or obtain a baby, due to the dreaded aphanisis. This left them with two choices, or two ways in which the libido could flow for self-expression. Either they must give up their erotic attachment to their fathers, or sacrifice their femininity. Either they must give up the object for another, or give up their desire for it. They must give up either their father and ultimately men, or their vaginas and femininity in an identification with father. Jones found three possible resolutions:

(1) women who identify with men, who convert their interest in father and men into a drive to be accepted as a man; (2) women whose sexual interest turns to women, enjoying femininity vicariously; and (3) women who obtain gratification of feminine desires through a female, utilizing a penis substitute, for example, finger or tongue. Jones concluded that this third type clinically appears completely homosexual but is nearest to heterosexual. The patient under discussion had clearly partially identified with father in her career, and for the most part, in her sexual relationships, resorted to the third solution Jones described.

Some of Bergler's conclusions regarding homosexuality (Bergler 1944, 1949b) also shed some light on this case. Bergler considered female homosexuality to be due to an unresolved masochistic attachment to the preoedipal mother. Although more detailed, this corresponds to Jones's claim of a strong mother fixation in the oral stage. He found the origin of homosexuality to lie with an unresolved oral masochistic conflict with the mother in the preoedipal child. He concluded that it was not libidinous but of an aggressive nature. Female homosexuals have a savage hatred for the mother, which is defended against by the libidinous, "I don't hate her, I love her sexually." This unconscious defense, Jones felt, is then shifted to other women. He described the following sequence: (1) the potential homosexual female is raised by an aggressive, domineering mother and a weak father; (2) the girl hates the mother but cannot free herself from the preoedipal ambivalent attitude toward her; (3) the oedipal complex never is full blown; and (4) masochistic tendencies predominate under an aggressive facade. Jones concludes that a woman who has to deal with an overwhelming, compensatory hatred of mother, covering a deep masochistic attachment, may choose homosexuality. This may explain a good deal of the picture with Ms. P.

Finally, Deutsch (1932) adds an element when she concluded, "All women have a primary homosexual attachment which may later be revived if normal heterosexuality is blocked." At pubescence, heterosexuality was certainly blocked in the case of this patient. The regression theory, as opposed to Bergler's feeling that the girl never freed herself from the preoedipal attachment, fits Ms. P. Furthermore, it is postulated that some homosexuals get close to women to obtain what they didn't get from their mothers, and remain angry when they find they are not getting the nurturance again. This, along with the masochistic attachment Bergler (1944) describes, more fully explains Ms. P.'s case.

To integrate the theories discussed above as they relate to the patient she, as Jones described, submits to women who serve as male substitutes to avoid "aphanisis" or destruction of her ego. Additionally, as Bergler describes, she has a strong hatred toward the mother she fears and a masochistic attachment to her. Ms. P. also was blocked in her feelings toward her father and men, and may have regressed to her preoedipal masochistic attachment to her mother with an accompanying unconscious claim, "Since I can't have men, I deserve from other women what I missed in the way of affection." This can lead to an unsuccessful search with accompanying anger. Ms. P.'s case is indeed multidetermined and demonstrates how theories focusing on only certain stages cannot alone explain many cases.

In her case, having a domineering mother and weak father led to a submerged ego and an incorporated parental pseudo-ego with a preoedipal masochistic attachment to mother, an only partially resolved oedipal solution, which fell apart at puberty, and regression occurred to a homosexual conclusion. Her lack of experiencing feelings in relationships was her pre-therapy solution to avoid overwhelming hatred with accompanying anxiety and guilt.

TREATMENT

See Chapter 3 for a general overview of treatment. The goal of treatment with Ms. P. was the freeing of the patient from the tyranny of the introjected parental ego as a pseudo-ego. In Ms. P.'s therapy, the attempt was made to achieve synthesis of various conflicting ambivalent attitudes, and to accent the submerged ego and to de-emphasize the pseudo-ego; to build the original ego and diminish the importance of the parental ego by allowing the repressed ego to emerge. The therapist encouraged the patient's repressed ego to new assertion. The therapist did not start by attacking the pseudo-ego, because the patient's security system depended too much on this incorporation. The therapist supported the submerged ego first, not setting about depriving the patient of her present adaptation until she had a more secure new one. The therapist was not initially concerned with interpreting the patient's hostility and hatred. It was important in the beginning to free the patient's own thoughts, feelings, perceptions, cognitions, functioning, and activity. This was achieved by helping the patient realize she was in a safe, neutral environment with someone empathic to her submerged true ego. This process strengthened her own ego enough to enable her to be angry with the parent. In the beginning, no insights were proffered other than how she had to spend so much time and energy complying and rebelling and never had time to know her own wishes and asking her if she would now like to discover them.

Another key ingredient in regard to the treatment of the submerged applied to Ms. P. was the expectation of ambivalent transferences including hatreds, until her own ego emerged. Then she was able to form idealized transferences to the therapist.

Plan of Therapy

In light of the above, Ms. P.'s therapist initially maintained an unobtrusive, noncontrolling stance in order to avoid too much closeness for her submerged ego defenses to handle. Initially, the sessions were almost monologues, with the patient acting as if the therapist were barely present. This wiping out of the other was her way of acting out her suppressed hatred and anger in a mother transference. She was afraid if she got too close, she might be murdered by her mother or murder her in the person of the therapist. She needed to feel understood and empathized with by a neutral noncontrolling other before she could become further therapeutically involved and an initial negative transference broken. She also had to feel that the therapeutic relationship was devoid of sexual threat.

When the initial anxiety and defensiveness were lowered, the therapist was able to encourage her to make connections between her present life and the past and to bring in and analyze dream material. Transferential relationships then began to develop. It was at this point that intellectual insights began to give way to emotional insight.

The therapy then involved a mother transference in which the patient attempted to work through a struggle and hatred of her mother, and at the same time, a transferential struggle with the therapist. Therapy involved effectively analyzing this struggle and the transference. This meant helping the patient reach a greater understanding of her anger, masochism, and need for homosexuality.

Later therapeutic planning came when the mother transference gave way to a more oedipal transference to the therapist. Here Ms. P. was helped to see her freedom to move to an oedipal resolution and to continue to see the limitations, yet the magnetism for her, in her old life-style. An idealized father transference had to be analyzed to allow her to realize that strong men exist and she could interact with one without diminishing him. This was not restricted in fantasy with the therapist and was supported in reality with other strong men.

Course of Therapy

The therapy can be viewed in three phases, with much overlap. The patient was initially cold and aloof, an initial transference to a fear of the hated controlling mother, and the sessions were almost monologues in which the patient came to some intellectual but not emotional insights. The patient attempted to work through a struggle with her mother, and at the same time, the transferential struggle with the therapist, which was effectively analyzed. Last, she had a more oedipal transference to the therapist as an idealized father figure, and began to date strong men.

Early Phase of Therapy

The patient was initially cold and aloof toward everybody, including the therapist who deliberately maintained an unobtrusive noncontrolling stance in order to avoid too much closeness for her submerged defenses to handle. Initially, the sessions were almost monologues with the patient acting as though the therapist was barely present. Having a steady, predictable person listen to her without controlling her or being bullied by her served to bring her out. Often the main intervention would be to assure her, after she described doing something her pathogenic mother might do, that she was not identical to her. However, she would always deny anger for her mother. As the months progressed, the patient began to interact more, and this was paralleled by reported greater affect out of therapy.

The patient spent this time describing in detail her childhood, except when in crisis, usually precipitated by a drunken phone call from her mother, needing money and criticizing her. Ms. P. would send the money, not talk back, and would often have a dream in which a plane would crash while she watched but experienced no emotion. The patient was eventually able to understand that the crashing plane represented her hatred for her mother. She was crashing her mother and her maternal introject.

As we explored her history, she came to these insights. When Ms. P. was a child, her mother never empathized with her feelings but did what pleased herself. Her mother resented her being pretty while she herself was homely. This brought forth in the mother feelings first aroused by the mother's attractive sister. The mother, from the time the patient menstruated, tried to keep her and the father from being close and, in fact, rejected all her boyfriends. The father also pushed her away in fear of the mother but also, perhaps, to control his own feelings. The parents were never happy. Ms. P. would arrive at these conclusions after sessions of detailing childhood incidents at various ages, as is done with submerged personalities without making direct interpretations which the patient might comply with or rebel against. During this time, her airplane dream was repeated seven different times, with herself always a spectator to a plane crash, but later experiencing some feelings about it in the dream. After its seventh occurrence, she made the association that the plane was her mother and her pseudo-ego.

An important point in therapy was reached when the patient, who had been out of touch with her angry feelings toward her mother, dramatically experienced her unconscious hatred during a session. She began the session in the following way:

P: Today is Mother's Day, you know? I really had to rush to get here. I just wired flowers to my mother and grandmother. My grandmother is at my mother's house, so I sent flowers to both of them. Here's what I jotted down to put on the card: "I hope you MOTHERS have a happy Mother's Day."
T: Would you say that again?
P: I hope you MOTHERS have a happy Mother's Day (laughter). Did I say it like that? You MOTHERS (laughter). You know I must be pretty angry at them, my mother, you MOTHERS (laughter again). Boy, I must be angry. Isn't that funny, and I didn't know why I showed you that card. Maybe I should talk more about my feelings toward my mothers, I mean mother. You know, my mother called last week.

The patient's first breakthrough of feeling out of therapy came when, after exploring her relationship with her mother, she began to experience what was at first nausea when her mother harassed her and later what she recognized and experienced as anger, an emotion she could only remember experiencing once previously in her review of her life. A tremendous struggle ensued with her mother, in which she began to work through her feelings and ultimately stood up to her mother. At that point, she even went back to her hometown, told her mother off, and returned, stating she was finished with her family problems and wanted to discuss her sex life. This sequence was frequently repeated in various ways thereafter. She then began to move toward independence in her relationship with her female partner as well. A verbatim session is available from this period and will be included to give the flavor of a typical early session.

P: I did not visit Stephanie [homosexual partner] last night. I'm sticking on my own. I did have a dream. I forgot it.
T: Oh.
P: I did something that was very meaningful. Always felt it was an escape. I

bought a television. I went through my priorities, time for me to have a television in preparation for more time by myself.

T: A way of moving away from some people.

P: I could only afford either a stereo or a television. I decided I could get more from the T.V. One of those little T.V.s. I took it home from the Hamptons. It gives me something I can do myself. I turn it on or off.

T: Does this have to do with independence?

P: Could be an escape, too. It is used by a lot of people that way. I watched the football game. I used to like watching football games with my father. I'm settling in for the winter. I don't want to do without people. One thing, when I was at home, I always felt guilty about getting things. Even things everybody had. My mother would want things that looked good to people on the outside, nothing on the inside. Even on dinner, she would spend lightly. I never got things for myself.

T: Held you back from getting T.V. before?

P: Limits all sorts of things. I'm always looking to someone to tell me what to get. Stephanie always did.

T: Did you feel that way before Stephanie?

P: At home they limited everything. My mother did, for everybody. God, I hate her. I could not even sit around the living room reading a magazine. That was frivolous. Funny, I remember coming home from school and reading geometry in an armchair in the living room, and my mother said, "That's not studying, that's relaxing," because I was in that chair. Stephanie wasn't that bad, but everything had to be her way. Limited even our conversation. I hope I'm not going to be a lonely person.

T: Wondering if you'll be lonely?

P: Maybe with this toy color T.V. Maybe it's a step toward breaking away (big smile).

T: Looks like you're happy about it.

P: I'm planning what I can do in March. Get all new furniture. It's got to be me. Even if I couldn't afford it, all the things. It's important for me to be myself. It's important I get it all.

T: This is the year for you to be yourself?

P: Yet it's hard for me to say I haven't had a lot for myself before. Got everything when I was growing up. I don't think, though, I got things important to me. A lot of things important to my family, not important to me. When I first came to New York, Mother visited and only wanted me to live on the upper East Side, to do everything properly. Only to go to stores where you can get things with monogramming. I wanted different things but I obeyed her. Sometimes I'm scared I actually am like her [the incorporated mother as a pseudo-ego].

T: How?

P: Her ideas and mine are very different, except I go along or went along with her, but not that I wanted to. In fact, I hated a lot of them. I was weak. I remember you said, "Just because you're cautious like your mother—or was it Stephanie?—that doesn't mean you're alike." I don't think she focused on who her family was or what they wanted, and when it came to show the public a facade, what they could afford, she made me part of that. Although I can be unrealistic, too. Unrealistic in different areas, but unrealistic or not, I'm going to be myself.

T: That sounds like a declaration.

P: It is. Perhaps homosexuality is my escape from something I always felt incapable of handling, others (the secondary mother). I still think that to a degree.

T: Escape.

P: At least it's my own world, except I let myself be controlled there too. Damn it, I got out from under my mother, but I let myself be controlled there too.

T: It sounds like you have some feelings about being controlled.

P: I don't think hiding in a homosexual relationship to be free will work, but I don't think I can change. I don't know what's right for me.

T: It's hard to size up what's right.

P: Here I criticize what others (mothers and mother surrogates) do when I don't know what I (her submerged ego) should do.

T: They can do what they want, and you do what you want, but first find out what you want.

P: I do not think less of people because they (her pathogenic mother) are not doing what I want to do. But since I'm in therapy, a lot of the things I do seem selfish (guilt over being autonomous and disappointing mother).

T: You feel too wrapped up in yourself?

P: Did you see the movie *Belle de Jour*? Stephanie and I used to feel associated to *Belle de Jour*. Her husband should have been rough with her. I did not associate myself with the rich husband and being bored. Stephanie said, "Let's go to the movie again," and I said, "No, I can't do it." She said, "You're being very selfish." One thing I want now is not fantasy. I want reality now. I don't want to go to gay bars. I won't go, maybe that's selfish. I used to go with Stephanie (the mother surrogate) out of guilt.

T: Guilt, is it making you do things now?

P: It's not that simple, either. I'm still calling up people I don't want to. I don't know why, I guess I want them to like me (trying to please the secondary mother, turning her into the primary mother, and suppressing her rage against the secondary mother). Maybe I'm going too far in trying to end friendships, but I need time to be alone to think. How far do I go?

T: Wondering where to draw the line.

P: This weekend worked better after I understood why I didn't want to be dragged to Fire Island. I didn't do anything different than last weekend, but I felt different.

T: It wasn't different in what you did, but it seemed less depressing.

P: Maybe 'cause of the T.V., too, but I didn't feel bad. Besides, I have already done a lot of thinking. A lot has happened since I moved. Maybe I'm more aware of people than I was before. I forgot, I got a letter from my mother. I told her that I had bought all this merchandise that sold the most. She couldn't say in her letter, "That's nice." She could never compliment me. It's just like when my father would bring some big news home. I make more money now than Father. Mother said in her letter she made $1,200.00 doing a survey. She thinks that it is just as important, and we were always supposed to compliment her.

T: She expects from you what she didn't give.

P: She gives me something, I'm supposed to thank her ten times, and I have a hard time complimenting her. I really have a hard time, she's very overweight and not physically attractive but I do it, oh God, I do it.

T: She can't do it?

P: She gives off an air of superiority, always has, as long as I can remember. Deep down, she doesn't think of herself as particularly superior. My father is a good-looking man. He always looks good whatever he is wearing, and I can do the same thing. She resents the fact that father is somewhat able. She strikes out whenever she can find a weakness. I can't believe he would be in the same shape if he had someone else to live with. She could be very vicious to my father and me. He spelled one word wrong and she went for it. She does it to lift herself, to make herself seem better.

T: You think superiority is a defense.

P: One arm is crippled since she was 12. Crippled since she was 12, and her father spoiled her terribly. Grandfather spent a lot of time with my mother. She always separated my father and me. She was close with hers.

T: She got from her father what she doesn't like you to get from your father?

P: She thinks her father is God's gift, and I was supposed to be named after him. He is on some pedestal in her memory. Mother spent her whole life thinking she was superior. It's a facade that's all, all phony. She's always telling me how she finished college, and I didn't. She's always topping me, but what did she do with her college?

T: You feel she's competing with you?

P: Yes, although I don't tell her what I'm doing. I go to the theater and they go to a little theater group. She describes it like it's off Broadway or better. She's always competing with me for Father's attention.

T: Competing for Father's attention?

P: Father and I always had an affinity for each other that Mother and I didn't have. Whenever I asked my mother whether she wanted a girl or a boy she said a boy baby, but she did say my father wanted a girl. Father was delighted I was a girl.

T: She wanted a boy and father a girl.

P: In seventh or eighth grade I asked her.

T: How come at that time?

P: I was a real tomboy and I played on the football team, and no girls in the neighborhood did. I was trying to be like my father. I was dressed in old clothes and Father's football helmet.

T: Who gave you the helmet?

P: I remember talking football with Father. I really didn't play with girls those couple of years; I'd forgotten about all those clothes.

T: Were you trying to please either of them?

P: When I was in ninth grade I was very shy. I'll never forget it. I had a boy's trenchcoat I remember not wanting. I remember mother said it was the latest style. She bought it for me. I remember walking home on rainy days getting wet, but it was not worse than the coat. I hated it, yet I never told her I didn't wear it. It gave me conniptions when I told her; she didn't remember. Definitely a boy's coat. By the ninth grade, I was against it.

T: Against boys' clothes.

P: Oh, I remember the dream. I was in Central Park but it looked like the park back home except surrounded by sky scrappers [slip of the tongue]— I mean scrapers, so it must be Central Park. I was walking across from the upper East Side to the West Side. I had to be somewhere when I saw a large black spider hanging from a tree. I was running through bushes and grass and I was scared to go on. It was hanging from a string like in Miss Muffet. I decided to sprint around it when my heart started to beat; actually, when I woke up, my heart was beating loudly.

T: How did you feel in the dream?

P: Frightened, I wanted to make it but I couldn't.

T: Have you felt that way recently?

P: Yes, that's how I felt last night. I didn't want to go to Stephanie, but I did want to go out but I couldn't get myself to call anyone new. Good thing I got the T.V.

T: Have you felt that way before?

P: Yes, the night before I went to Louisiana. That's it, that spider is my mother or Stephanie. They both want me to stay like I was, and I want something new.

T: What do you want?

P: I'm not sure, but it's not Stephanie. Maybe to be free.

Another important step in therapy occurred when the patient, at the end of a session, began to describe sexual fantasies she had about her father. She described:

P: I've never told anybody this, but sometimes, when a woman is touching me, I pretend it's a man. I guess I just don't feel I could hold up my end of a relationship with a man. But it's more than that: sometimes I pretend it's my father.

She spent the next several sessions talking about the fact that, for financial reasons, she would have to cut down on sessions. The therapist finally identified the resistance and got below manifest statements with the following intervention.

T: I wonder if your wanting to cut down has anything to do with what you talked about at the end of the session, a few sessions ago?
P: You mean about my father. . . . I think that's right. I guess I should talk about that.

In her further exploration, she was able to see the connection between her own confused sexual role and the relationships in her family. She could only enjoy sex with women while fantasizing she was being loved by a man. In her relationships with women, she would only let them touch her while fantasizing being touched by a man. This represented her struggle with the mother, where she would submit to the mother in exchange for being allowed her incestuous fantasy. In some of the fantasies, the man was, in fact, her father. She, at that time, recalled adolescent sexual fantasies about her father that she had forgotten.

It was noticed by the therapist following these sessions that, after every crisis when the patient had acted dependent on the therapist, she would suddenly want to cut down to one session in a reactivation of the transference to the hated mother in the therapist (when the analyst was experienced as the feared and hated spider that might kill her or be killed by her). After every business trip to an exotic place when her mother would want to go along, she would return to the female partner, the mother surrogate. This, along with expressions that she wanted to be more independent and didn't need therapy, were finally understood by the patient as part of the transference to mother. It was handled by the therapist after the transference was clear by leading the patient to explore her relationship to the therapist, and by her eventual insight and interpretation that, "I'm fighting you like my mother but you're not like my mother." This sequence was subsequently repeated often. My not punishing her expressed hostility toward the mother and her sexuality toward the father and not undercutting her assertiveness while not being weak or wishy-washy either was indeed a new experience.

Later Phase of Treatment

A new phase began when the patient began to date men again, but all weak men. After a series of such affairs, and after analyzing her dating choices in men in the past, she was able to see her repetition compulsion to date weak men like her father or as she put it, "men two steps in back of me." Also, she was able to see her mother's part in preventing genital primacy by interrupting possible marriages. She also reported the following dream:

P: I am walking in Central Park, and I come to a gazebo [her central, submerged, feminine ego], and a black man is in it, and it is like I am going to meet him 'cause I go right in and we take off our clothes to make love. A whole bunch of women are outside having tea on the lawn. Suddenly, its like a small-town tea party and I am thinking, "What will they think when I come out? They will know what I am doing," and then all of a sudden, I am out in my underwear, waving a scarf, and I am really enjoying shocking them. I guess I knew it would get to my mother. It's funny how my dream is both in Manhattan and back home at the same time. Then the park seems hazy and I am looking for you at the tea party when I realize you are in the gazebo.
T: What do you associate with the dream?
P: I am beginning to enjoy men's attention on the street, often black guys give me the eye, but other men notice me too. But I just look down.
T: How do you feel in the dream?
P: Good, but scared of what people would think.
T: Which people?
P: My mother.
T: When did you recently think, "What will they think?" forgetting the dream?
P: I was thinking what would you think of my having this dream. What you would think of my liking catcalls.
T: What do you think?
P: I don't know. Maybe you'd look down on me or maybe you'd think that's progress.
T: I guess you're not sure if I'm in the tea party or the gazebo.
P: (laughing) That's right!

Subsequently, she began to laud therapy, marveling at any interpretation. She simultaneously began to date some stronger men and fantasize about strong men while dressing more femininely for sessions. This, however, was not consistent, and particularly after a series of sessions missed for business trips, the mother transference already discussed would reemerge. Parental transferences had to be worked through further. In her last airplane dream she was not only emotional but was an active participant, saved by her latest boyfriend from a crashing airplane (her mother). One of the earlier dreams and her latest will be presented to illustrate the contrast.

Airplane Dream Three

P: I have had this dream many times before. I am standing alone in a sandy desert and I see a large plane overhead, and it begins to fall and crashes right at my feet. What gets me is I do not feel any emotion at all. The plane is full of foreign men who I can tell are dead because they don't move, but what I notice is the interior decoration of the plane. It's pale blue upholstery and green rug and gold curtains. Maybe 'cause I'm a buyer and deal in decorating. A plane crashes and I feel nothing. I think there is something wrong with me even as I tell you this about myself. I can almost hear myself say it, but I don't feel it.

Airplane Dream Seven

P: I am at the airport when a plane crashes on the field, and my girl friend and I have just gotten out of a plane. The airport is like a war, full of fires and shooting Arabs. I get caught up in the excitement and I am running, holding hands with my friend, when a man sweeps me up and carries me to safety behind a locker. I don't know what happened to Stephanie. It's funny, I knew somehow that the plane would kill me and I had to escape. [The bad mother plane is aiming at her and kills all the fathers. She is saved by a strong man from the destructive mother and the weak father.]

After the last airplane dream, her association was, "I think I am interested in men now, but this time they don't have to be a step in back of me."

She identified the man in the dream as a boss at work whom she had started to date.

As Ms. P.'s relationships with men improved, she was able to resume a relationship with her parents. Her father visited her in Manhattan, and she took him out to dinner. She started to talk with her mother again by phone, but felt she was free of her mother's control and consequently relaxed in talking to her and was not so easily upset. She also began to relate to her brother as an adult, not as if he were her son.

In her almost four years of treatment, Ms. P. had made tremendous progress. She had been supported in her need to express her feelings in the sessions, as well as in her life. She became far more open with her family and friends. Her success in business had not been curtailed and she had, in fact, been promoted. She seemed to be enjoying life, feeling more independent, experiencing emotions, and dating more freely. She had moved beyond submergence with hatred to freedom. Ms. P. terminated therapy when she was promoted to the highest job a woman has ever reached in her company. She left with very positive feelings toward therapy. Further analysis of her preoedipal submergence and hatred of her mother had led to genital primacy, including dating a male executive in her company.

SUMMARY

The patient was seen for nearly four years for a total of 277 sessions. She had gained many deep insights, her affect was remarkably different, she had come out from under the yoke of her mother, and was, for the first time, choosing involvement with strong men. In the past, she had relationships with men, but usually men like her father, who would confirm her attitude toward men. But she had avoided strong men, emotionally unable to share in a relationship of that kind. This progress involved the resolution of a mother fixation in the oral stage with a corresponding unresolved masochistic attachment to the preoedipal mother. The patient had to work through the anger and hatred toward the mother she feared and was masochistically attached to in order to obtain genital primacy, and for her submerged ego to emerge.

DISCUSSION

Therapy with Ms. P. had consisted of an initial phase, where an initial mother transference was worked through largely due to the therapist's unintrusive neutral stance, and his making all interpretations in the form of questions, not statements, for her to comply with or rebel around. A middle phase of therapeutic alliance between the patient's submerged but emerging ego and the therapist followed, due to the therapist's having carefully avoided any alliance with pseudo-egos. In this phase, Ms. P. was able to realize that her energy need not go into rebelling and complying with the other but rather into discerning what she was and what she wanted. Therapy culminated in her submerged ego completing her developmental growth to genital primacy, with the therapist in an idealized father transference that was eventually replaced by healthy, developing relationships outside of therapy. For the first time, she had worked through and resolved oedipal issues.

6

A Depressed Patient

Jeffrey C. Greenberg, Ph.D.

> *There are many who dare not kill themselves for fear of what their neighbors will say.*
>
> —Cyril Connolly

Submerged patients are those who present a specific developmental pattern with a resultant specific intrapsychic structure. This intrapsychic structure manifests itself through a constellation of symptoms and behaviors. While such a constellation of symptoms may also be indicative of other characterological disorders, Chapter 2 had as its goal to differentiate the submerged personality from other entities based on environmental conditions present throughout the process of ego emergence. In this chapter, the treatment regime in working with a depressed patient whose intrapsychic structure is submerged will be highlighted and discussed. A case study will be presented, which focuses on characterological symptoms, behavioral manifestations, developmental issues, and general therapeutic considerations, including the importance of neutrality in working with patients in this diagnostic group. Since much of the therapeutic work is centered on the treatment relationship, transference and countertransference will be examined, as well as their impediments to the treatment process. Additional concepts will also be discussed as they related to submergence and this specific case.

A NOTE ABOUT PSYCHOTHERAPY

Psychotherapy is a process dependent on a multitude of variables, occurring intrapsychically as well as interpersonally. While this process occurs in the therapeutic relationship, work with patients and investigations into the understanding of human behavior confirm how influential past environmental experiences are with regard to behavior and emotional processes within and outside of a psychotherapeutic relationship. As such, a cohesive and clear understanding of a theoretical framework, based on drives, relationships, and on developmental processes, should guide the clinician in his psychological treatment of a patient. The word "guide" is used because a balance should occur, with theory not blinding the therapist to the individuality of the patient but rather being used as a backbone in understanding the patient's pathology. Seeing the patient within his/her individualized context should be the body of good therapy. This case study will be presented with this in mind, integrating the therapist's understanding of the patient's psychopathology as well as therapeutic issues pertinent to the submerged personality.

THE PATIENT AND SIGNIFICANT ASPECTS OF HER HISTORY-IDENTIFYING DATA

Data

Maria has been in psychotherapy for twenty months. She is a very attractive 29-year-old Caucasian female of Protestant faith and American parentage. Her family is of Italian origin. She is of medium height, slender, and well developed. Her black hair is long, usually worn away from her forehead. Her dress varies from casual to professional and is always stylish. She is neat and appropriately groomed. She has a high school diploma and has been married for nine years, although for the past two she has been separated from her husband. Currently she is living in a two-bedroom apartment with her two children: a son who is of primary school age and a daughter who will be entering school in the fall. Maria and her husband, Jerry, separated twenty months ago. Maria is currently employed as a bookkeeper with a construction company.

Reason for Seeking Treatment

Maria sought professional mental health treatment through referral by her family physician after she complained of feeling lonely and depressed, with vague suicidal ideation. Precipitating factors included separating from her husband and quitting her job because she could not concentrate on her work. She reported feeling tense and anxious. She elaborated on these feelings in terms of feeling shaky, cold, having numerous crying spells, and "butterflies" in her stomach. Maria also reported that she felt like a failure, was having sleeping difficulties, chest pains, shortness of breath, frequent headaches, and gastrointestinal problems. Furthermore, she complained that everyone always tells her what to do, and that she wanted therapy to feel better and decide what she wanted to do with her life.

Summary of Previous Treatments

Maria had minimal prior involvement with the mental health system. Some years ago, after feeling depressed, she sought the help of a local psychologist in a CMHC (community mental health center). Seeing him for only a few sessions, Maria thought he was helpful in suggesting things for her to do, but that therapy was not for her. Shortly prior to her present therapy, she began seeing her family physician for medical problems, which included feeling "jittery" and having gastrointestinal problems and heart palpitations. Numerous medical tests were performed on her as an in- and outpatient, with results being negative in regard to medical causes of her physical disturbances. Her physician concluded that her problems were psychological, and five months prior to the start of her current psychotherapy, he put her on Valium 2 mg BID.

History of Presenting Problem

Although Maria's current psychotherapy was initiated by a separation from her husband and by her employment, her presenting problems developed over many years. Maria has described feeling depressed and "empty" numerous times in her life. One of her strongest recollections centered on her mother returning to school part-time when Maria was in her early school years. She recalls feeling lonely and upset, with these feelings present for a few days. A few years later these feelings recurred when her mother was abroad for a few weeks. Throughout the years, Maria recalls having strong butterflies, stomach pains, and dizziness whenever people were angry or disapproving of her. Maria's feelings of loneliness, depression, and nervousness, as well as her gastrointestinal problems, backaches, headaches, and severe dry skin became exacerbated shortly after her marriage and particularly after moving out of state. During this period, Maria reports feeling unhappy with her living situation and crying about it frequently. Six months prior to beginning psychotherapy, after moving back to her original locale and taking residence with her in-laws, her depression and physical symptoms subsided. This period of symptomatic remission was brief, in that her prior feelings and physical symptoms returned. While manageable, particularly with the Valium, these symptoms intensified about ten days prior to the beginning of therapy after Maria left her husband.

Developmental and Personal History

Maria's personal history was obtained throughout the course of treatment, although a modest amount of information was gathered in the initial session. Many background highlights unfolded in treatment as initially she had difficulty recalling or elaborating upon prior events.

Maria was born and raised in a suburban town that was predominantly middle class. She is one of three children. The children and both parents comprised the family constellation. Maria is the youngest child, with a brother and sister respectively three and four years older. Maria notes that she was a full-term baby with developmental milestones reached at appropriate ages. She was never severely ill and never had a serious injury.

Her parents were married eight years before her birth. Her father, a high school graduate, married Maria's mother in his early twenties after discharge from the service. He is currently retired, due to a shoulder injury from a fall. He was a detective. While he spent long hours working, Maria reports that he was a family man. He is described as conservative, strict, and authoritarian. Although usually quiet and reserved, he was outspoken when the children stepped out of line. Maria reports that he was the "muscle" in making sure the children obeyed their mother. When angry, he had a strong temper and used a belt, shoe, or hand for discipline. Maria reports that she loves and admires him, although she never feels comfortable when she is with him.

Maria's mother, a high school graduate, married Maria's father in her early twenties. Maria describes her as warm, caring, concerned, and "motherly." She also is described as hypersensitive, anxious, and overly involved with the children and family. She has worked part-time as a lab technician, starting when Maria was in her elementary school years. Nevertheless, she was quite involved with the children and household, with the house kept in "immaculate condition." Maria also reports that while caring and warm, her mother was demanding with the children, "always putting her two cents into everything," and that "the only right way is her way." Although Maria's father is described as the disciplinarian, her mother is described as an "expert in administering guilt." When upset, she would become either hysterical and emotionally "wound up," or withdrawn and depressed. While Maria's father was regarded as head of the household, her mother was viewed by Maria as the center of it.

Regarding her brother and sister, her relationship with them has been mixed. Maria has positive feelings toward her brother, to whom she was close as a child. In Maria's early teenage years, they grew apart due to his inability to get along with their parents. He began spending more time away from home, got married in his late teens, and moved out of state. Maria views her sister as being close to her mother and being her mother's "eyes and ears." When Maria misbehaved, her sister would report it to her mother, even fabricating stories at times. Maria feels her relationship with her sister has always been poor. As teenagers, each had separate friends, and they rarely did much together. Currently, Maria's sister is divorced. She and her children reside in Maria's parents' home..

In the social domain, Maria had a group of girl friends during her childhood and teenage years. A few of these girls Maria considered to be close friends, spending much time with them. Maria reports that her friends appeared happier and more outgoing than she was, and she always thought they were more attractive.

Growing up at home, Maria reports that she was usually well-behaved and compliant. She reports the house as being "warm," with Maria getting along with her parents, particularly her mother. She notes that she usually followed her parents' wishes and this allowed for a comfortable relationship. Nevertheless, she recalls a few occasions when she became "fed up" with their demands and acted directly against their wishes. She recalls one incident when her parents would not allow her to sleep at a girl friend's house. In opposition, she slept at another girl friend's house for the entire weekend, facing harsh consequences when she returned home. During adolescence, Maria reports, her parents became more strict and concerned about her. While she reports that her friends disapproved of drug and alcohol use, her father was always concerned about her male friends, since he assumed that they "only had sex on their minds." He did not allow Maria to date until she was 17, and before her marriage she had an early curfew. In spite of her parents' views, Maria dated during high school years without her parents' knowledge.

Maria reached puberty at about age 12. She first experienced sexual foreplay at age 15 and did not engage in sexual intercourse until age 19. This occurred soon after her father wrongly accused her of going to bed with many of her male friends.

Educationally, Maria reports that she was an A student. Her parents were strict about grades, and she worked hard in school. She reports that her teachers liked her and she was never a behavioral problem.

Upon graduating from high school, Maria enjoyed working as a waitress for a year. During this time she met her future husband in the restaurant she worked at. He was a few years her senior, had just graduated from college, and seemed sexually attractive and financially well off. After a very short courting period, against her parents' strong objection, they eloped across country and got married. She recalls feeling very ambivalent about this, but remembers feeling attracted to him and wanting to leave her parents' household. On returning, they lived at her in-laws' house because her parents wanted little to do with her. Maria reports feeling upset in this house as Jerry and his parents gambled heavily and engaged in drug abuse. After a few months with Jerry still an unemployed accountant, they borrowed money from his parents and moved out of state with the prospect of a good employment opportunity. Maria was upset by this move and felt "it was for him." At their new residence, Jerry was rarely home. Often, he came home in the morning hours in an impaired state from marijuana and cocaine use. Refusing to spend much time with Maria, he spent many nights "around town" with friends. Communication between them became nil except when he wanted sex, which she resented but with which she complied. Maria felt very lonely and spent her time doing housework, working as a waitress, or favoring the company of a few girl friends. After two years of marriage, she became pregnant. While this was unplanned, she felt she always wanted children and that having a child might change Jerry. After the birth of her son, Maria stopped working and felt more alone. In spite of some satisfaction obtained from motherhood and the developing relationship with her son, Maria's loneliness and depression increased with the birth of a daughter two years later. After this birth, Maria began having an affair, which she halted after a short period. Although depressed, Maria reports working hard at caring for the children. She reports that frequently she would become intolerant of them or angry at their demands. While Maria still desired Jerry's support, his involvement with the family remained minimal. When under the influence of drugs, he often became verbally assaultive toward her. Her response to this was usually crying and occasionally screaming at him. At times, particularly when upset, Maria went on eating and spending sprees, buying clothes for the children and herself, which only upset Jerry more.

During their first six years of living out of state, Jerry was frequently unemployed due to his drug use, gambling, and overall noncommital attitude toward his work. Nevertheless, with borrowed money, they moved out of an apartment and bought their own home. After a short time, with the house near foreclosure, Maria convinced Jerry to move back to the East. After moving back with his parents, Jerry continued to abuse drugs. While Maria found employment as a cashier, she reported that Jerry and her in-laws continued to criticize her and provided only mediocre care of the children in her absence. After some months of tolerating this situation, Maria and the children left Jerry, moving back with her parents against her sister's wishes. With difficulty sleeping and concentrating, and feeling more depressed, she followed her physician's advice and sought mental health services.

THEORETICAL UNDERSTANDING
OF THE PATIENT

Psychotherapy begins with the therapist having a broad understanding of theoretical issues and etiology of psychopathology. As the therapeutic relationship develops, more precise theoretical understanding of the patient should ensue, with resultant tailored treatment.

Clinicians note (e.g., Boyer 1980a, Giovacchini 1979b) that similar symptoms can be characteristic of many types of mental disorders. True understanding of the patient develops over the course of treatment as the therapist obtains a total picture of the patient's intrapsychic and interpersonal functioning. The therapist "has to be able to tolerate and sustain ignorance" (Giovacchini 1979b, p. 12). Understanding the patient develops through hypothetic formulations and reformulations, with the therapist using theory to anchor his confirmed hypothesis into a larger, more complete picture of the patient. As Giovacchini (1979b) states: "A sound and scientific clinical picture requires a consistent conceptual background. It must be supported by theory which permits the observer to make sense out of an array of data which otherwise would be chaotic and overwhelming" (p. 11).

As understood through the treatment process, Maria's major dynamics and personality structure is submergence. Simplified for brevity, her issues appear centered on an unavailable and suppressed ego, overshadowed by a need to comply with others, and yet a need to rebel against them. Maria has submerged her own ego and incorporated her parents' wishes and symbiotic demands through developing a pseudo-ego compliant with their views, which, however, she opposes through the development of a rebelling pseudo-ego. This internalized conflict is repeated in other significant relationships. Incorporating the opposing pseudo-egos affects her ability to integrate interpersonal relationships into a whole. Her protecting the primary (prerapprochement) mother from contamination by the secondary (postrapprochement) mother exacerbates this condition. Thus, significant people are perceived by Maria as good or bad, usually ambivalating between the two. With dependency needs great due to a loss of self and prior rewards for regressive behavior, relations focus on recapturing the nurturing and accepting object. Yet, with Maria having experienced the emergence of the secondary mother, all relationships become suspect. Although Maria desires intimacy and sexual contact, these feelings are threatening to her. Gratification is hindered by anticipation of a rejecting object and by the fact that oedipal issues are not resolved. Maria forms close heterosexual relationships with individuals who are demanding and unable to meet many of her needs, thereby completing the repetition compulsion and confirming the secondary mother's message that autonomous behaviors lead to negative consequences.

With regard to acting out, as is common with the submerged personality, Maria has engaged in numerous rebelling behaviors, for example, drinking, eloping, and having an affair, which are particularly noted when complying behaviors do not result in need-gratification. While at times Maria's frustration tolerance is low, this is not surprising when complying has not had the expected payoff. Furthermore, low frustration tolerance develops when the self has experienced intense frustration in childhood.

In terms of self, Maria's perceptions are negative, highlighted by feelings of insecurity and inadequacy. With parental figures unable to accept her emerging autonomous self, cause and effect are noted. Furthermore, feelings of abandonment, isolation, depression, and depersonalization develop out of the loss of self and frequently emerge into awareness when involved with significant others as secondary objects are anticipated and psychically reexperienced. With regard to the self-object dyad (see Chapter 2), Maria is experientially focused on objects with minimal awareness of self. Objects are psychically experienced as strong and powerful, with the self not only experienced as negative, but as relatively weak. Any emotional strength that Maria experiences occurs when she perceives herself as an extension of an object (in the form of a pseudo-self). In addition, with the expression of anger unacceptable in the formative years, and with the rejection of her own ego creating tremendous rage, underlying this depressed shell is an enraged woman with discharge occurring through somatization. Somatization also symbolizes Maria's conflict. It expresses her inner pain and simultaneously confirms the parental introjected message of weakness and vulnerability. Also, with submerged ego, the intensity of her anger is a threat to her. As such, diffuse anxiety is better tolerated while acting as a signal that the self is in danger.

In spite of Maria's symptomatology, conflicts, and rebellious behavior, a healthier but submerged ego is present and evidenced when Maria is not involved in rebellious behavior. The primary object, stability, and many positive factors in the home account for this situation. Indicative of this intact ego is an intact observing ego that allows Maria to judge her behaviors, perceptions, and others with relative accuracy, although she is not always able to convert this information to the emotional sphere. Also, Maria is very personable, has developed some stable peer relationships, has adequate daily living skills, possesses a variety of mothering skills, has adequate work-related skills, and outside of conflict areas, sees life in a more integrated format. Further indications of the presence of a more stable, less damaged ego are noted when Maria is under stress. While an exacerbation of symptoms occurs, with some regression noted, reality testing and stable ego boundaries never give way to a psychotic thinking process.

TYPE OF TREATMENT CHOSEN AND EMPLOYED

The main thrust of a psychoanalytic approach is focusing on the therapeutic relationship and its developing transferences (and countertransferences), relating the past to the present, with emphasis on insight, interpretation, and understanding the patient from many levels. As Giovacchini (1979b) states: "The psychoanalytic method is an in-depth approach and can be compared to a microscopic examination" (p. 7). Technically, analytical work with the ego-submerged is constructive. The primary work is constructive in allowing the ego to emerge and replace the pseudo-egos. Reconstructive work also occurs in focusing on prior experiences and their distortions, and because once the ego has emerged, it is weakened and may require some structural change. Overall, with a borderline the therapist is attempting to reconstruct the ego, whereas with the submerged he is allowing the ego to emerge and strengthen. While the main thrust of treatment with the borderline is toward increasing integration and organizational processes of the ego, as it is split and composed of organizational malformations, with the submerged, the emphasis is on ego-enhancing techniques to foster emergence of the patient's own ego as opposed to reconstructing it. As such, while many clinicians have introduced numerous parameters (Eissler 1953) in working with borderline patients, including confrontation (Kernberg 1975, Masterson 1976) and purely supportive approaches (Zetzel 1971), these are contraindicated with the submerged. The difference between ego-enhancing techniques and supportive psychotherapy is that the former is making an appeal to and alliance with the submerged ego while the latter can be more nurturing, gratifying, and/or controlling. The former fosters autonomy, the latter, dependency.

In order to allow the patient's own ego to emerge, treatment must be conducted in the most orthodox manner with regard to what Freud (1958) termed relative abstinence. Failure to remain abstinent can be viewed by the patient as an alignment with either pseudo-ego, resulting in treatment failure or termination; this results from the patient feeling a loss of self or primary object. Particularly, being directive, supportive, or nurturing can create problems in that one might unknowingly either support a pseudo-ego, or else foster a transference in the patient's complying to obtain acceptance, with unforeseen results.

While abstinence has implied passivity, neutrality is more accurate, whether the therapist is passive or active. Neutrality does not mean "listless indifference" (Freud 1963), but rather "a sufficient degree of objectivity combined with an authentic concern for the patient" (Kernberg 1979a, p. 296).

Also of importance is that neutrality is in the eyes of the patient, not the therapist. As Kutash and Greenberg (1986, 1989) have discussed, the activity level of the therapist may affect the therapist's being perceived in a neutral manner. This is dependent on environmental conditions that the patient has experienced. If a patient comes from a family in which parents were withdrawn and emotionally unavailable, a passive therapist may produce a strong negative transference, as the therapist's stance will not be experienced as neutral. In addition to examining the structural aspects of the patient's psyche, particularly the ego, the patient's sense of self-object (i.e., how he experiences objects and self) also needs to be addressed.

In working with Maria, being too active would overemphasize the object element in the self-object dyad, which could lead to negative transferential problems. This is because in Maria's formative years, affirmation of objects occurred in that they were emotionally available (as long as compliance occurred) and experienced as all important, as opposed to the self being affirmed and experienced as important. This may also exacerbate her self being experienced as weak, and the object being experienced as strong and overpowering. Also, as Maria's mother was warm and involved with her when she was compliant, a negative transference could occur if the therapist was too active and available, for the patient may anticipate "a price to pay." On the other hand, by not being active enough, Maria may experience overwhelming anxiety as the ego and sense of self are weak and only allowed to exist as extension of the object (structurally, in the form of a complying pseudo-ego and experientially, in the form of a complying pseudo-self). Furthermore, being too passive may be experienced as withdrawal or rejection, heightening a negative transference, as this occurred when her own ego attempted to emerge. In order for Maria to experience the therapist as neutral, the therapist needs to be moderately active, with a focus on Maria's own thoughts and perceptions in which she can experience her own true sense of self, and her sense of self can be experienced as strong as her sense of object.

These are the therapeutic guidelines used in treating Maria. In addition, and most important, "The therapist must be a real person" (Masterson 1976, p. 90). Thus he must be himself and transform a procedure to his own style. The therapy employed is not only geared to the dynamics of the patient, but also to the therapist's style. Therefore, the therapist's training, style, and experience also set the treatment parameters. With Maria, the treatment approach has been psychoanalytically oriented psychotherapy, with the goal of allowing her own ego to emerge and strengthen. This should decrease her anxiety, depression, underlying anger, and somatic problems, and increase productive behaviors and positive self-regard. The treatment frame consists of face-to-face treatment in a low-lighted room twice weekly for 45 minutes a session.

PSYCHOTHERAPY WITH MARIA

Psychoanalytic psychotherapy is usually separated into three components: initial, middle, and termination phases. With Maria's treatment currently in the middle phase, focus will be on initial and middle phases. The opening phase of therapy had as its main goal understanding the presenting and underlying problem, evaluating her potential for establishing a therapeutic alliance, detecting anxieties and resistances to treatment, stabilizing emotions, and obtaining personal information. The first impressions of Maria centered around her overall appearance, as she was well dressed, appeared well controlled, and had an air of pleasantness. Once in the office, this appearance diminished, giving way to a distraught, helpless, sobbing individual who felt alone and frightened by her current state of affairs. While organized in thought, her affect was intense as Maria told her story about separation and job loss. At times in the initial sessions, she appeared over-whelmed with emotion and the need to tell her story. This overwhelm-ing feeling was instilled within the therapist and was understood through the mechanism of projective identification (Leboit 1979, Boyer 1982). Maria was allowing the therapist to experience what she internally felt. Also, the strength of her affect and need to "spill" her story gave the impression of trying to "steamroll" the therapist. Because of Maria's need to protect herself, this behavior appeared to keep the therapist at a distance. With treatment just beginning, initial transfer-ences develop as the therapist is perceived in an uncertain manner. Paradoxically, Maria also appeared to make some contact, as noted in her leaning forward. She appeared caught between wanting contact and being fearful of it.

Although Masterson (1976) and Kernberg (1982) use supportive techniques throughout treatment with "primitive" patients, the guide-lines of Boyer (1961, 1980b), Eissler (1953), and Langs (1973) were used. Supportive psychotherapy can be warranted in early treatment to foster a therapeutic alliance and emotional containment and to help the patient deal with a crisis, but it can then be removed, once these objectives are met. While initial therapy was mildly supportive, the stance was still neutral with the therapist being nondirective and withholding judgment or advice. Therapy initially focused on making Maria feel understood, allowing and fostering appropriate emotional discharge, providing some optimism for the future, helping her focus on how she was feeling (because many emotions were blurred), and helping Maria engage in a healthy therapeutic relationship, which treatment could build upon. Control over her life and feeling under-stood appeared particularly important to Maria, as she repeatedly noted that people do not understand her and she always has to do what others want to do. This was understood to be her "prescription" for her treatment within therapy. Much of her early treatment was directed toward providing a "holding environment" (Winnicott 1960) in which she could feel some reprieve from her daily interpersonal experience and also provide some structure for her feelings. Ego-enhancing techniques were used to give Maria more control over her feelings, for example, "While I understand how upset you feel, these feelings can act as a force to help *you* find a way to resolve the situation *in a manner that's best for you*." The neutral stance was particularly helpful during these initial sessions in that, as noted, closeness appeared to be a concern of Maria's. Neutrality allowed Maria to feel understood in a nonthreatening way, as well as giving the therapist time to understand her issues and dynamics clearly without interrupting her projective field.

Testing the therapist and strong transferential reactions usually appear in the initial phase of treatment. This was evident in treating Maria. Although therapy was structured with reference to the frame, Maria had control over the content and direction of her sessions. Yet Maria would start many sessions by asking the therapist what he wanted to talk about. While therapy was directed at helping Maria focus on whatever she wanted to, the scenario outside of treatment became evident within the therapy as Maria would discuss specific problems and then ask: "So what should I do?" Although she felt helpless, this was also viewed as an attempt to prove that the therapist was like others in her life: to please them, one must submit to their control. These situations were explored, helping Maria look at various alternatives and allowing her to decide what she wanted to do. At times she was given a neutral ego-supportive statement, such as, "As we continue working, you'll figure out what's best for you." While usually appearing content with this approach, on occasion she would get anxious or withdrawn. One hypothesis is that when she complied, acceptance of her by parental figures was forthcoming. The neutral stance prevented complying and may have evoked a feeling of object loss, as was the case in prior situations when Maria did not comply with others' wishes. She remained somewhat active but neutral in an attempt to reduce abandonment depression, but on one occasion countertransferential issues interfered with therapy. Giovacchini (1979b), Shapiro (1978), and Searles (1979) noted that, with more regressed patients, countertransferential difficulties are greater, due to these patients' emotionally heightened, less integrated impulses, and feelings of helplessness. In needing to be the "helper" or "giver," on one occasion when Maria asked what to do, a suggestion was given by the therapist. The following week Maria missed her appointments under a pretense. The therapist's suggestion may have been experienced as controlling, aligning with the secondary mother, as well as making her feel more helpless. Reexperiencing the transferential mother may have evoked a loss of self, with anger being expressed through withdrawal and rebelling from treatment. Therapeutic recovery occurred in that neutrality was reinstated. This interruption was accepted by the therapist, making Maria feel she could make decisions without consequences. Testing continued to occur, with Maria asking a few sessions later how the therapist feels when she cannot make an appointment as scheduled. Exploration of these feelings occurred with therapeutic neutrality maintained. Therapy in this and other situations was ego-enhancing, allowing Maria to focus on how she felt, or what she wanted to do in a given situation, whether her feelings were similar to or different from others, whether she felt she was acting or reacting, and allowing Maria to decide what was best for her.

Maria's response to interpretations was similar to her response to suggestions that led to the initial diagnosis and treatment plan. Although Giovacchini (1979a), Kernberg (1979a), and Leboit (1979) view interpretations as the crux to analytic treatment, soon after therapy began it became evident that Maria could only make minimal use of interpretations presented by the therapist. This is congruent with the Blancks' (1979) and Leboit's (1979) position that with preoedipal conditions, interpretations are contraindicated in early treatment. Maria had difficulty incorporating the most ego-enhancing and horizontal interpretations. While she would comply in accepting them, internalization or focusing on them appeared minimal. She appeared to view them as the therapist's and not hers. It appeared that "digesting" was difficult for her in the fear of greater loss of self. Thus, therapy was established with Maria exploring what the given manifest content means to her, and treatment progressed with having Maria develop her own insights and interpretations. This was accomplished through Maria and the therapist exploring events, feelings, and occasionally dreams. The conclusion of this exploration was left to Maria, with the therapist at best elaborating or fine-tuning her insights. On occasion, when an interpretation was given, it was presented in question form, allowing for dismissal.

Dealing with the therapist's transferential issues was especially important during these months. In the early months of treatment, Maria was feeling more helpless and negative with regard to her view of self. While well contained, the therapist's need was not only to change Maria's view of self, but to do it in a timely fashion. Introspectively, these therapist transferential issues and their potential effects were explored in consultation. Dealing with these transferential issues allowed the therapy to proceed unhindered, as going against Maria's feelings would also go against the parental message, and this would be a threat to Maria, because the message has been that she needs them. To feel more autonomous would also create greater feelings of abandonment and depression because the secondary mother emerges when these autonomous feelings are felt. Furthermore, "persuading" Maria that she should feel better about herself might make her feel that she cannot be herself in therapy, creating greater feelings of anger and inadequacy, as well as confirming the parental message. Also, change could be perceived as the therapist's agenda and not hers, with Maria complying and then rebelling against therapy. While Maria was very repetitive in her feelings and concerns, this was understood as indicating her need and concern in being heard, as well as a test to see if the therapist could be accepting of her or would become the secondary mother, presenting his own agenda. It became apparent that the impetus for change would be the development of the transferential therapeutic relationship from which the therapist could be accepting as Maria's ego emerges and strengthens. This strengthening of her own ego is of critical importance as a submerged ego, by definition, is in part analogous to a negative, helpless view of self.

Crises presented themselves in treatment, and these were evaluated and dealt with within the therapeutic frame. One concern was Maria's suicidal potential, which took priority above all issues. A concern in initially treating Maria was her statement in one of the early sessions: "I can't go on." While any indication of suicidal potential must be therapeutically addressed, careful evaluation of the situation is imperative, since over-reacting can have a negative therapeutic effect. To overreact with Maria could create a negative transference in which the therapist would be perceived like her mother, who was hysterical, overly concerned, and protective. This would further confirm parental messages that Maria needed to be controlled and guided. In addition to exploring Maria's statement, Shneidman's (1980) risk factors of suicide were used, including evaluating concreteness of plan, history of attempts, and impulse control. Maria did not appear to be in actual danger. Maria's statement appeared to be a cry for help and a message of the pain her inner self felt. This evaluation of the situation was also confirmed by a consulting psychiatrist to whom Maria was referred so he could evaluate and titrate her Valium use, as well as confirm her physician's findings that her physical ailments were psychosomatic. Another situation that had therapeutically destructive po-tential and was dealt with in treatment concerned Maria's parents, who called the therapist "so maybe you can put some sense into her head." This situation was handled in a tactful manner, insuring that the parents would not disrupt treatment. It was made clear that treatment is confidential; Maria was informed of their call in order to prevent a perceived alliance between therapist and parents.

The middle, or working, phase of therapy began in the latter part of the first year of psychotherapy. It was highlighted by a reduction in somatic symptoms, depression, and anxiety. A positive transference developed, in that Maria appeared to enjoy coming to her sessions and was able to relax more, feel less threatened by the therapeutic relationship, and apparently feel some emotional connectedness between herself and the therapist. During this phase of treatment, the supportive parameter was reduced, with the therapist becoming less active, remaining neutral, and guiding Maria to her own insights. Although Maria frequently came to her session feeling anxious, as the session progressed she would feel more relaxed, sometimes having difficulty terminating the session. This appeared as a result of not knowing which mother might emerge in the session, since away from therapy, the image of the therapist became more ambiguous. Through the session, the secondary mother's not emerging made Maria feel more relaxed with an attempt to hold onto the primary mother through delaying termination of the session. The sessions always ended promptly and in an ego-enhancing manner, for example, "If you like, we could pick that up next session."

During this middle phase of treatment, although Maria still had days when she felt very depressed, she also had some positive days, which appeared to be slowly increasing as treatment progressed. Maria's most difficult days appeared when, in overt conflict with family members, she would feel more alone and depressed. On the days she felt better she would still describe herself as feeling empty, for example, "Something's missing within me," as the self was still submerged. Nevertheless, these contrasting periods were used to help guide Maria to an understanding of issues, conflicts, and their effects on her daily functioning. During difficult periods, focusing on the prospect of the recurrence of better days was also ego enhancing, in that it allowed Maria to soothe and comfort herself within her own thoughts as opposed to getting these needs met externally.

As Maria's ego was strengthening and emerging, it allowed her to continue to have more positive days, but this ego emergence also appeared to increase the conflict she was having with family members. Not only did the conflict appear to increase, but the nature of the parents' response toward her changed, presenting a hardship for Maria. It appears that as Maria was making genuine autonomous and independent strides, her progress became a severe threat to family members. While a secondary mother response (rejecting, critical) is the usual course for dealing with strides that go against parental wishes or demands, a shift in general responding appears to occur when this action does not bring the child into compliance. This shift is seen through the emergence of a tertiary parent. For Maria, the appearance of the tertiary mother occurred when her parents became critical of all her behaviors and actions. Although the secondary parent confronts the child's (or adult's) initial strides for autonomy through the implementation of a negative consequence such as withdrawal, anger, or punishment, which is usually replaced by acceptance, warmth, and closeness, once the attempt is thwarted, this is not true when the tertiary mother emerges. The tertiary parent, in her threatened state, continues to apply the negative response, regardless of whether the child or adult has ceased in his or her striving for autonomy, and even when the person attempts to reconcile through other actions designed to please the parent. The emergence of the tertiary mother appears to result from the parent experiencing the child's emerging self so intensely that one or more psychological processes occur within the parent. The parent may experience such an intense loss (e.g., severe narcissistic injury) that emotionally she perceives the child as deceased. As such, regardless of what the child does, it is unacceptable, as if it were too late. Also, the emergence of the tertiary parent may be unconsciously designed to heighten the child's feeling of helplessness, confusion, and fear as a final attempt to psychologically bring her back home. Furthermore, emergence of the tertiary parent makes the feeling of autonomy and separation more pronounced, which may be a maneuver to redirect the child toward compliance, as if to say, "See how it's going to be like being on your own."

For Maria, the emergence of the tertiary response from parents appeared to be quite disturbing. She experienced feelings centered around intense helplessness, inadequacy, and confusion. This appeared to heighten her feelings of loss and aloneness as well as guilt in not being able to please her parents. Also, "look what I've done" type of concerns were elicited from Maria. Yet, emergence of her own ego and sense of self was evident in that she had days in which she felt very angry at them, as indicated by responses like: "I'm sick of them treating me like a doormat," and "Who the hell do they think they are?" In fact, emergence of the tertiary parent appeared to heighten the contrast between days when she felt depressed, lonely, and negative, and other days in which she felt angry, strong, positive about self, and needing to find her own way. It was frequently noted that on these positive days, while still unsure of herself, Maria appeared to "glow" with a sense of self admiration in her ability to use her emotional strength still to focus on and move toward her own goals in spite of the strong objections she felt from home.

Throughout this period, the therapist's response was still neutral, with an alliance maintained with the emerging self. While this was nondirective in approach, Maria felt respected and understood by the therapist. This appeared to affirm her developing self. The content of the sessions was still geared to areas of importance to Maria. While the conversation frequently centered on difficulties with family, therapy allowed her to articulate and sort her feelings out, to "center" herself with regard to actions, desires, and thoughts, as well as allowing her to understand the change at home in her own framework, with some input from the therapist. Again, interpretations by the therapist were mild, in question form, and tied to Maria's own perceptions and understanding of the family situation.

A central issue for Maria that emerged as therapy progressed was her disproportionate concern with what others thought of her and her actions. These concerns were a defensive operation geared to protecting herself from the potential for future rejection, and related to a complying pseudo-ego. In addition, these concerns are indicative of both her historical experiences and the submergence of her own ego and its perceptions. Treatment focused on Maria's being the judge of her own behavior (as well as incorporating the therapist's acceptance of the emerging self). A condensed dialogue of this type of treatment approach is presented below:

Maria: I feel like I would like to go out with this guy at work, but I do not know if I should do it.

Therapist: Do you feel you do not know what to do, or is something else preventing you from making a decision?

Maria: I would really like to date him to see what it's all about again, but what would others think in that I'm only separated from my husband.

Therapist: What do you think others would think?

Maria: That I'm doing something wrong.

Therapist: What does it mean to feel that someone thinks you're doing something wrong?

Maria: . . . That they won't like me, that they'll think something is wrong with me.

Therapist: If whatever you decided to do you knew that people would agree with you, any thoughts about what you might do?

Maria: I would go out with him.

Therapist: What would you think if a friend was in the same situation and asked you what to do?

Maria: I would tell them they have to do what they think is best.

Therapist: What if your friend was concerned that what they thought might not be in line with what others thought?

Maria: I would tell them that they have to do what they feel is best as they probably wouldn't be happy until they did what they wanted to do.

Therapist: I know you mentioned that with regard to yourself, a concern would be that others wouldn't like you. Would you feel this way toward your friend?

Maria: No, even if I disagreed with them, it would have nothing to do with friendship. I always feel that people should have the right to disagree, even though I'm scared if they disagreed with me that they might not like me. . . . That's how it was at home. If you disagreed you got your head chopped off. . . . If only I could be a better friend to myself.

Therapist: Is there any way that you can be your own friend?

Ambivalence was quite evident during this phase of treatment. It was evident not only in relation to making decisions, as this was a new experience for Maria, but also with regard to significant people in her life. In terms of her parents, she would ambivalate between viewing them in a positive manner some sessions, and other sessions feeling very negative towards them. Yet, in this phase of treatment, an observing ego was evidently allowing her to perceive parents and others in a more integrated and realistic manner. However, she had difficulty translating these observations to the emotional level. Integration of feelings was fostered through focusing on the polarity of feelings Maria highlighted in previous therapy sessions. Certainly, the need to ambivalate will be diminished as Maria's ego emerges and she can tolerate not needing the primary, accepting parent nor strongly experiencing the secondary, critical parent due to a submerged ego.

While Maria's seeing the therapist as the all-good accepting primary mother was quite apparent, there was simultaneously a negative view of self and a fear of the therapist's becoming the secondary mother. At times, Maria would remark: "You must think I'm nuts," and "How can you put up with me?" Therapy would focus on exploring these feelings and having Maria evaluate her thoughts, concerns, and behaviors. Occasionally, treatment focused on examining where her negative feelings may have come from, but in a nonthreatening, neutral manner, for example, "Did you feel that anyone else had difficulty putting up with you?"

Of particular difficulty for Maria in the emergence of her own ego is fear of the critical mother emerging. This was apparent in her dreams and her daily concerns. One dream that exemplified her fears regarding the emergence of her own ego as well as other submerged ego issues was centered around Maria swimming in a lake wearing a heavy overcoat (her pseudo-ego) saturated with water. While trying to keep her head (ego) above the surface and gasping for air, she constantly had to duck as a motorboat (secondary mother) kept heading toward her.

With regard to daily events, no matter how well she was doing—she obtained a new job, enjoyed dating—Maria would focus disproportionately on negative events from the past, for example, having a brief affair and going on shopping sprees, which occurred a number of years before she began therapy. In incorporating the complying pseudo-ego, Maria appeared to punish herself for her nonparentally approved successful strides, and also viewed herself negatively. Interventions were again ego-enhancing, allowing Maria to develop her own insights, for example, "Recently you've been feeling more comfortable with yourself. Do you think focusing on these past events is a way to take some of your enjoyment away?" With her response towards the affirmative: "Any idea of why this would occur?"

Introjection of the secondary parent's message was also seen when at work. Maria was fearful that she was not as good as the other employees (sister transference), that the boss did not like her, and that she would lose her job. (Rebellious behavior was also noted in that while she was performing well, her performance would deteriorate, particularly when the boss was present.) Other feelings toward self were noted: she had a fear that she was schizophrenic, and she was fearful of losing her hair, something that had occurred years before. Concerns with schizophrenia appeared to be centered on whether she was the "sick one" and recognition that her feelings towards others were ambivalent. Hair loss was symbolic of the loss of self as a grown woman, as well as proof that she was the "sick one." Again interventions were neutral but ego enhancing. The focus was on exploring her feelings and allowing Maria to develop her own insights into these concerns.

Regarding treatment, her testing the therapist through acting out presented therapeutic problems that were explored in treatment. During a four-week period, Maria became very ambivalent with regard to her fixed appointment time. Maria would ask for a new appointment slot, but when it became available, she would ask for a different one, and so on. It appeared that Maria, in addition to resisting treatment for fear of her true self emerging, was rebelling against the therapist in having to comply with the therapist's schedule; after finding she could have her way, she began testing the therapist to determine if the secondary mother would emerge. Other behaviors with similar latent content also surfaced on occasion, such as Maria coming to her appointments late and being tardy in her payments. Therapy would focus on exploring this behavior in a neutral, nonthreatening manner, discussing associated feelings and other related situations in her life, allowing Maria to develop some understanding of her present behavior. Maria usually came up with her own insights. Any interpreting by the therapist was done in question form, allowing Maria to reject the interpretation.

Another major issue taking place in treatment, which produced countertransference issues, occurred during the seventeenth month of therapy when Maria left treatment to enter a drug program. Maria was doing well at her job, becoming socially active, feeling less depressed and anxious, and had reduced her Valium to 2 mgs/day, with some days taking none. Nevertheless, the fear of the self emerging and fear of further rejection from her parents were too great. In needing to see herself as the weak one and as the "problem," she entered a drug program that had many secondary parents (very harsh and confrontative). Paradoxically, while complying with her parents' message, this entry into the program became a form of rebellion. Although Maria first had reservations about her entry, this quickly changed as her parents attempted to convince her that she did not have a drug problem. With the secondary parents in charge of the program, Maria found many ways to rebel. She began calling the therapist, staying up past curfew, and socializing with males, all against the program's rules. During phone conversations with the therapist, Maria was ambivalent about staying in the program. While it was made clear that she would be accepted back into therapy, neutrality and an ego-supportive position were maintained, with Maria having to decide what was best for her. With regard to therapy, Maria's entry in the drug program may have been another test of the therapist's acceptance of her autonomy: checking to see if the primary or secondary parent would emerge. With neutrality still maintained by her therapist, after six weeks she rebelled against the program by leaving prematurely, and resumed her individual psychotherapy. This situation was used in treatment as a "vehicle" for Maria better to understand herself; it helped Maria to use the feelings in this situation to understand her

feelings in other situations. Again, the approach was discussing the events
and feelings, with Maria developing her own insights and awareness.
While Kernberg (1979a) and Masterson (1976) discuss confronting the
patient, particularly when acting out behaviors occur, my therapy has
followed the position that confrontation lends to compliance but not to
changing internal emotional structures. Furthermore, opposition by the
therapist to either pseudo-ego can lead to further complying and rebelling
behaviors. Of course, the therapist can allow the patient to confront him/
herself in a neutral ego supportive way, for example, "What do you think
would be best for you in the long run?"

Currently, therapy continues to focus on allowing Maria's own ego to
emerge and strengthen. This process will be facilitated as the transference
with the therapist becomes stronger and Maria experiences the fact that
she can truly be herself without rejection occurring. As complying behaviors are reduced, in that Maria realizes she can be herself, so should
rebelling behaviors be reduced, as the need to rebel will be diminished.
While many more treatment obstacles and "tests" are expected, these
should diminish as the therapist continues to remain neutral and allows
Maria's ego to emerge and strengthen. As her ego emerges, and as Maria
learns to evaluate her own behaviors and decide which are acceptable to
her, complying and rebelling should ultimately be reduced. This is because
these defenses will no longer be needed as Maria can tolerate not having
the accepting mother, and can become the judge of her own behavior. At
this time, the relationships that she develops should be more fulfilling,
since they can develop by choice as opposed to need, and Maria can
tolerate closeness better. Furthermore, as Maria's ego emerges and strengthens, interpretations by the therapist will be better tolerated and digested
with the working through process facilitated. As the ego continues to
emerge, Maria should feel more comfortable when her desires coincide
with significant others. Currently, when this happens, as Maria is used to
complying, the other person's desire overshadows her own with a reduction in desire or satisfaction noted.

Concerning specific issues, at present Maria has not been able to
express anger, particularly at its source, for fear of further loss or rejection
as well as concern about her own self tolerating these emotions. As Maria's
ego begins to strengthen and the therapeutic relationship and transference

continue to develop, anger towards the therapist should emerge. As her view of the therapist as primary mother is reduced, seeing the therapist as secondary mother is expected to occur, especially when she wants to be gratified but is not. Integration with others should be facilitated as therapy allows Maria to see the therapist as he is, as opposed to either the primary or secondary mother. Integration should also be facilitated as Maria discovers that the therapist can tolerate and accept her anger and other negative emotions, thereby allowing her to integrate better and express her emotions appropriately. This should further reduce misdirected and often self-destructive rebellious behaviors, as well as somatic complaints. Other major issues to be dealt with as therapy progresses are oedipal issues. Problems in this area further contribute to heterosexual difficulties. A difficult relationship with father, lack of separation from mother, and a submergence of her own ego have interfered with the oedipal process and resolution.

7

A Schizoid Patient

Daniel P. Juda, Ph.D.

The only man who is really free is the one who can turn down an invitation to dinner without giving an excuse.

—Jules Record

Ego-submergence, as described by Wolf and Kutash (1984a, 1985) and Kutash and Greenberg (1986, 1989) is predominantly an object-relations theory. As such, its roots lie with early comments by Freud (1923), who spoke of the ego as the repository of abandoned objects. This notion led to the idea that there exist specific intrapsychic structures (as an aspect of ego organization) that develop as a result of our interactions with significant others, and our constitutional tendencies to form attachments with others—the mental representations of self and of other. As Phillipson (1955) wrote: "This (internal) world is basically the residue of the individual's relations with people upon whom he was dependent for the satisfaction of primitive needs in infancy and during the early stages of maturation." The process of making that which was once external a part of the self is called the *internalization of object relations.*

Specifically, when we come to studying the etiology of a pseudo-ego, we see the major writers again and again refer to the mothering matrix to account for its development. (See Wolf 1956, 1980, Kutash 1984b, and Wolf and Kutash 1984a, 1985, and in this volume, Chap-

171

ters 1 and 3.) Winnicott (1965) describes how the mother serves as a bridge between the child's experiences of self that originate within him and those that originate in the external world of reality. As such, her interventions make possible the consolidation of a reality-related self-representation, that is, an identity based on a real self. When the mother fails in this function, the real self is cut off from reality and may be organized delusionally. The false-self identity is the consequence of the failure of the mother to bridge these two worlds adequately.

Kohut (1971, 1977), in his major works on the self, carefully explores how the failure to organize all aspects of ego functioning within the self-representation is viewed as a manifestation of pathology of the self. Mahler (1952) believes that some infants are constitutionally unprepared to form attachments to others—which leads to primary autism. (This view is also supported by the work of Bowlby [1969].) When the child is otherwise prepared to form these crucial attachments to others, sometimes his environment is grossly pathological. When this is the case, this external inadequacy may disrupt the organizing tendencies of the child and there may result, she writes, a retreat into secondary autism. If these vital symbiotic attachments do develop but are disrupted later in development (usually around the second year of life when the child begins to manifest strong tendencies towards individuation), then defensive or compensatory structures are built (Kohut 1977).

The work of Harlow (1958), Spitz (1965), and Ainsworth and Bell (1969)—indeed, the now substantial body of infant research as a whole—leaves the clear impression that the maternal matrix (both the infant's and the mother's personalities) will be the crucible for the child's future sense of self. The impinging, nonempathic mother (or the child constitutionally predisposed to not attach himself to the mother) will result in a pathological self—possibly a false self.

Winnicott (1965) describes a continuum of false-self organization. The earlier its place in the developmental continuum (that is, the earlier the child needs to behave purely reactively to the impinging mothering), the greater the pathology. Horner (1984) describes these five levels of false-self development as follows:

1. If it is forced to develop at the earliest stages of development, the false self is all that the child has experienced. To all appearances, it *is* the real person. Spontaneity ceases to be a feature in the living experience of the child (Note: Mr. L. entered treatment because he felt he "lacked spontaneity"), and the self-as-reactor to a chronically impinging environment is central to the developing self-schema instead.

2. Less extreme is when the false self protects and defends the true self. The individual is aware of a true secret self that is allowed a secret life. In treatment, this patient might experience panic at the possibility of discovery of the true self by the therapist, as though it might lead to annihilation of the self. A correct interpretation may evoke a negative therapeutic reaction, being experienced as a violation of boundaries and an assault on the real self [Horner 1973, also, Wolf and Kutash 1985, who write: "With too emphatic or enthusiastic encouragement, or signs that the patient is daring to recover his suppressed self, the patient feels the therapist is appropriating him and that the surrogate parent in the therapist is getting too much pleasure out of the treatment process. The patient then becomes too eager to frustrate the stand-in parent, tries to deny him the satisfaction of any accomplishment, and suppresses once more the glimmer of his creative ego functions" (p. 526)]. (Note: This was repeatedly experienced in the treatment of Mr. L., especially during the first five years of silence when the therapist was rarely able to provide insights regarding the patient's behavior; the patient would withdraw deeper into himself and even leave treatment for a few sessions—sometimes even a few months.)

3. Still healthier is the individual who uses the false self to search out conditions in which the true self can come into its own. The false self protects the true self from hurt or insult. (Note: This, I believe, is what was happening with Mr. L.'s use of silence and withdrawal in his sessions; it was his way of protecting his true self from hurt or insult or further contamination

by others' needs and demands.) If the therapist shows an overly positive response to the false self, this patient is likely to hide his true self. If the therapist shows pleasure about the false self, the assumption is made that he would show displeasure of the self-representation; analytic neutrality is critical here. This type of false self is not an integral part of the self-representation. Rather, it is a socially derived role identity to satisfy an environment that fails to support an autonomous and spontaneous self. It develops after differentiation, but before object constancy in the rapprochement subphase (Mahler et al. 1975). This type of patient is likely to be aware of being fraudulent, with the conviction that the fraudulence is the price of love and acceptance.

4. Winnicott writes of the false self that is built upon identification. This sort of false self is reinforced by parents who take excessive narcissistic gratification from the child's normal imitative and identificatory behavior, while failing to reinforce and support the child's other spontaneous expressions of self.

5. In the healthy individual, the false self is an adaptive social behavior—by politeness and behaving in ways appropriate to the situation. This person can accept and experience the limits of society without threat or the loss of the true self.

Both Wolf (1956) and Winnicott (1985) believe that for the purposes of planning treatment, the recognition of the pseudo-ego's (Wolf and Kutash) or false-self personality (Winnicott) is the most important aspect of the diagnosis. From their writings, it is imaginable that an entire treatment might unfold in which what is treated (by an unwitting patient and/or analyst) is the pseudo-ego false self, while the submerged ego or true self remains unanalyzed. Perhaps this is why some patients appear to be ready to terminate treatment, but discover all too soon the need to return.

I believe that Mr. L., the patient I will present, began treatment in stage one (above), managed to put up with my technical errors (e.g., overexcitement in uncovering, etc.), and moved into stage two toward the end of the first five years. What we see in the brief excerpted session notes that follow is his move from stage two to stage three. It would be interesting to find out if others have experienced this same progression from stage to stage—as if up the developmental ladder of true-selfhood—or, if instead, they found their patients moving from whatever stage they entered treatment in to ego-emergence or true selfhood more directly.

In an earlier paper (Juda 1983), I reported the case of Mr. L., in which I discovered (for myself at least) that "it might be more fruitful to reconstrue the repetition compulsion as *primarily* a healthy function of the cohesive self, and (in rare instances) as *secondarily* a maladaptive resistance. The repetition compulsion is now understandable as almost always the self's adaptive attempt to make sense out of its universe by either (a) seeing the universe as a comprehensible and coherent system, even by distorting otherwise unaccommodatable evidence, or (b) 'playing' with the new unaccommodatable data over and over again (when it is not construable or distortable into preexisting schemata) in an effort to discover new schemata" (p. 361). In this paper, I conclude that the way to work with powerful and stubborn repetition compulsions—in the case of Mr. L., his years of silence and painful withdrawal from others and from life—is to "form an alliance with the patient's repetition compulsions by indicating to the patient—in his or her own laws and language—that we can understand and construe their inter- and intrapersonal universes as they do. . . . A failure to understand and ally oneself with the patient's repetition compulsions is to leave the patient feeling alien, misunderstood, mistrustful, and abnormal" (p. 367). The paper concludes on a rather optimistic note, with the patient's suicidal ideation all but gone, his severe headaches abating, and with his beginning ability to talk with the therapist for the first time in a flowing and consistent manner. What I have since discovered about Mr. L. is the subject of this report.

I am now convinced more than ever that Mr. L.'s silence and profoundly withdrawn persona (his repetition compulsion) not only was a "healthy function of a cohesive self," but most likely saved him from becoming much more seriously disturbed than he already was. What I discovered was that Mr. L. was protecting his true self from being extinguished and engulfed by his negative pseudo-selves (Wolf and Kutash 1984a). His "repetition compulsion" was his heroic effort to fight off singlehandedly the attempts of those around him to create him in their own image of who he should be. His only defense against this onslaught was to insulate himself from it by moving into himself; that is why he guarded his privacy so tenaciously—not because of a "death instinct" (Freud 1920), or as "man's rebellion against reality and his stubborn persistence in the ways of immaturity" (Silverberg 1948). It was precisely his need to cling *to* reality—*his* reality as opposed to his parents' reality—that led to this extraordinarily lonely stand. It was to ward off succumbing entirely to ego-submergence (Wolf 1949) that Mr. L. kept hidden from the world, as I hope this brief follow-up study will reveal. First, I will review Mr. L.'s history and early years of treatment (the fuller account may be found in the 1983 paper); then I will present the last two years of his treatment with abbreviated process notes so that you can follow the discovery of the submerged nature of Mr. L.'s disorder for yourself.

HISTORY AND EARLY TREATMENT OF MR. L.

Mr. L., a college graduate and former military officer, was earning a good living when he entered treatment in his early thirties. He sought help because he was unable to socialize and became deeply withdrawn in the presence of others. This, in turn, made him terribly anxious and inhibited him from seeking out the company of others, which, in its turn, left him feeling still more withdrawn, isolated, and lonely.

Mr. L. is the oldest of three children; he has two younger sisters with whom he says he never played. His father and mother, still living at the time of treatment, also did not play with him when he was a child. His only reported contact with his father occurred when he helped in the family business; Mr. L. never spoke about his mother. At the outset of treatment, his only other early childhood remembrances were of (1) his father fighting with his sisters, his hating these scenes, and withdrawing from the three of them; and (2) visiting his paternal grandparents' home, where he remembers always playing in a room by himself.

Throughout high school, his military experience (he worked with sophisticated electronic equipment in Vietnam during the war), and college, the pattern of his early childhood repeated itself. His life was void of meaningful object relations, empty, and lonely. However, in college he did meet and was able to form an important connection with a woman who was in love with (and eventually married) another man. When they parted at graduation, the patient was genuinely saddened. She was the only person Mr. L. remembered caring for very much and being cared for by.

The patient moved from one job to another, leaving them when he became successful, and found himself in positions of responsibility which required increasing interaction with others. In spite of his successes, Mr. L. complained that he was never listened to by his employers. "No matter what I do, I never seem to get what I want; no one ever seems to listen to me. Nothing I do seems to make any difference." His jobs never satisfied him and always left him feeling used.

In his first session, Mr. L. recounted the following incident: "I know you're going to think this is very important, although, after thinking about it a long time, I don't. But I'll tell you anyway. When I was 12 years old, my father and I were driving on the highway when our truck got a flat tire. It was still dark out and my father asked me to take the flashlight and go down the highway to warn the cars to slow down and move over. The next thing I remember was a car had hit the truck. I ran back to the truck and saw my father's leg lying a few yards away from him. Someone had stopped and covered him up and told me to run back down the road to a phone and call for help, which I did. That's all I remember." No attempt was made to discuss this incident in this early session, as it was evident that L. did not wish to explore it further at that time. It was not mentioned by L. again and was talked about only when the analyst resurrected it later on, as will be discussed later. Except for this incident and the few bits and pieces of information presented above, the patient did not speak of any family history for more than a year. Instead, the sessions were dominated by a profoundly disturbing and persistent silence, or by the analyst's speaking. The patient virtually never began a session verbally. During his sessions, L. would invariably withdraw deeply within himself if an attempt was made to focus on feelings, or even if the silences continued for too long a time. One could visibly observe him withdraw at these moments. If the withdrawal was pointed out, the patient would withdraw still further (as I see now, to hide still further from the analyst in order to prevent his fragile sense of self from being contaminated by another). If the analyst began to speak about a neutral subject, L. would shake his head as if he had just been awakened. Frequently, he would report splitting headaches at these times. If asked to describe what he was thinking, he would state that so many ideas were going through his mind that he could not focus on any one of them. (I see this now as his following the paths of his pseudo-selves' reactions to events, trying to sort them out, and getting lost in the process.) Often, he reported feeling as if his brain was "detaching itself from [his] head and moving inward."

If the analyst directed the conversation away from feelings to more general topics—such as sports, movies, politics, or job duties—the patient would sometimes join the conversation. But the instant L. was asked to talk about a feeling relating to these various topics and subjects, he would freeze and withdraw. If the therapist did not attempt to engage Mr. L., silence would follow. On one occasion the analyst allowed the silence to continue and L. did not break it once during the entire hour, although intense eye contact was sporadically achieved. In the following session, L. reported that he would leave treatment if this silence continued because "it doesn't do me any good to just sit here; that's what I've been doing all my life. It's too painful for me to realize how hopeless I am. I know I have to talk if you're going to help me, but I can't." Efforts to continue investigating his feelings about this declaration were met for session after session by silence. The patient was simply not able to answer questions, except sometimes to say, "I don't know"; otherwise, he would sit silently when asked a question. This fascinating pattern, of saying something very revelatory and then remaining silent for many sessions afterwards, repeated itself again and again in L.'s treatment. After a year, L. reported feelings of despair. Nothing was changing. Since therapy was not helping, he felt even more miserable. His last hope was gone. Suicidal ideation entered the sessions.

Around this time, he learned that his old college girlfriend was divorcing her husband. The patient called her and they agreed to meet. The patient's entire affect changed; he became involved, talked about his feelings for her, and even his wish for marriage. For six months they could not find a time to meet, although they lived only a short distance apart. Finally, after much soul-searching and agonizing on both their parts, they met and things went very well. The patient could hardly stop talking in his sessions. Then, after only a few meetings, the woman withdrew and would not see or talk to the patient.

For the next year the patient lived on the hope and fantasy that she would "open up again to me. I know she is like I used to be before therapy [his first statement indicating that therapy had helped him, albeit an indirect one], and it's only a matter of time before she tries again. I'm going to wait for her." When L. was finally convinced that she was not going to come back to him, he became severely depressed, even more withdrawn, and more clearly suicidal. He threatened to run away and live "the rest of my life alone. I'm going to sell everything I own and disappear. I'm worse off now than I was when I first entered therapy. Before I had learned how to live alone without too much pain. Now I feel even more how alone and hopeless I am."

FORMING AN ALLIANCE WITH
THE PATIENT'S REPETITION COMPULSION

It may be useful at this point to review what I wrote in my earlier paper (1983) regarding my early failures to form a working alliance with Mr. L., and how I sort of stumbled upon the technique of forming an alliance with his repetition compulsion. This is what I wrote:

In the first few months of treatment, the therapist attempted to establish a mirroring transference (an idealized transference was not possible, even if indicated, since the patient could not yet openly or privately recognize the analyst's existence). It was hoped that the damage from early empathic failures would be gradually ameliorated by such an approach (i.e., via transmuting internalizations), as Kohut (1971) had suggested. But, it soon became apparent that mirroring silence was not experienced as an empathic intervention or transference; rather, it was experienced as a recapitulation of L.'s earlier traumatic removal from others. The patient, not surprisingly, responded by withdrawing more deeply within himself and spoke more frequently about terminating treatment and even of suicide.

When this approach failed, the analyst attempted to analyze the resistance, as suggested by conflict theory. The father's accident was revived by the analyst and interpreted as having profoundly affected the patient's self-confidence. Guilt feelings surrounding the patient's wish to hurt his father for having abandoned him and used him were explored. The patient was even able to recall—apparently for the first time—the large amounts of blood at the accident: "My God! I can't believe this is the first time I remember seeing all that blood." He also remembered how he felt while running down the highway to the phone. It was as if "I were in slow motion, like I had entered a different time zone." Yet in spite of these interpretations of conflict and memory recoveries, the patient's depression and withdrawal deepened.

Progress was not made with L. utilizing the traditional and neotraditional means of "exorcising" his repetition compulsion of severe withdrawal and private rumination, accompanied by depression, despair, and feelings of hopelessness. Progress occurred only when the therapist abandoned his attempts to work around, work through, or interpret away the repetition compulsion. . . . Indeed, the analyst's own feeling that he was failing to help the patient contributed to the despair L. was experiencing. It was as if all the analyst's tools (i.e., techniques) to help unblock L. had failed and there was nothing left to do but hope that, in time, he might enter "remission."

The analyst finally learned that he had to form an alliance with the patient's repetition compulsion in order to further the treatment. This idea came about more by trial and error than by planning. The analyst had no idea, at the time, that this was precisely the approach needed in this case, since it was the equivalent of validating the true self of the patient—as we shall see. The analyst pointed out to L. that withdrawing was a vital part of his personality, something to be cherished for all the good it had done. It had helped him survive the excruciatingly painful experiences of his childhood, and the adolescent and adult recapitulations of these experiences. It had helped him to survive loneliness, guilt, and shame. The important thing, then, became how to utilize this successful way he had of keeping himself functioning as well as he was to help develop *additional* effective coping behaviors. After the analyst stumbled upon this approach—after painfully learning that a mirroring transference could not be established with a silent patient, and after repeated failures of trying to analyze the resistance—the therapy began to move into its second phase. The patient began to talk. We take up Mr. L.'s treatment beginning with his session of March 27, 1984, with the following abbreviated session notes.

However, before beginning with these sessions, I wish to present the reader with a series of comments by psychoanalysts regarding ego-submergence, or the development of a false self, so that these sessions might be more fully understood. If the reader will utilize these comments by referring to them from time to time while reading the patient's and my comments, I believe he or she will be better able to understand the material and follow the fascinating emergence of the true self in Mr. L.

I will begin with a few remarks by R. D. Laing (1959) from his book *The Divided Self*. He writes:

Every man is involved personally in whether or to what extent he is being "true to his nature." In clinical practice, the hysterical and the hypomanic person, for instance, have their own ways of not being themselves. The false-self system to be described here exists as the complement of an "inner" self which is occupied in maintaining its identity and freedom by being transcendent, unembodied, and thus *never to be grasped, pinpointed, trapped, possessed. Its aim is to be a pure subject, without any objective existence.* [My emphasis.] [pp. 94–95]

And again:

We said that the false self arises in compliance with the intentions or expectations of the other, or with what are imagined to be the other's intentions or expectations. . . . This consists in acting according to other people's definitions of what one is, in lieu of translating into action one's own definition of whom or what one wishes to be. It consists in becoming what the other person wants or expects one to become while only being one's "self" in imagination or in games in front of a mirror. . . . In the schizoid person, however, the whole of his being does not conform and comply in this way. The basic split in his being is along the line of cleavage between his outward compliance and his inner withholding of compliance. [pp. 98–99]

And finally,

The "inner self" is occupied in phantasy and in observation. It observes the processes of perception and action. Experience does not impinge (or at any rate this is the intention) directly on this self, and the individual's acts are not self-expressions. Direct relationships with the world are the province of a false-self system. [p. 99]

Compare these remarks with those of Wolf and Kutash (1984a):

Di-egophrenia develops before the age of two under the influence of a controlling and domineering parent, usually a mother who does not see the infant as an individual, separate and different from herself. The infant, seeking her approval, if not love, and fearful of her disapproval if he or she does not submit to her will, denies his own perceptions and abides by her judgments. To the extent that the infant submits to mother's persistence, he suppresses his own ego and incorporates her views as a negative pseudo-ego against which he repeatedly and compulsively rebels with an equally protesting pseudo-ego. Thereafter, the child and later the adult, with these two superimposed pseudo-egos separate from his own real self and oppositional to each other, is ambivalent about any suggestion of another person, projecting on him or her the original mother or parenting figure. This ambivalence between complying and rebelling leaves little time or energy for the expression of an individual's own genuine ego, own perceptions, judgments, appreciation of reality and his or her own creativity. [p. 12]

And Wolf and Kutash in 1985:

The first milestone for the di-egophrenic comes when he is able to accept insight. He has spent so much of his life utilizing most of his energy either conforming or rebelling around introjected parental values and has never truly found himself. . . . At this point the di-egophrenic . . . needs psychoanalysis in groups to discover further his complying and rebelling, so he can ultimately resist either side of this coin and be himself. The patient's transference to the therapist can become sufficiently diluted in the group to allow the acceptance of interpretations around his ambivalating within the group. [p. 526]

With these brief remarks in mind, I will present (relatively uninterruptedly) the brief notes from some of Mr. L.'s sessions over a two-year period:

3/27/84: Patient able to admit feeling totally unable to "interpret" others' behavior. He feels that he (1) overreacts to them—hoping to form a deeper emotional liaison than the circumstances warrant, or (2) underreacts, or (3) does not react.

Patient says he doesn't know if anyone likes him or not, that he can't make this determination. He isn't sure how the therapist feels about him and "I'm not sure how relevant your feelings about me are to me anyway."

4/3/84: Why patient hasn't committed suicide: "I don't have an answer for why I haven't done it."

Patient in a project at work with thirty-six others: "They all work in groups, but I work alone."

4/10/84: "I once saw, in Hong Kong, this ivory sphere. Within it was another ivory sphere, and within it was still another and so on until there were about seven to eight in all, all able to rotate totally independently of one another. I always wondered how anyone ever made anything like that."

5/3/84: Patient expressed great anxiety about admitting how ignorant he is about sex. Patient feared "what the other person [i.e., the woman] would think of me for being so unable to please her."

5/8/84: Patient feels he "never got feedback from anyone about what I felt or believed. So, everything was like a fantasy—it was never based on real life experience. I feel like I live in clouds."

Therapist: Fantasies came to be the same as actions?

Patient: No . . . I believe my actions to be reality. My mind's eye feels that my fantasies are real. Oops! I guess that's a Freudian slip.

Patient feels the result of this upbringing is: "I developed a very solid sense of myself, only it was a negative self."

5/25/84: Patient received a substantial bonus at work for his excellence there. His parents showed no reaction when he told them. "I was hurt. I realize they just *expect* me to be excellent at everything so I can never do well enough to get their praise."

5/31/84: Patient feels safe in his depression—it is a smoother "sign wave," a known way of being. His depression is seductive.

His coming to treatment, though a "sanctuary," also makes him "hurt" more which "probably means the treatment is working."

6/5/84: "I can't take the responsibility of letting people who are dependent on me down."

6/12/84: Patient said that for the last five minutes he let the therapist run the session instead of talking about what he wanted to talk about. "Last Thursday's session was *very* important to me. Remember when I said, 'I wouldn't be here if I didn't want to be?' Well, I realized there is a part of me that cannot let me go back to withdrawing that far away anymore. I felt so good about that all week. You remember how I used to feel like the pressure in my head was pushing *inward*? Well, last Thursday I felt the opposite—like the pressure was pushing *outward*. I felt energized. I know that you helped me bring about this change, but what I realized was that it was in me, not in you. It was my change."

7/17/84: "My parents always said what great 'potential' I had and never realized I *was* expressing my potential in reality in *my own way*. Because it wasn't their way, it didn't exist. I learned to answer questions by myself and in my own head—otherwise, I wouldn't have had the answers to any questions. In school, I processed the information given to me, all right, but in my own way. So, that when it came time to give the information back, it came out having been changed by me, and, therefore, in an unrecognizable form."

Patient wants to write a letter to his parents to tell them: "I am not their son, their little boy anymore; I am a totally separate person."

8/14/84: Whenever the patient expressed his feelings, his parents (1) ignored him, (2) were hurt, (3) were frustrated, or (4) told him how he *should* feel instead.

8/28/84: Patient lives in a tension state between: "the reality of what my mind is telling me and the fantasy of what was created for me. I'm afraid to look into myself because I don't know if I can find that anyone is there. I can't sit down and write my parents who I am because I don't know."

9/4/84: Patient wants Miss H. to love him, but he doesn't know how he would feel towards her if she did. When pressed about how he would feel towards her, the patient looked embarrassed (i.e., he has very negative associations about exposing himself, especially the feeling of humiliation).

9/25/84: Patient wants to terminate treatment.

"I cannot change. I feel I do not have a self and it is too painful to keep trying to discover who I am in therapy. I choose to live alone. I'm going to quit my job in a month and a half."

10/23/84: Patient sets up traps for others. Because he cannot tell himself if another's behavior is genuine towards him, he tests them by not letting them know at all what he wants from them and sees if they give it to him "spontaneously" (i.e., "genuinely"), because, to tell another what one wants is to contaminate their response (i.e., one can no longer know if they responded because they wanted to or because you wanted them to. That is, people can manipulate others' feelings). Patient remembered (1) his mother's mother died, after a long illness with cancer, when the patient was two months old. (i.e., Mother's unconditional love was not available and the patient developed a need for others' unconditional love); (2) his sister was born ten and a half months after he was born—so, again, mother was removed from him; (3) his other sister's birthday is "back-to-back" with his, with his at the "tail end of the back" and "we couldn't have two parties in a row; so, my birthday was always ignored compared with hers."

10/26/84: Patient had an excellent review at work, received a pay raise and bonus plus the promise of more money later. He also won an award at work which entitles him to a night out on the town "with a guest."

First time patient told the therapist his pay level. Began four and a half years ago at $11,000. Went to $13,000 a year later. Now is $35,000 and going up again in January.

10/30/84: Patient is interested in group therapy. Patient is "interested" in the paper the therapist wrote about him and is "happy" that it was helpful to other therapists.

11/2/84: Says he once had a college class regarding group therapy and was able to "intellectualize extremely well," so much so that others admired him for it, while he felt, "I was merely showing a false facade."

Patient hasn't been able to write a letter all year because whenever he tries, he writes things that feel like a facade—he doesn't know how he feels, he says.

"I have some trepidation about group, but I don't feel against it at all anymore."

11/16/84: "You have told me for years that I am cut off from my feelings. Today, for the first time, I *feel* how I am cut off from my feelings. It irritates me that all along *you* have had the key to accessing my feelings and that *I* haven't. I want the key for myself. . . . I guess my saying this means I am accessing my feelings. (Note: The therapist and the patient cry together). . . . We both have April showers. It feels good. Coming here today I *felt* how beautiful the day felt. Now, I feel that here with you too."

Patient met with the two recommended group therapists and liked them both.

11/20/84: Patient tending toward the female-led group. Anxious and excited about going into a group.

Patient excited about going home for Thanksgiving and told mother over the phone: "It depends on who's doing the judging," when she tried to lay down the law on some subject. "That stopped her dead in her tracks," the patient said with obvious pleasure.

11/30/84: Patient remembers nothing of grades one through three except that he kicked his third grade teacher in the shins (i.e., he felt his teacher's incompetence). By the fourth grade the patient was put in the "slow" class (i.e., teachers' incompetence misjudged the patient as "incompetent," which further disturbed and alienated him).

12/7/84: Patient afraid to "commit" to group for a twelve-week period.

12/11/84: Patient went to an office party and for the first time in his life he told two people what he thought of them—both the negative and the positive. Amazingly, he not only did this in a very constructive manner, but, also, was able to clearly see how one person's response to him was *her* problem (and, in fact, illustrated the very criticism that he had made of her; i.e., that she cannot admit her own problems).

Therapist: You say you don't make progress, but you wait to act until you understand *so* much about something that it seems as if you're not changing when you really are. You remind me of the type of child who doesn't speak until he can speak in whole sentences.

Patient: I was. I didn't speak for a very long time, I was told, and when I did speak, I spoke full sentences.

1/8/85: Patient feels defective (i.e., he was unable to make his parents love him at Thanksgiving again, and, therefore, he feels helpless, ineffectual, and inconsequential).

1/11/85: Patient: Do you think that I had to give myself the love that I never got from my parents and that this drained me?

1/29/85: Patient takes care of others' problems so that *their* pathology will not surface and threaten his own destruction.

Patient interested in being a therapist, but is afraid he cannot go to school because "I cannot retain information in reading and cannot write now."

2/5/85: Patient met with the group leader and she told him (1) People in the group are interested in him; (2) they are concerned that he wants to leave group already; (3) others might think he was "arrogant"; (4) it was OK if he wished to remain silent.

2/12/85: Patient very excited about group again, and about work.

"Things have eased up a lot at work. I am giving people back responsibilities that are theirs. It's like when I went home and realized I could never change my parents. I could still change myself and people here *are* able to change, too!"

2/22/85: Patient has preserved a purity and naïveté regarding his feelings—as if they were in a capsule insulated from radiation contamination—and he is slowly opening the capsule up for scrutiny in therapy.

3/1/85: Patient feels like withdrawing from group because he doesn't know how to "socialize in groups."

3/5/85: Patient's views about Vietnam War: "The leaders are greedy and too stupid to see that there are different ways of looking at things. If I had it to do over again, I would tell the government where to go and I'd go to Canada."

3/8/85: Patient says he is going to leave group without telling the group and without telling the group leader. "I don't want to be persuaded not to leave."

Patient feels he cannot express himself in group. Patient's self is engulfed by (1) other group members' needs; and (2) his own empathic skills, which make him feel like he's taking care of others and not himself.

3/22/85: Patient able to tell group he cannot open up his feelings there as yet.

3/29/85: Patient feels "comfortable" for the first time in a group, as of last Tuesday's session.

4/5/85: (Extra session called for excitedly by patient a few hours after his early morning session.)

Patient: My mother was able to be herself with me, and we had to keep this a secret from my father. This taught me to tape record—in my mind— all conversations I had with others, so I would never forget who said what to me and, therefore, would not betray anyone's secret.

4/23/85: Patient frightened about "taking the next step, of rebuilding myself from the top down or from the outside in. I built myself from the bottom up, and I'm afraid what might happen if I try to rebuild myself."

4/26/85: Patient feels his mood states alter—like Billy Mulligan's—without his control and without his knowing why. [Note: The patient lent the therapist a copy of the book *Billy Mulligan* because "there is something about him that is like me; I don't know what exactly."]

5/3/85: Patient says he used to steal money (first coins, then small bills) from his parents and hide them in a "false binder" on his book shelf.

Patient had been stealing food from grocery stores (especially inexpensive meats) until two years ago, when he was caught and "talked my way out of it" and "realized that the attention I needed I was getting in therapy, and I didn't need to steal anymore." [Note: The patient had never mentioned his stealing before in treatment.]

5/17/85: Patient described his self as being locked away safely inside a "safe" which has a "secret combination which even I have forgotten, so I can't give it away even if I wanted to."

5/24/85: Patient wants to leave group because (1) "I don't want to give strangers ammunition to hurt me with; people can be cruel and I can't stand it; (2) "I'm afraid I could destroy them with my words"; (3) "If you tell them something about how you feel about a devastating event—like my father's accident—they will categorize you. It's phony."

5/25/85: Patient says that there have been several key sessions for him this year in therapy:

The first was to realize he had a right to have his own feelings.

The second was to realize he had a right to have his own thoughts.

The third, Friday, was that his insights were often correct, even though others could not see or understand what he saw and understood.

7/9/85: Patient feels he has reached a turning point in his therapy where the "journey in" has become the "journey out." He feels excited and scared that his life is now under his own direction. He feels that the "trickle of hope" that always existed in the past is gone and has become his whole self, or at least "huge."

7/12/85: The patient gave the therapist a copy of a letter he wrote recently to an old male friend who had advised him to seek therapy years ago because "you seem to not connect to people." The following are excerpts from this letter:

Dear Mr. X.,

The time has come for me to go public with the *New* L. Being that you spurred the emergence, you get the first announcement. This Personality Under New Management and Open to Life. Since our last visit I have experienced extreme changes in my life. The walls of Jericho have come tumbling down in succession. . . . My years of therapy for a long, long time were a crawl through the desert in search of water. The years were meager in return on investment as Dan, my therapist, attempted to breach my often formidable defenses. What you had experienced and fortunately pointed out to me. After years of Dan and me dueling, his professional skills and compassion against my defensive maze-building and distrust of people's intentions, we slowly created an infrastructure for support of external pressures (i.e., negativity, impressed thoughts and ideas, bad communications). This support allowed the me that is me to separate from all the bad input that had been layered on year after year of my life. The infrastructure began to hold out the repetitions of the bad input. My personality glass house grew slowly but mostly steadily over the last six years. The flip side of the cliché "people who live in glass houses shouldn't throw stones" is that a person in a glass house can see out or in clearly. Looking back, I see that in November . . . is when the house was completed but missing certain important features—a heating and cooling system, telephone, and the niceties of being a home. The last few months have been a bumpy juggernaut that in succession has given me the reality of the rights to my own feelings and beliefs (heating and cooling), why I was so secretive (communications), and the knowledge and ability that I can be me (homeliness). For the first time in my life my personality is mine without other people's stamp. My being is my home. And the mortgage is fully paid for. From here on, therapy is for remodeling, expansion, and maintenance. Eventually all the tools become mine and I become both architect and contractor. My house of glass allows me to see those old problems as they approach and then react and relate to them. My house has also been built with numerous doors so I can venture forth to find experiences that don't come *to* me. . . .

Love, L.

7/12/85: Patient remembers something else about his father's accident. When the repair truck came, the patient was sent with a flashlight to warn the oncoming cars. The patient remembers the driver asleep at the wheel before he crashed into his father. The family lawyer told the patient *never to tell anyone* what he had seen because the driver did not have insurance. The patient remembers being told that, if he ever told the truth, his father would suffer greatly.

7/26/85: "I'm going to start the session today! I realized after the last session just how good a therapist you are. You were able to pinpoint exactly what was making me depressed. I talked with my boss, Mr. U., yesterday and told him that I didn't trust Mr. Z. [the patient's immediate superior] and, also, that he—Mr. U.—was also part of the problem. I didn't say *I* had a problem; I made sure not to say that."

Summer break: Patient feels very vulnerable with his newly found "New L.-self" and is given the name of an analyst to call if he feels the need while the therapist is on vacation. [Note: The patient did not call the covering analyst, but did call the group therapist for an individual session during this break.]

9/10/85: Patient is angry with the therapist for abandoning him at a critical stage of his therapy, but is unable to express this anger towards the therapist and does so only against himself. The patient is regressed and withdrawn again.

9/17/85: Patient continues to express anger towards himself for "not being able to take care of myself."

9/24/85: Patient wants to leave his job, leave therapy, and leave New York City again. "I can't fit into society. I do not want to be dependent on you or anyone; I need to be independent." [Note: Dependency needs are experienced as loss of self, while independence is fantasized as equivalent to the existence of the true self.]

10/1/85: Patient enrolled at a university and is taking ten credits after all. Patient withdrawing from group because "groups are not trustworthy."

10/11/85: Patient feels a "clear shield or wall" lies between him and the group, but he can now see the wall more clearly and can see that the group wants him to join them, not only out of their needs, but for his sake and pleasure as well.

10/15/85: Patient feels a "block" at school; he can't remember things he knows he knows. He remembers his parents became "frustrated" with him for forgetting on tests what he knew at school.

10/22/85: Patient experienced "all my energy going to building a *concrete* wall" in the group therapy session last week and "seeing myself doing it—like an observer." At the same time the patient visited old friends and was able to be "spontaneous" with them in a way he had never been able to be before.

11/5/85: Patient feels a great calmness coming into him as "the pieces of my self seem to be strong enough to fight off the old pieces of my self."

11/8/85: Patient returned for a second session on this day at his urgent request.
Talked about his last sexual encounter (one of his few sexual experiences): intercourse with a woman he had dated a few times only. Patient was able to have an erection and orgasm, but "I didn't know if what I was doing was right. I touched her rib cage, breasts, vagina, clitoris, but then I pulled away. I don't know if what I was doing was making her happy or not."

11/12/85: Patient not doing schoolwork; dropped one of three classes.

11/19/85: Patient believes he is not showing the group his "new personality" because he wants to use the group to work on problems regarding his family and the old family dynamics.

11/26/85: Patient feels his self-worth vis-à-vis his accomplishments (e.g., at work or at school). However, at the same time he feels he does these things to please his parents. Thus, he does not allow himself to feel good when he succeeds, since this success comes from a false self. This trap makes it very difficult for the patient to feel a development of a positive true self.

12/3/85: Patient talked with his youngest sister and became depressed. He "fought" with her when she asked him to do something for her and he said, "No," and she hung up the phone. Sister's affection for him is couched in what he feels are demands, and he needed to free himself from this by saying "no"; yet, at the same time, he was punished by his sister by her removal of her attention and affection from him for refusing to do what she wanted.

12/6/85: Patient quoted the therapist's paper about him in his group, regarding his opening doors to people and then seeing if they pass his secret tests, and when they fail (inevitably) these secret tests of their "true" characters, he closes the door on them again. The patient chose to go to group last time rather than stay at a business party. "I wanted to be with the group because I enjoyed being with them, I didn't want to miss a group session."

12/10/85: Patient's lack of follow-through at work and at school relates to his determination to develop his true self undiluted by the demands/wishes of others.

12/13/85: "I really trust you," patient says to therapist for the first time.
Patient thinking of leaving group again because "I really want to make a commitment to myself." Patient feels he doesn't want to concentrate on others' problems, but only on his own.
Also thinking of dropping out of school for a while and taking a leave of absence from work—for the same reasons as leaving group.

12/17/85: Patient is going to leave group again.
Patient's favorite poems are Robert Frost's "The Road Not Taken" and Dylan Thomas's "Do Not Go Gentle into That Good Night."

1/7/86: Patient returns from visit to parents over Christmas holidays; he feels OK about the visit but has decided he doesn't want to see them much anymore. Patient asks: "I wonder why no one wondered how the accident [of his father's] affected me?"

1/14/86: Frequent headaches still. False self versus true self. How to be himself amidst others—at work, school, group, in therapy.

1/17/86: Patient left group finally. "I don't want to take care of people now; I want to be selfish and concentrate on myself. The monolith [Note: as the "wall" came to be called by Mr. L. in his treatment, named after the block-wall in the movie *2001*] is no longer between me and other people. It has moved and is intrapersonal now. I can't access my own feelings and memories and dreams now."

2/4/86: Patient's headaches cleared up after the last therapy session when he realized that the therapist felt he was strong enough to leave New York City for three months and, therefore, to leave therapy for three months. Patient feels sad about the possibility of terminating therapy: "It was the one constant in all of this time."

2/7/86: "The happiest moment in my life may have been last session, when you intimated that you believe I now have all the pieces I need to live my life happily. I cannot tell you how happy that makes me feel."

2/11/86: Patient able to say he masturbates and looks at pornographic magazines and reads pornographic books. But he is not able to talk about his fantasies in this area as yet.

2/14/86: Patient was granted a three-month leave of absence from work and will be going to a southern location. Meanwhile, the patient took on the new job of assistant stage manager in an Off Broadway theater production— something he has never done before. Patient seems happy and excited.

2/18/86: Patient feels he has learned in therapy to no longer let other people's problems become his problems: "I'm like the new anti-graffiti trains—they can write all over me, but it comes right off."

2/25/86: Patient feels "sad" about leaving friends at work for three months, and about leaving therapy. He also expressed his fear of sex and not knowing what to do to get over this fear.

3/7/86: First week of his "liberation," and the patient regressed. He feels the "shoulds" dictate what he should be doing, and so he "doesn't do anything." The therapist's interpretations seem "contaminating" to him as well. Patient wants to do things completely on his own now.

DISCUSSION

Mr. L.'s need to go on long breaks from treatment has been consistent throughout the years. Before this last stint, from March 27, 1984 to March 7, 1986, Mr. L. left treatment for a six-month break. He later explained that he felt these breaks were as important to his treatment as the treatment itself. He believed he needed to get away from the therapist in order to consolidate all that had occurred while in the treatment proper. One is reminded of Wolf's (1959, 1960) concept of the "alternate session" in group treatment where the patients in a group meet alternately with the group leader and without the group leader. The belief here is that patients benefit from being removed from parental figures in the development of their autonomous identities and true selves. Mr. L. seemed to have discovered this for himself.

Wolf and Kutash (1985) warned that placing submerged patients in groups—though often very helpful because "the patient's transference to the therapist can become sufficiently diluted in the group to allow the acceptance of interpretations around his ambivalating within the group (p. 526) "—can sometimes also prove ineffectual. They write: "The di-egophrenic may sit in silence in the face of a group propelled by the therapist who chooses to emphasize overpowering group process and group dynamics, a silence that is manifestly submissive and latently rebellious and hostile, in which he endures his own solitude as the group must endure it" (p. 525). Earlier (1984a), these two authors warned of the hazards of group for certain submerged patients: "A danger for the di-egophrenic in group psychotherapy is that he may simply continue to submit and rebel in the face of group pressures, of group dynamics, or under the influence of members who are more outspokenly forceful" (p. 14).

In Mr. L.'s case, he certainly did relapse into his silent persona in group, and he was certainly ambivalent about it throughout his exposure to group.

However, this experience was not reported by Mr. L. as a "danger"; rather, he found it invaluable. He was able to see himself much more clearly in the areas he was most interested in working on: his true self versus his false self. By discussing this issue privately from time to time with the group leader, and regularly with his therapist, Mr. L. was able to experience this core issue from various perspectives other than his own. Furthermore, the issues were fresh and recent and vivid and unrelenting—they pressed for working through. His very decision to leave group—in order to demonstrate to himself his "right" to his own feelings, thoughts, and behaviors— also helped him to see that he had the same right in his therapy, at work, and at school. The patient was able to practice this independence in a benign environment (which work and therapy were not, since he depended on them far too highly to risk losing them forever). Furthermore, although Mr. L. did not show his "new personality" to group members, he did show it to his friends as he never had before. That is, Mr. L. says that his newly experienced "spontaneity" with his closest friends resulted directly from "what I learned in group about myself. I couldn't use it there— I think because the group members don't mean anything to me really; but, I was able to use it with my friends. As a result, my friendships—for the first time—seem to make me feel really close to people and really good inside."

8

A Paranoid Patient

Kenneth Wald, C.S.W.

Anyone can do any amount of work, provided it isn't the work he's supposed to be doing at that moment.

—Robert Benchley

E go-submergence is a construct with useful applications that cut across various diagnostic categories. In this chapter I will show its application to an aspect of treatment of a chronic paranoid psychotic condition.

Submergence, as Wolf and Kutash (1985) describe it, is characterized by the development of two pseudo-egos in conflict with each other, and the submergence or suppression of an intact ego, called the "submerged ego," that is in "a state of partial arrest." This patient primarily introjected her mother's unconscious paranoid demands, which formed the core of the paranoid maternal pseudo-ego. Following this, as a defensive measure, the patient's ego formed a second pseudo-ego whose purpose was to protect the submerged ego and oppose the paranoid maternal pseudo-ego in such a way as to maintain the connection with the mother and thus avoid the threat of abandonment and retaliation that the patient felt her autonomous development would precipitate. This was due to her mother's powerful narcissistic need to maintain a symbiotic relationship with her daughter. This assisted her paranoid mother in maintaining her own maximal possible cohesive sense of self, temporal stability, and positive affective coloration of her self-representations (Stolorow and Lachman 1980, p. 10). This pseudo-ego is called the rebellious pseudo-ego, since its primary purpose is to oppose, either overtly or covertly, the paranoid maternal pseudo-ego.

For this patient one of the essential tasks was to resolve her ambivalence, thus allowing for the further development and emergence of her submerged ego, with its synthetic and adaptive functions and perceptions of reality more intact. In order to accomplish this, the nature of the relationship of this submerged and paranoid psychotic patient to her pathogenic parents, especially her mother, had to be reworked.

She had to learn to accept her parents for the way they really had been, including their limitations. She had to learn to develop the capacity to see past the gross distortions of reality that she introjected from her paranoid psychotic mother and cold and removed father. Between her two parents, they created a sensed state of relationships in my patient that was charged with paranoia and rife with ambivalence. She was compelled to deny her own perceptions and abide by the judgments of her parents, especially her mother. She submitted to her mother's perceptions of the world as dangerous and to her father's coldness and distance, which also pushed her deeper into the paranoid maternal orbit. Due to the perceived threat of harsh parental retaliation in the form of punishment or abandonment, her own perceptions of reality were defensively suppressed by her own ego. Her own ego became submerged, and in its stead the two pseudo-egos emerged as the observable and dominant structures in her psychic life. The first pseudo-ego was an introjection primarily of her mother's dangerous paranoia and need for a symbiotic relationship with her daughter, which was also markedly increased in power by the cold remoteness that she felt characterized her father's relationship with her. Because her father's role in the creation of the first pseudo-ego was secondary in the sense that he did not appear consistently to oppose his daughter's autonomous development, this pseudo-ego is referred to as the paranoid maternal pseudo-ego. To dethrone the pseudo-ego that emerged out of the parents' relationship to my patient, it was necessary for her to understand and gain a feeling for her mother's real, albeit distorted, love and concern for her as well as her father's detached and cold concern, which she later realized was not really directed at her. Rather, it was a result of profound trauma secondary to war combat suffered by her father, from which he never recovered.

Change was initiated by establishing a new kind of relationship with the therapist that made it possible for the patient to risk expressing her own felt problems gradually, and her own perceptions and thoughts about her problems, which led her to challenge the previous supremacy and accuracy of her pseudo-egos. As this process proceeded over a two and a half year period, the patient's submerged ego gradually emerged from being dominated by the introjected paranoid maternal pseudo-ego and the patient's often covert but rebellious pseudo-ego.

The patient's paranoia and ambivalence were diminished by interrupting the usual course of her psychotic process. The therapeutic entry point was for the therapist to intervene actively in a verbal and empathic way as soon as silences developed, which were early in treatment almost always representative of the psychotic process and the paranoid maternal pseudo-ego. Active interaction by the therapist with the patient interrupted the psychotic paranoid process and assisted in the emergence of the submerged ego and its more reality-based perceptions.

HISTORY

The patient, Ms. D., is a married woman in her fifties with grown children. She has been psychotically paranoid for over twenty years, but never hospitalized. The psychotic break occurred in response to her husband's loss of work and alcoholism, the patient's assuming all responsibility for managing the family with its attendant stress, and the family's going on welfare, which was intensely humiliating to the patient and resulted in her withdrawing from others and accepting her mother's paranoid representation of the outside world as hostile and inimical to her. She has a history of intense interpersonal fearfulness, going back to early childhood.

When the patient was a child, her mother was at times observably psychotic at home, but was initially able to hide this in public. The mother had been perceived as odd by family members since my patient was a child. She was guarded, suspicious, and secretive, as well as being afraid that outsiders could see what she was doing, or even read her mind, and harm her or family members, particularly her children. She was also at times impaired in her judgment and ability to take care of her children adequately. This is linked to the patient's hiding her being on welfare, and her own and her family's difficulties from others. When the patient was in early adolescence, her mother was eventually permanently hospitalized, after she ran out of her apartment in her nightclothes, screaming that something horrible was chasing her. It became apparent at this point that the patient's mother was a chronic paranoid schizophrenic with persecutory delusions and visual and auditory hallucinations.

It seems to be typical of pathogenic mothers to invest themselves inordinately in their children (Wolf and Kutash 1985, p. 523), and this is what the patient's mother did. Much of the patient's mother's limited ability to regulate and maintain a cohesive, stable, and positive affective coloration of her own self was derived from her role as a mother. She sought to keep the patient close to her and dependent on her. One way in which she achieved this was by inculcating in the patient her own (the mother's) paranoid fears of others. She succeeded in doing this and the patient was, as a child, adolescent, and adult excessively fearful, distrustful, and eventually paranoid toward others. So the mother's paranoia created a fear of the external world in the patient that pushed the patient closer to the mother, making her even more dependent upon the mother's perceptions and resulting in the introjection of a paranoid maternal pseudo-ego and the development of a defensive rebellious pseudo-ego. The mother was threatened by any of the patient's movements towards autonomy. The patient's earliest memories of her own intense fearfulness and her mother's bizarre and frightening actions go back to as early as 3 years of age and represent a screen memory of other earlier and later traumatic events that were gradually recovered, often in fragments. However, there were also unshakable positive feelings towards her mother. The patient always felt that initially she had had a very close relationship with her mother. However, she observed throughout her life how her mother needed to foster a symbiotic relationship both with herself and with her younger brother. She felt that her mother had been like this with her until the brother's birth when she was 3 years old. She had rebelled against his birth and recovered memories from when she was about 4 years old of thinking to herself that she could push him out of the window and be rid of him and his interference with her closeness to her mother. She recalled in therapy how heavy he was as she carried and dragged him to the window. Her mother stopped her by asking her what she was doing, not realizing her daughter's intention. The patient felt she had been found out by her mother. Later on, she was horrified by the thought that she could come so close to being a "murderess." However, the birth of her brother fortunately produced a separation between her and her mother that appears to have fostered a rebellious spirit (the rebellious pseudo-ego), less dependency, hatred of her mother, and less absorption of her mother's toxic paranoia and need for symbiosis with her daughter. Her brother was less fortunate. He was mildly retarded and taught to be almost totally dependent upon his mother, her paranoid perceptions, and her need for an exclusive symbiotic relationship with him.

The patient's mother, because of her own needs, had to maintain an exclusive symbiotic relationship with her son, as she had tried to do initially with my patient. The son was kept at home throughout his life and prevented from doing anything outside the home. When he became seriously ill in early adulthood, the mother could not permit someone else, even a physician, to treat him and thus break into the exclusive mother-child relationship. Lacking medical treatment, he died. My patient experienced this event, even in her fifties, as a "horror."

DISCUSSION OF THERAPEUTIC ISSUES AND TREATMENT TECHNIQUE

At the beginning of treatment, a salient piece of information emerged. Out of a detailed exploration of the patient's past therapeutic experiences, the basis of the therapeutic approach to dealing with the patient's psychotic paranoia was formed. The silences that developed in past therapies as well as in the present therapy emerged as the symptomatic expression of the patient's psychotic paranoia. A decision was made at the beginning of treatment not to allow silence to develop in the sessions. This approach was decided upon because in prior therapies, silence on the part of the therapists resulted in the progressive development of strong fears that the therapists would do some unspecified harm to her. Because of this, she had to break off past therapies. This was an explicit example of intense paranoid projection arising from her introjection of her mother's paranoid fears in the form of a paranoid maternal pseudo-ego.

An investigation of the circumstances in which the paranoia developed to unbearable proportions, forcing her to terminate therapy, revealed that her therapists would frequently remain silent in session. The intense meaning of the silence to her is illustrated by a memory she had later on in treatment. She said, "I was three or four years old; my mother put me in the corner of the apartment's hallway, she kept the lights off, put one finger to her lips, and said, 'Shh, don't make a sound,' and then left the apartment. No one else was there. I was terrified that something awful was going to happen, I didn't make a sound or move. It was dark, there was a window at the end of the hall, far away, some light was coming through it. I wanted to go there but I was scared to move. I didn't make a sound. I didn't know if she'd ever return or if I'd remain there alone forever."

My active interaction in the form of talking and relating to her current feeling state, as well as reality events that could be "checked out" by her interrupted the development of the paranoid process and her behaving from the perception of the paranoid pseudo-ego implanted by her mother, or from the fear of abandonment by her mother or significant others in the present. It also permitted the emergence and further development of the reality-oriented perceptions of her submerged ego rather than further strengthening her rebellious pseudo-ego, which would have been to the detriment of her autonomous development. This permitted the emergence of both present and past psychotic perceptions linked to the maternally derived paranoid pseudo-ego of the mother within a reality-oriented matrix established and maintained by the therapeutic relationship. This was facilitated through the positive transference relationship. The patient saw the therapist in a variety of roles that were affectively stimulating and warm to her. She often related to me as a warm paternal figure, a replacement for her dead father who she had felt had been cold and remote but "normal," and she began to remember in therapy that he had even been occasionally friendly and warm to her when she was a child. She also related to me at times with the friendliness she felt towards her children and this, too, stimulated the emergence of her own warm feelings and a greater sense of identity.

Material, that is, paranoid perceptions of reality that had been bound to (or by) the introjected paranoid maternal pseudo-ego, was ventilated and transformed in ways that allowed its integration into the developing and more emergent submerged ego in the sessions. The patient's submerged ego became progressively more adaptive at transforming and integrating the paranoid functions of the maternal pseudo-ego and the defensive functions of the rebellious pseudo-ego. Over time, she was able to accomplish this more and more outside of sessions and away from the analyst. The patient's need to submit to the mother and her internalized representations were much enhanced by the lack of warmth, the feeling of distance from, and lack of support from, a father she had felt was remote and unavailable. That left only her mother to relate to, and she felt pushed by her father into this relationship as well as pulled in by her mother.

So, in this case, for this psychotically paranoid patient medicated with various antipsychotic medications, as discussed, silence on the part of the therapist was contraindicated. My original reasons were that her anxiety level increased to unmanageable proportions when I was silent. Also, she desperately needed the object relationship in the form of words she could hear—a consistently friendly, warm tone of voice—and my relieving her of the pressure of speaking. Thus, I took the role of a parent who actively interacts with a child verbally and seeks to engage and develop the child's capacities to relate to others, develop and test out her perceptions of reality, be soothed by ventilating her anxieties, and act as a counter to the introjected paranoid maternal pseudo-ego. In this way, the patient's submerged ego was encouraged to emerge and develop in a reality-oriented way and challenge the dominance of the pseudo-egos.

In the psychoanalytic literature (Pressman 1960) are many references to the negative impact of the therapist's silence that relate to this patient.

These include the danger of increasing the patient's resistance, thus impeding the therapy. The above did occur in prior therapies and was a striking factor in the failure to continue to make progress in previous therapies. The patient was able, with the help of prior therapists, to become more active outside the home, but the paranoid ideation remained intense, frequent, and of long duration. Also, silence on my part would have represented a repetition of a traumatic infantile experience. To this patient, silence represented the return of the trauma of the transmission of her paranoid mother's fears into her, as well as the feared loss of her mother as an object to relate to when the patient was a child. As previously mentioned, the memory of the dark hallway, her mother "shshing" her and leaving her alone, is one example of this. In the therapeutic interaction, periods of brief silence were followed by a loss in the patient's adult abilities to observe herself, and also by the patient's chit-chatting, a nervous replay of the day's events much to the detriment of the expression of her emotions and thoughts. This strengthened her defenses in a maladaptive way and increased her anxiety. Rapid interaction between the therapist and the patient, without permitting the silence to develop, resulted in the patient probing into her fears and increased the strength and warmth of the patient–therapist relationship.

The marked increase in her verbal communications also obviously relieved and relaxed her, as some anxiety was discharged through the motor action of speech. Also, in response to the therapist's active interaction, the patient became more expressive, gesticulating with her hands and arms, moving about more in her chair rather than sitting very still, also making eye contact more frequently, and overall, displaying more and more over time a genuine affective expressiveness in place of the paranoid fearfulness or quiescence.

Therapeutically, silence was also viewed as placing too much pressure on the patient, which generated excessive anxiety. This had caused her to leave two prior therapies. The excessive anxiety caused by extended as well as brief moments of silence resulted in her becoming either more fearful and paranoid or more detached and depressed, with a flat affect and a diminished connection to her own perceptions. This represented her way of defending against the overwhelming paranoid fears that developed in response to the silence. At the beginning of therapy, before a positive transference had developed, the patient was more vulnerable to bouts of severe depression than she had been in the past. These depressions sometimes lasted for weeks at a time, reducing her activities outside of the home to minimal levels. At times, this resulted in her missing therapy sessions in spite of her fierce determination to overcome her illness.

Silence also increased an already severe superego reaction. After about twenty months in therapy, some silences were allowed to develop and her feelings in relation to the silences were explored. She felt she would be condemned during the silence by the therapist as she had been by her mother. A previously repressed childhood memory of her mother condemning her for killing a kitten in the street by stepping on it emerged. She remembered feeling terribly guilty that she had "murdered" the kitten. She also remembered her mother pulling her rapidly away from the scene of her crime while muttering that people would see that she had killed the kitten. She then remembered that she had been terribly fearful of what the adults on the street would do to her if they realized she had murdered the kitten. She felt they would kill her as she had killed the kitten. She felt grateful that her mother had protected her by quickly pulling her away from the scene of the "crime," and then with a startled expression as she related this previously untold crime of hers, she realized she hadn't killed the kitten. She realized it was her mother's fears when they were on the street exposed to the eyes of others that had created this fantasy that the kitten was dead and that a fearful retaliation would take place.

In the months following her remembering the "crime" of the murdered kitten, which represented a screen memory, her fears of people, really the dreaded adults of childhood, receded and she recovered a crucial memory about wanting to push her brother out of the window of the apartment and her feeling that she was a "murderess." This memory and the previous memory of the kitten represented a major positive shift in the therapy that included both a lifting of the repression and a strengthening of her submerged ego, which eventually resulted in her fears toward her mother, in the form of the introjected paranoid maternal pseudo-ego, diminishing to manageable and nonpsychotic proportions.

Prior to these childhood memories being recovered, the silence of classmates, fellow members of the singing group she had joined, her husband, mother, and father, as well as fears of her own silences, had

arisen as clear and compelling current issues that contained many paranoid fears that others disliked, hated, would punish, or think bad things
about her, or make sexual advances to her, or leave her alone in a cold
world had repeatedly come up and been dealt with often in a reality-based
way. As the patient at this time was actively psychotic and often felt that
others could read her inner thoughts, including her heterosexual, and
worse yet, occasional homosexual fantasies, lack of active intervention on
the part of the therapist until her ego functioning had markedly improved
was avoided. Silence also represented others being hostile and unresponsive to her. She felt this way with a varying degree of intensity toward
virtually everyone she met. This included even those who she thought and
felt were genuinely friendly to her, including the therapist. However, she
did increasingly develop her own perceptions of what was really happening, even though at first she was unable to act upon these perceptions, but
rather continued to react to others according to the paranoid, maternally
induced pseudo-ego or the alternately rebellious or seemingly compliant
defensive pseudo-ego.

Additionally, reality testing and the use of the therapist as a "real object"
were necessary to counteract excessive regression and a loss of reality. Also,
silence evoked a loss in the patient's capacity to be cooperative as it ran
counter to her obvious need for active input and sometimes even direction
by the therapist. She had frequent dreams that indicated the need for
direction by a friendly person. In her dreams she would start off in a
familiar place and then begin to wander around; but then something
terrible would happen, as when her mother ran screaming out of the house
in a psychotic paranoid frenzy, and the patient would run away until she
found herself in totally strange territory, lost, and looking for someone to
help her find her way "back," an expression of her need to find a lost object
relationship with her mother, as well as create a new one that was more
adaptive, reality oriented, and warm.

Last, silence interfered with the patient's ability to free associate, come
in contact with and express fantasies and dreams, and develop a fuller
transference that could be expressed and worked through. The patient
would free associate only in the context of my not permitting silences of
any length to develop. She remembered and naïvely spilled dreams and
fantasies like a child. These were sometimes deliberately not interpreted by

the therapist in order to avoid the patient's attempts to get the therapist to take responsibility for her life, thereby encouraging the persistence of the patient's ambivalence and the continued suppression of her ego (Wolf 1980). Also, interpretations early in treatment, if made too frequently, would have been experienced as intrusive to the patient, the danger being that the interpretations would have resulted in an increase in anxiety and hence an increase in defensive maneuvers that were connected to the patient's pseudo-egos and the ongoing paranoid process. This therapeutic procedure allowed the maternally derived paranoid pseudo-ego to be punctured by reality, and enabled the submerged ego to develop greater capacity to adapt and emerge as the primary ego with its perceptions, reality testing, and ability to act intact.

Ms. D. also needed to develop the capacity to ventilate her genuine affects, which had been dammed up by the paranoid fears associated with the introjected maternal pseudo-ego and the defensive maneuvers of the rebellious pseudo-ego. Her experience of both hearing her own expression of her affects, as well as experiencing harmonious and gratifying interaction with the therapist, libidinized her verbal capacity to express herself, which counteracted the regressive pull to her mother's paranoid perceptions. Hence, it was often more beneficial not to interpret her productions but to do whatever was necessary to encourage them and thus encourage the emergence and development of a positively libidinized submerged ego. Later on in treatment, after her productions had been sufficiently libidinized and the paranoid maternal pseudo-ego reduced in its hold on the patient, silences were gradually permitted to take place. By this point, the patient's reaction to silence was not automatically paranoid. The paranoid feelings were being more successfully bound by her internally. She now felt that silence was a "blank." The therapist pointed out that silence was not just the blank she now consciously thought it was, but rather had a lot going on in it. The patient then began to look in a focused way at what was contained in the silence with a sense that she could master this, just as she had previously partially mastered her paranoid fears in a variety of social situations. She could now reflect on unpleasant material that was not reality based. Eventually, out of the silence, highly eroticized feelings toward the therapist, both conscious and in dreams, emerged and were interpreted. This led to the further emergence, development, and strengthening of the submerged ego, and to a further reduction of her need to align herself with the introjected paranoid maternal pseudo-ego or her rebellious but often seemingly compliant pseudo-ego.

While Ms. D. continued to repress and defend herself against a great deal, what was more important was that, in spite of this, new material was brought up that she could gain insight into, assimilate, act upon, construct a meaningful sense of life history from, and relate to in later sessions that reduced her paranoid fears and the power of the paranoid maternal pseudo-ego and moved her toward the development of an adaptive functioning ego.

The patient primarily brought up her paranoid fantasies about what others in the present would do to her. These fantasies were laboriously "checked out" by the patient. She is a very courageous woman without even realizing it. This was stated directly to the patient, as her courage represented a function of her submerged ego that, like other adaptive functions of her submerged ego, had not adequately been brought into conscious awareness. She experienced a greater sense of self as aspects of herself that had not been validated by her parents were validated by the therapist. The patient regarded her own perceptions with a great deal of suspiciousness as she identified with her mother's view that any separation from the mother, that is, that autonomous adaptive functioning on my patient's part would not only be a betrayal of the mother but also dangerous to my patient. Her mother gave the daughter a powerful message while she was alive—"never leave me." This message, as well as the mother's perceptions of the world and relationships and her paranoid behavior, were introjected by my patient. While she rebelled against this, she was not able to free herself from it until she gained an ally in the form of psychotherapy. Then she began to "check things out" rather than accepting the dictates of the introjected paranoid maternal pseudo-ego.

For example, she began to ask people with whom she associated for feedback and validation about herself and what she was thinking, feeling, or doing. She asked members of the singing groups she belonged to if they liked her, what they thought of her performance, whether they would like to sit with her, if she could have a ride home with them, what they thought about some specific incident, and so on. These were all things she had not done before, but now she was feeling able to accept or reject their views.

Ventilation of the paranoid fantasies of the present was a major contrib-
utor to her ability to recover childhood memories, some of which had been
repressed, and others that, while conscious, had never been related to
another human being. The transference implications, and implications for
the lessening of resistance, of my not being silent, began to emerge after a
period of time in which I would not always immediately respond to her.
She came in with the following dream. There was a man in a corner, a
bright window to his right, a desk and chair in front of him. He was
standing. She went over to him, put her arms around him, and kissed him.
Her first associations to the dream were of her husband, but she stated it
didn't look like him at all. I asked her to describe the man. She did: he was
tall, broad-shouldered, and had a beard and mustache. She looked at me,
blushed, and said, "It was you." She was infused with various emotions and
sexual feelings. She was embarrassed but talked about her feelings and was
fairly assertive, saying, "It's my right to have these feelings; this is therapy!"
It was the therapist in the dream. It was a dark room except for the light
coming in the window, and she had herself and me in the corner together.
She was no longer in the dark hallway of her apartment, with the only light
coming through a distant window, alone, lonely, fearful, and silent. In the
dream she was quite actively kissing me—a new edition of an old memory
that was linked to recovery of previously repressed positive memories of
her father, and a more reality-oriented and sympathetic evaluation of him
that had developed during the course of treatment. This also represented
her growing capacity to pursue vigorously what she needed and wanted,
while maintaining an acute awareness of her fears, which no longer
overwhelmed her. Her dream of kissing and hugging was not representative of a pseudo-courage but represented a growing linkage to and emergence of her submerged ego and a developing personal creativity and
capacity to lessen the tyranny of the pseudo-egos.

Concurrent with the movement of the patient toward the further development and emergence of the submerged ego, the introjected paranoid
maternal pseudo-ego was largely disincorporated. It lost much of its power
to organize the patient's perceptions, thoughts, feelings, and behavior
around paranoid themes and the unconscious fears of maternal abandonment and retaliation as the price of separating from the mother and
developing an autonomous self. Additionally, the alternately rebellious and

compliant defensive pseudo-ego progressively lost its functions to the now strengthened "liberated" (Wolf and Kutash 1985) and previously submerged ego that was now dominant. The defensive pseudo-ego was progressively being disincorporated as it was now unable to drain energy from the more "liberated" ego, which emerged as a more personally creative and adaptive structure that henceforth acted as the executive agency of the patient's psyche. As the treatment proceeded, the patient's diagnosis was revised from that of a chronic paranoid psychotic disorder to a paranoid personality disorder. The patient no longer had chronic persistent persecutory delusions; she was less fearful, more socially active, and more in touch with her internal feelings, including those of an unpleasant nature.

She remained moderately suspicious and hypersensitive, which she was aware of and able to deal with reasonably well. Her affectivity was also now only moderately restricted.

In conclusion, the psychotic nature of the patient's disorder and the unique meaning of silence to the patient necessitated a treatment that was somewhat different from the treatment for other patients. This was particularly noticeable in the handling of silence. Silence is typically used in analysis to encourage free association and facilitate the emergence of unconscious material, filling in infantile amnesias, ventilating affective states, and producing dreams and fantasies. However, in this case, from the history of previous therapies, I hypothesized early in treatment that silence had a detrimental effect on the patient's previous progress in therapy, which would be repeated unless I adopted a different and much more interactive approach. This approach, which initially did not allow for the development of silences in the therapy sessions, interrupted the usual development of the psychotic paranoid process and established in its place a warm therapeutic alliance with multiple positive transferences that allowed for the strengthening emergence and "liberation" of the patient's submerged ego.

9

An Oedipally Conflicted Patient

Arnold Wm. Rachman, Ph.D.

The submerged personality patient's mother's position on abortion is that a fetus is a fetus until it graduates from medical school.

—Irwin L. Kutash

THE NEED FOR A HUMANISTIC DIAGNOSIS

I would like to share with you my clinical work with a fascinating individual I have been seeing in what might be termed a "humanistic analysis" for about twenty years. I have come to speak of this individual as "Oedipus from Brooklyn."

There are many theoretical vantage points from which to derive meaning for this individual's emotional problems and their amelioration. As I will outline in the next section, this analysis has been based upon certain tenets of humanistic psychology. I have always felt that the traditional diagnostic categories and evaluations have a pejorative, nonhumanistic quality. They don't describe the assets and potential of the individual as much as they focus on his psychopathology. As such, they seem to be used to "damn" an individual with a diagnosis, and give little hope either to the clinician or the individual for change and personal growth. If one were to read and take at face value the detailed diagnostic reports of a psychiatric, a psychosocial, or projective test evaluation, one would often conclude that an individual was so intrapsychically disturbed that it would be a miracle that he could cross the street by himself, until the demographic data revealed that the individual in question is the president of a major business, head of a university, or a trainee in psychoanalysis.

In 1956, Alexander Wolf introduced his notion of the submerged personality, which has appeal as a humanistic way to view emotional disturbance. In particular, it may provide an interesting and helpful way to view Oedipus from Brooklyn's psychological history and the development of his serious emotional problems. It also may provide an optimistic, humanistic view of the analysis of such an individual.

THE DEVELOPMENT OF THE SUBMERGED PERSONALITY

The concept of the submerged personality was developed by Wolf (1957, 1980) and elaborated by Wolf and Kutash (1984a), Kutash (1984b), and Wolf and Kutash (1985). It is an alternate humanistic framework for understanding and treating the development of psychopathology in the early period of mother/child interaction. It addresses the blocking of creative potential in the individual.

A submerged personality usually develops before the second year of life, when the psychosocial interaction between mother and child is characterized by the mother's control and domination. The mother does not view herself as separate from the child. The child is in a precarious emotional position with such a mother. If he does not submit to her will, he runs the risk of losing her approval and love. If he submits, he may lose his emerging sense of identity. In order to survive, he must construct some emotional compromise. Usually, some portion of the individual's ego is suppressed. A pseudo-ego develops, separate from his own real self. Underneath the submission lurk resentment and anger. A severe oppositional tendency develops. The tragedy that emerges is that the individual is emotionally drained of his creative energy by the ambivalence experienced between complying and rebelling.

The individual with a submerged personality problem must go beyond the struggle of negative parental transferences to the inner struggle of maintaining compulsive defenses against submission or rebellion. Wolf and Kutash (1984a) state "It is only when the unplanted parental seed dies that the creative ego can bear fruit" (p. 13).

We now turn to the development of the submerged personality adaptation in the individual I call Oedipus from Brooklyn.

THE DEVELOPMENT OF EGO-SUBMERGENCE IN OEDIPUS FROM BROOKLYN

Oedipus from Brooklyn is a white, middle-class Jewish male who was in his mid-twenties when he began analysis about twenty years ago. An honors graduate from one of the most prestigious colleges in the United States, he was in a state of social isolation and withdrawal, severe depression, and decompensation at the time of consultation. He was unemployed and living at home with his mother. His father had died several years before. Days were spent sleeping, smoking, listening to the radio, and masturbating.

His pseudonym derived from two essential identifying ingredients in his special life story. He was born and spent his formative years in Brooklyn, New York. Brooklyn also had the very special association to him as the psychological place where "the crimes were committed against him" by his mother. As a result of his analysis, he had to return to "the Brooklyn in his mind." In doing so, he began the process of identifying and working through the crimes of childhood, gaining control of these ghosts of the past and healing his psychic wounds.

The Oedipus part of the pseudonym identifies this man's fascination and obsession with the ancient Greek language and Greek mythology. For about a three-year period during the analytic phase of therapy, he was devoted to studying ancient Greek, which he taught himself. This was both an intellectual and emotional experience. When he had mastered ancient Greek, he read the original *Oedipus Trilogy* by Sophocles. His Greek studies and the desire to travel to the ancient world were an attempt to unravel his own oedipal conflict. From then on, he became "Oedipus from Brooklyn" for me.

THE THWARTING OF THE CREATIVE SELF

The story of Oedipus from Brooklyn's early childhood is the key to an understanding of his psychology. During his first year (perhaps as early as 4–6 months), Oedipus experienced a series of traumas when his emerging creative self was seriously thwarted, from which he did not begin to recover until recently. From the age of roughly 6 months to the present, Oedipus suffered intense emotional pain because he felt his mother had destroyed his natural desire to create. Instead of being a creative, happy individual, he was forced to work at an uncreative job he hated. Hopelessness, passivity, and resignation pervaded his existence.

The development of his psychopathology was inevitable in the family psychodynamics. His mother was a controlling, seductive, intrusive woman who saw herself as a "professional mother," a woman who lived and breathed for her children.

In his dreams, Oedipus depicted her as a "giant mole," an animal-like creature who bored her way into every cell of his body and mind. He experienced her aggression through her determined, insistent manner of being the controlling, all-hovering mother. Perhaps that is why as a child he would wake up in the middle of the night feeling that his parents were out to kill him. His father was the accomplice because he did nothing to stop the aggressive mother.

Oedipus's father was an emotionally distant, self-absorbed man whose twin sister had been hospitalized most of her adult life for mental illness. In Oedipus's dreams, his father was depicted as a cloud. He remembered him as an uninvolved man who would drift off into his own thoughts when Oedipus tried to make contact. He longed for fatherliness. His father's inability or unwillingness to curtail the poisonous effect of his wife's interaction with his son engendered a great deal of anger in Oedipus.

His younger brother was an object of his rage, one reason for which was the brother's usurping of his dominant position with the mother. The birth of this brother and the subsequent intense sibling rivalry was eventually to become a life-saving device for Oedipus. His brother's presence moved his mother's focus away from him, and the intense anger fueled the separation process. By withdrawing, Oedipus allowed a symbiotic-like connection to be formed between the brother and the mother, resulting in a homosexual somatic adaptation. The brother gave in and submitted to the mother, whereas Oedipus always resisted submission. (For a fuller description of his psychodynamics consult Rachman 1976, 1981, 1986.)

Oedipus's particular psychodynamics produced a pathogenic experience. His relationship with his mother brought about an early suppression of his creative self through her intrusive, controlling, unempathetic, narcissistic behavior. In all likelihood, his nurturant, nonconflicted period was very early and short lived. According to his report, she was never a nurturing mother. His unavailable father left Oedipus with nowhere to turn. With no one in the family to liberate him, Oedipus was overpowered by his mother. The only avenue for escape was withdrawal into his own world of fantasy and suppression of his creative self to protect himself from further invasion.

THE BUILDING BLOCK TRAUMA

Although Oedipus's entire childhood was marked by a continuing controlling intrusion, there was one experience that symbolized for him the loss of his creative self. Sometime during the first year of life, probably at about 4–6 months, Oedipus had an unforgettable experience. As he was able to recall and reexperience it under analysis, the following event appeared to take place:

One day, he was busily engaged in playing with building blocks. He was completely absorbed in building a structure, perhaps a building. He had his back to his mother, completely ignoring her, as he was totally involved in the adventure of creating a structure. He was enthralled. His mother, either intentionally, or by accident, reached over his shoulder and knocked the blocks over. Oedipus was surprised, but picked the blocks up and proceeded to rebuild the structure. The blocks were knocked down again. This time he was frustrated and angry. He tried to stop the invasion by moving into a corner of his playpen and hovering over his building. Once again, he returned to his building construction. This time, when his mother knocked down the blocks, he crawled into a ball and gave up. He did not try to build his structure again. Apparently, the mother, resentful that her son was more interested in his own creation than in her, struck out at him and tried to force him to pay attention to her. Oedipus did not experience it as a playful gesture between mother and child, but as a destructive act. He never forgot and never forgave it.

PSYCHOTHERAPY AND THE SUBMERGED PERSONALITY

The psychotherapy employed in this case was developed, in part, as a response to this individual's needs. This psychotherapy, which I have come to label *humanistic analysis*, is an attempt to integrate a particularly rich and innovative tradition within psychoanalysis of active and humanistic interaction, exemplified by the ideas and clinical practices of Sandor Ferenczi and the Hungarian school of psychoanalysis (Alexander, Balint, Coq Herron Group, DeForest, Deri, Herman, Lorand, Gedo, Thompson), and the contemporary developments in humanistic psychotherapy, exemplified by the work of Carl Rogers and the person-centered school of psychotherapy (Butler, Charduff, Gendlin, Rogers, Shlien, Truax). The integration of psychoanalysis with humanistic psychology is beginning to find adherents. In an initial attempt, Stolorow (1976) found similarities in Kohut and Rogers's formulations on empathy. Kahn (1985) has written a comprehensive review of the similarities and differences in Kohut's and Rogers's work, in which he states that "Kohut has succeeded in integrating many of Rogers's concepts of humanistic psychology into his version of psychoanalysis" (p. 893). Unfortunately, neither Rogers nor Kohut has paid tribute to the pioneering work of Ferenczi, who is the precursor of their thinking. A very specific connecting link between Ferenczi and Kohut will be presented here (Rachman and Wayne 1986, 1988).

HUMANISTIC ANALYSIS

Here is a brief outline of some basic tenets and practices of humanistic analysis as they were applied to the psychotherapy of Oedipus from Brooklyn to help him liberate his creative self. This clinical framework and practice may also have relevance for the psychotherapy of submerged personality, borderline, and so-called difficult individuals.

Humanistic analysis is an interpersonal/relationship-oriented analysis emphasizing the creation of an emotional encounter between analyst and analysand for the purpose of the patient's self-actualization. The relationship is intended to provide a corrective emotional experience with a caring, empathetic, demonstrative, parental figure to work through the traumas, conflicts, and anxieties of childhood, adolescence, or adulthood. Psychotherapy is seen as a holistic synthesis of *feeling*, the experiential component in the interaction, *knowing*, the value of understanding and developing insight into the origins of one's conflicts and their manifestations, and *doing*, the capacity to translate one's feelings and thoughts into creative action.

Such a synthesis occurs in three phases throughout the course of psychotherapy: (1) the empathic phase, in which the focus is the establishment of a relationship based on accurate empathetic understanding for the purpose of entering the internal frame of reference of the individual; (2) the analytic phase, in which the analysis of early recollections, fantasies, dreams, and transference material predominate; and (3) the action phase, in which the emotional experience of the empathetic relationship, the understanding of the psychodynamic material, and the insights developed from both the uncovering process and the encounter in the therapeutic relationship are translated into sustained, creative action. The action occurs both within the therapeutic sessions and in daily life. Many creative parameters are introduced, when appropriate, to aid the translation of insight into action. The major parameter in this case was group therapy, but others were also employed (see Rachman 1981).

The analysis of Oedipus from Brooklyn will be discussed in the three phases outlined.

The Empathetic Phase

Humanistic analysis follows the Rule of Empathy originated by Ferenczi (1928) and elaborated by other psychoanalysts (Rachman and Wayne 1986, 1988) and humanistic psychotherapists, such as Rogers (1951, 1959, 1961, 1967, 1975, 1978, 1979, 1980, 1986). The psychotherapeutic relationship is built upon the bedrock of empathy. The analyst's attention is focused upon a special empathetic listening that suspends all value judgments, theoretical assumptions, and preconceived notions regarding the meaning of the individual's behavior. What is listened to is the analysand's "phenomenal experience," his being-in-the-world. The analyst listens to how the analysand feels, thinks, behaves, and creates meaning in the world, not to how the analyst interprets the meaning of the analysand's behavior. The challenge is to stay focused on the analysand's experience of the world, no matter how contrary it is to the analyst's experience.

Empathetic responding is the active dimension of empathy. The analyst "comes forward" in the relationship by demonstrating the inner sense of empathy directly to the analysand through accurate empathetic understanding (Truax 1966, Truax et al. 1971).

When dealing with an individual with severe psychopathology and a difficult way of relating, the use of empathetic responding is a crucial dimension in the therapeutic relationship. Empathy, therefore, formed the basic means of responding to Oedipus during the first year of analysis. Whatever material Oedipus presented to the analyst, the intention was to respond with accurate empathetic understanding. Whether Oedipus presented his diminished life functioning, his paranoid interpersonal feelings, his resentment and frustration toward his mother, his depression, or any dreams, early recollections, fantasies, or transference material, the analyst would search for its meaning in Oedipus's phenomenal world.

An example of the analysis of interpersonal issues from the accurate empathetic understanding viewpoint occurred in the fifth session (10/21/64). Oedipus talked about the difficulty he was having in social relations on a job he had just begun. He had been unemployed when he began therapy a month before. He was happy to be working, feeling comfortable, and beginning to look around for some kind of social contacts.

He was attracted to a woman at work. Oedipus expressed what the analyst sensed was a very painful emotional experience. Thus, when Oedipus said he was afraid to make contact with the woman because she wouldn't find him attractive, the analyst responded, "Your feeling of rejection is *so real* that before you've spoken to her, you feel it's already happened."

Oedipus verified this empathetic response by going on to discuss his masochistic feelings of rejection. But what is more significant, he began to acknowledge that making contact with a woman was emotionally connected with his seriously conflicted feelings about his mother.

. . . [a] girl . . . would pull me away from my mother. Hot area. Having sex with a girl frightens me. Bad thing, dirty, animalistic. Bad because sex is connected with my mother. Be horrible to think of having sex with my mother. Get signal about these thoughts, push this down. Having sex with a girl would be like having it with my mother.

Further on in this same session, Oedipus also uncovered an early recollection from when he was 4 years old. He exclaimed that his early childhood school experiences were so disturbing that he felt "like a student in one of Dickens' stories."

Although one accurate empathetic intervention usually doesn't produce such rich uncovering, it can do so because the interaction between analyst and analysand is centered on empathy. A sense of understanding, trust, caring, and decreased defensiveness develops. Since human beings have a natural need to be self-disclosing, empathy creates the corrective emotional climate to encourage openness.

There was additional objective data to verify that empathetic understanding was helping Oedipus. After one month of analysis, he responded
to a questionnaire monitoring the progress of the relationship between
analyst and analysand with the following:

The main reason I like my analyst is that he seems to realize how serious my
condition is and how important some of the apparently inconsequential things I
say are to me. [session 10/21/64]

The Analytic Phase

This second phase of humanistic analysis is characterized by an intense
focus on the analysis of dreams, fantasies, and early recollections. During
this phase hundreds of dreams were reported and analyzed. We would
discuss two and three dreams at a time, and we would not proceed until
we had analyzed each one. For months on end, entire sessions were
spent in the sharing of his unconscious world.

Oedipus had a natural affinity for dreams, fantasies, early recollections, and linguistics (use of metaphors, puns, symbols). The analysis
of dreams showed the same perfectionistic and compulsive attitude
that characterized his general functioning. It belied a deep sense of
inadequacy, the feeling developed in early childhood that he had to
drive himself with his intellect in order to gain self-esteem, protect
himself from his mother's emotional intrusion, build a wall to guard
against rejection, and gain mastery over the environment that he
perceived as so hostile.

When a dream was analyzed, the emphasis was again on empathetic understanding. A dream was a means of entering his phenomenal world. It presented an opportunity to respond in an empathetic
way to unconscious material. It could convey to Oedipus that the
analyst was aware of the emotional struggle at the most basic level of
his existence. Empathetic understanding of preconscious and unconscious expressions conveys a deeply felt sense of trust and oneness.

The feeling of really being understood or of finally being understood is a profoundly corrective emotional experience.

Dream Interpretation Session

He began telling me a dream that he felt was important (session 4/27/81):

You and I had sessions in someone's office—*Syrene Grissenthal's*. She had tapes we made. Called her to get the tapes. Can't get through to her, wrong number, out of order, etc. Sylvie in group says she knows her. Gives me phone number. I can't remember it. I say it over and over, but when time comes, I don't remember it.

Oedipus's special capacity for the Greek language is illustrated by referring to some of his associations to the dream. He began to separate the elements in the dream as if they were part of a secret code from the ancient world:

Syrene: That's Greek, makes me think of *sirens*, women in the Odyssey singing, sailors would be hypnotized, crash into rocks and die.

Selene: Goddess of moon = Sylvie, don't know why.

Grissenthal: Thal = valley in German Swiss. = area in Swiss.

Grisson: Grey = gris in French.

Gr: Animal growling

gl/rl: Related gl = connected with light in European languages—gleam, glow, glisten.

The associations now became more revealing as they were connected to positive parental figures and he began to reintegrate something positive about them.

Siren, causes damage, that's my mother.

Grey is my father, glowing.

German name means restraint. Jews who came from Germany, aristo-
crats.

This is from my father's family. I associate myself with aristocratic
Europeans.

The person in the dream may not be one person. To get better I need to
get in touch with the good part of my father and the good part of my
mother.

Although I connect my mother with danger, I also connect her with
Athena, goddess of sun. Confusing.

The analyst practiced empathetic listening while Oedipus continued
with his revealing associations. Empathetic listening is present in the
accumulated empathy in the relationship as well as in the facial and body
language that conveys, "Although I am not speaking, I am with you while
you struggle to understand your dream. I will not intrude upon your
associations. When you need help I will talk to you." Empathetic listening combines with a natural human desire to self-disclose, to produce a
therapeutic effect. The best indication that empathetic listening was
producing a positive effect was the continued unfolding of associations
and the development of insight that occurred.

I have another association to the dream.

Gris: French word = my obsession with my age; my hair is turning
grey. Time is running out and I'm not getting what I want.

Oedipus had begun to develop the insight that his creative block was
associated with his emotional relationship to his mother. Further on in
the analysis, he was able to become aware that creativity was as-

sociated with fear of homosexuality. Homosexuality meant giving in to his mother. Creativity meant letting go, and being emasculated by her.

Transference Reaction

During a dream analysis session, the analyst focused on Oedipus's sense of despair, which had appeared in the analysis as a signal that he was struggling with change. In the following session his despair, its relation to change, and his transference reaction to the analyst as the agent of change were explored:

OFB: You said we'll talk about changing.

AWR: Change means giving in.

OFB: It's true, my mother was so stubborn in wanting to do things her way, I had to defend myself by not doing it.

We had an interchange where he expressed a negative reaction toward my not understanding him. The analyst realized that Oedipus was in a heightened state of anxiety. The dream and the reworking of his feeling of being controlled by his mother made him vulnerable to the analyst, whom he perceived as trying to change him. At the same time, the analyst was annoyed at the assault. Speaking from a counter-transference reaction (the unappreciated good mother), he reminded Oedipus that it was the analyst who helped him understand his sensitivity to control. Oedipus admitted he was unfair in his criticism. The analyst had gotten him to retract his negative reaction and praise him, another countertransference reaction. The analyst continued when the countertransference interlude was finished.

AWR: You have been imprinted with the feeling of *being forced*, you can't experience freedom as deeply.

OFB: Yes, that's it!

AWR: You are afraid of some basic, ultimate control.

OFB: I'm afraid I'll lose control. Life will be out of control. You say I'm afraid of some ultimate change; my mother will capture me again.

AWR: How will it happen?

OFB: In order to change, I have to give up my defenses. Let things flow. Be vulnerable to her.

AWR: It's a Catch-22.

OFB: That's how I feel.

There is a very important point to make regarding the phenomenon of empathetic lapses and the resultant countertransference reaction. A neverending empathetic connection in human relatedness is a fantasy, even in the earliest years of life when it is more likely to occur. The mother of an infant may be tired, preoccupied, resentful, or narcissistically absorbed at a given moment of infant need. Such unavailability for empathetic response is, after all, only human. The difficulty would arise when a mother is more likely to be unavailable for empathy, is unaware of her child's need for empathy, is inconsistent in empathetic responding, or does not have the capacity for empathy.

In all probability, Oedipus's mother had the severest of empathy problems. She was unaware of her nonempathetic impact upon him, and either lost or had little capacity for an empathetic connection to him. At one point in the analysis I spoke to her about her relationship to her son. She was genuinely unaware of the connection between her behavior and his and that she had had an intensely negative impact upon him. She believed his problems were constitutionally inherited from his father. She also seemed unaware, or denied, that Oedipus's brother was homosexual and suffered from conversion hysteria. Apparently, massive denial and a narcissistic preoccupation with protecting her image of "professional mother" was paramount. It allowed her a sense of integration and positive identity. What was a lifesaving device for the mother turned out to be a lifethreatening device for the child. This is likely to occur when the mother has a serious problem in empathy, or when there is a lack of emotional synchronicity between mother and child.

At a point when he was feeling vulnerable, Oedipus became critical of the analyst. This feeling of vulnerability reminded him of his mother's controlling, intrusive, seductive behavior, which enraged him. The analyst was caught off guard for the moment because he was feeling good about helping Oedipus. What he wanted to hear from him was something like, "I really appreciate your helping me. You are helping me understand why I am feeling despair and how I can change." The assault on the analyst produced resentment, thereby preventing an empathetic response.

The curative emotional experience in the analysis for Oedipus was the empathetic relationship with the analyst. Such an experience can be curative in and of itself. But the analysis went beyond this, by using the empathetic understanding to analyze his severe emotional conflicts. The analyst's empathetic lapses were natural breaks in connectedness that occur when two people are involved in an ongoing, committed, mutually responsive emotional relationship. They can be compounded when dealing with such a difficult individual. The empathetic lapses are signs that the analyst is emotionally involved, that the analysand's interaction with him reaches him deeply. These lapses are not seen as therapeutic errors.

We need to distinguish between momentary and lasting empathetic lapses. The analyst's empathetic lapses with Oedipus usually did not produce an adverse effect for longer than a portion of a session. In the example cited, the negative effect lasted for several moments; then the analyst recovered and the empathetic connection was resumed. (In some difficult stages in the analysis, there were longer periods of empathetic lapses that lasted for several sessions or more.)

There was greater likelihood for a negative therapeutic effect to occur if the analyst did not understand and analyze his own behavior. The analyst needed to practice self-empathetic understanding—that is, to be nonjudgmental and nonpunitive about his empathetic lapses. It was important to accept that empathetic lapses are more likely to occur with a narcissistic, borderline, or difficult individual. What proved therapeutic was to develop an accepting attitude toward the empathetic breaks. There is also a mandate that the analyst must accept when working with a difficult patient. He is having a personal as well as therapy-induced emotional reaction to the individual and he needs to examine the meaning of the reaction for his own personal functioning as well as his functioning as an analyst.

In this case, ongoing countertransference analysis enabled the analyst to keep unempathetic lapses to momentary rather than permanent breaks in the therapeutic contact.

The Active Phase

The third phase of the analysis aims toward action. Empathetic understanding, the bedrock of the relationship, allows for a sustained sense of trust so that the analyst can introduce parameters to aid the translation of insight into action. Material uncovered during the analytic phase becomes the focal point for the active working through of conflicts.

It is during the action phase that group analysis is introduced. The use of group coincides with the individual's needs, resistances, and willingness to confront personal issues in an interpersonal setting. Alive, emotional experiences with group members trigger a series of parental transferences that stimulate the working through of core conflicts.

The Group Analysis

Oedipus needed a group experience to become more humanistic. It was with some trepidation that the analyst placed him in a group. Because of his severe interpersonal difficulties, his rigid defenses hid an ever-present fear of intrusion, seduction, and abuse by his mother and women he perceived as mother. Furthermore, there was a serious lack of cathexis for interpersonal relations or group affiliation. He was hypercritical and demanding, and he often maintained hostile prejudicial feelings toward certain people, especially blacks.

A combination of factors led to Oedipus's success in the group. (For a fuller discussion see Rachman, 1981, 1986). They were: the extended period of empathetic analysis that built a sense of basic trust in the analyst, softened Oedipus's negative feelings toward others, and allowed the analyst to become a transitional object for expanded interpersonal relations; the liberal use of parameters; the special techniques of screening the potential group members and assimilation of a deviant group member to help Oedipus join and maintain himself in the group; the introduction of action technique that encouraged projective contact with deep-seated primitive material; the group's positive response to Oedipus's leadership; and the analyst's encouragement of peer-to-peer interaction.

Group and the Creative Self

The emergence of Oedipus's creative self began when the additional parameters of the Intensive Group Experience (IGE) were added as an adjunct to the group analysis (Mintz 1971, Rachman 1979, Rogers 1979). For the purposes of the present discussion, I would like to trace the awakening and display of his creative impulses to several key incidents in the action phase of the analysis: (1) IGE No. 4: The building block encounter, (2) dreams about becoming an architect, (3) exploration of a course of study to become an architect, (4) drawing courses that indicated an inability in skill and perceptual-motor functioning, and (5) photography as the form of creative expression.

Prior to the fourth IGE, Oedipus was able to confront material about his relationship with his mother and he began a working-through process designed to liberate him from her historically seductive and controlling influence. The ability to confront his mother's seductiveness freed Oedipus to deal with his creative urges (Rachman 1976, 1981b, 1986). The analysis became focused on the central issue for his personal growth—the ability to create. Historical material emerged as a result of the special experiences that were explored in group sessions. His inability to be connected to a meaningful career and to be creative was his greatest source of pain. He blamed his mother's intrusive, seductive, controlling behavior for his incapacity. He began to recall a hazy memory from childhood of being thwarted in an attempt to play or create. There was a hint that his mother interfered with his attempt to build something one day while he was playing in his playpen.

As a stepping stone to the next IGE, an unusual session was planned with Oedipus's mother. The exploration of his early history left him dissatisfied. He felt we had not pinpointed the exact factors that caused his creative block. The analyst also felt the need to know more, since the analysis had not produced a clarification of the exact influence of the mother's personality and behavior on the development of her son's psychopathology. As is often the case with an individual who experienced such a troubled childhood, there was the search to know who was responsible for the "craziness." Was Oedipus crazy—or was it his mother? We decided, therefore, that it would be instructive to have the therapist interview his mother, go over his history, and attempt to discern the locus of psychopathology.

Two consultation sessions were arranged with Oedipus's mother. A tape recording of the sessions was given to a colleague who was an expert in early mother–infant behavior. After listening to the tapes, she concluded that the mother's voice quality, manner of relating, thought processes, emotionality, and level of denial suggested a borderline adaptation. Although these personality characteristics were not as apparent in the face-to-face interviews, they were discernible when the therapist also listened to the tapes. What became clear in trying to reconcile the discrepancy between the consultant's and the therapist's assessment of the mother's functioning was that being in the mother's presence may have had a "seductive" effect on the therapist. Her vitality, eagerness, and willingness to please and cooperate created the expectation that significant material was going to be forthcoming. She did reveal meaningful historical material. However, she practiced almost total denial when the therapist attempted to link two significant childhood experiences to Oedipus's adult personality problems.

At first, a detailed inquiry into the possibility of the occurrence of the building block experience yielded a total lack of recall. When the issue was pursued more vigorously, she responded, "It may be possible; I don't remember anything like that, and, I ask you, Doctor, do you think I would do something like that to my son? Never!"

Through contact with the same colleague who listened to the mother's tapes, Oedipus and the analyst were able to view research films of negative mother–infant interaction. The film we viewed was of an intrusive mother with an 18-month-old child. Through exploration of the film, Oedipus revealed that he was emotionally touched by the experience and identified strongly with the infant. He thought that the mother was intrusive, but that his mother was still more intrusive. Now he was satisfied that the proper diagnosis had been made about his mother and that he was the victim of her intrusiveness and control. He was once a curious, adventurous, and potentially creative child who was thwarted.

IGE NO. 4: THE BUILDING BLOCKS ENCOUNTER

After the discussion of the interview with his mother, it was decided to go ahead with an encounter that would attempt to encourage a fuller recall of the trauma that interfered with his creative development.

The scene was set by excluding all outside stimuli; the shades were drawn, the lights were lowered, and an area was cleared for the encounter. The group surrounded Oedipus to form the walls of a symbolic playpen. He sat on the floor, playing with the pillows from the couch. The pillows functioned as symbolic building blocks. A group member role-played the intrusive mother. Each time Oedipus built a structure with the building blocks, the member came from behind without warning and knocked it down. This was repeated several times. With each interruption of his attempt to build a structure, Oedipus became more frustrated and withdrawn. Finally, he sat immobilized, unable to continue. The encounter ended. Oedipus and the group reported that a profoundly moving experience had occurred. He was convinced that he had reexperienced a basic event of his early childhood in which his mother intruded her presence into his physical and emotional space, forcing him to pay attention to her, rather than to be left free to create. The experience was a basic way of behaving for his mother. In sessions to follow, we were able to discern that he chose to withdraw from her in frustration, rather than give in to her demands for attention. He developed a protective outer shell to fend off her intrusiveness. His withdrawal into a private world of fantasy became a lifesaving device. In his private world he was free to create, safe from intrusion. Although the flame of creativity could not burn brightly in a protective shell, the light did not go out, waiting for some event to rekindle it. The group experience began to melt the protective shell and the flame began to burn brighter.

EMERGENCE OF THE SUPPRESSED SELF

As a consequence of the continued analysis of the emotional meaning of the building block encounter, Oedipus had a dream that signaled the next stage in the rekindling of the creative self. He dreamed about becoming an architect: "I am an architect. Sitting in a studio. The light is coming through" (session, 1/22/81).

Upon hearing this, the analyst could hardly contain his excitement. He noted to himself that this is the sign that both had been waiting for, that Oedipus was beginning to reintegrate his suppressed creative self. Oedipus had great difficulty telling the dream and expressed a sense of depression, as if he was preparing himself for a crisis. He said, "Feel like I had a breakdown when I first started therapy . . . smoking, staying in my room, whacking off. Now I feel I will have another breakdown before I finish." However, this breakdown, if it came, could be the letting go of ancient defenses against maternal seduction in order to be free to create.

At first, Oedipus accepted this most literal interpretation of the architecture dream. The dream signified a coming out of the darkness caused by his mother casting a giant shadow over his original attempts at creating a structure in his playpen. He fell into darkness from that and other similar occurrences. With the corrective emotional experience in his analysis, he was beginning to see the darkness lift. A light was shining through and the light was the reawakening of his creative self. Since infancy he had wished to become a designer of buildings. Now he could try to be the architect he was not previously free to become.

With some prompting, he inquired about a course of study for architecture. In order to be able to study it, he needed the technical skills of drawing and drafting. Unfortunately, he found a drafting course very difficult, and he had neither the eye-hand coordination nor the artistic talent to perform the drawing tasks. A temporary sense of despair and depression set in. He returned to his lifelong lament that his mother had robbed him of his creative potential and he would never recapture it. He was emotionally stuck between despair and rage.

The analyst had maintained since Oedipus began his analysis that his creative self had not died—it had been suppressed. It was time to allow the flame to burn brightly again. It was suggested that Oedipus channel his newfound motivation to create into an outlet he could master. From time to time he had expressed an interest in photography. He had a camera, had taken pictures, and had exchanged ideas about photography with some group members. It was time to use photography as the creative focus. The analyst exerted some therapeutic pressure, focusing on suggesting photography as the creative outlet, and actively interpreting resistance to it.

Oedipus slowly but surely began to devote time and energy to photography. He shared his new interest with his wife and his therapy group. Everyone rallied behind him. He began to spend weekends taking pictures. His analysis and his search for meaning became interwoven with photography. He planned a return to Brooklyn for a weekend where he photographed scenes of his childhood. The photographs demonstrated a warm, sensitive feeling. He, his wife, and the group were all pleased and excited.

Photography began to fascinate Oedipus and he developed plans for photography outings. He also enrolled in an undergraduate degree program in photography. During this three-year period, he developed a modification of the Diana camera, a camera with special lenses. He also learned very sophisticated methods of developing and enlarging pictures, and he mixed his own chemicals. His pictures took on a very special, idiosyncratic quality, reflecting his talent as well as his psychological preoccupations. For example, he spent one period of experimentation photographing statues and then applying oil paint to accentuate a particular feeling tone. The statue photographs appeared to express his preoccupation with blacks, whom he saw as prototypes of his own "intrusive, sexual, dumb, uncontrollable primitives." A second series of statue photographs were of a sensual, seductive woman, also a symbol of his mother.

After graduation, he decided to become one of the first candidates for a Master of Arts degree in photography in a special dual program between a university and a photography institute. His undergraduate photographic portfolio was the test of entry into the graduate degree program, and he passed with flying colors.

At present, he is finishing the M.A. program and he plans to exhibit his photographs at a show. He has developed several new photographic techniques. Recently, he devised a way of developing photographs that links historical works of art with live model studies. This technique promises to be the beginning of a unique style in which he communicates beyond his personal preoccupations and demonstrates artistic and conceptual talent.

10

A Dual Borderline/Submerged Personality Patient

Steven Dranoff, Ph.D.,
and Irwin L. Kutash, Ph.D.

The nature of the infant is not just a new permutation and combination of elements contained in the natures of the parents. There is in the nature of the infant that which is utterly unknown in the nature of the parents.

—D. H. Lawrence

Diagnostic categories are, at their best, guideposts for treatment. However, treatment would seem to be more complicated and difficult if an individual's behavior, symptoms, and dynamics fall within the borderline and submerged categories. For example, what if an individual has the damaged split ego of the borderline, but the damaged ego with problems in drive regulation becomes submerged? Does the therapist treat the individual using more structure and confrontation, as he would with a borderline patient, or a neutral stance, as he would with a submerged personality? The patient presented in this chapter poses such a dilemma.

DIAGNOSTIC CONSIDERATIONS

Mr. M. possessed many features that correspond to the clinical picture of the borderline patient. His life history revealed the presence of an inconsistent mother, leading to chronic depression, poor anxiety tolerance, difficulty with impulse control, and poor subliminal defenses.

His reality testing was impaired, especially in the area of object relations. His relationships with people were characterized by suspicion and mistrust; he viewed women as inconsistent and controlling and men as dictatorial and abusive.

In contrast, Mr. M. also displayed characteristics of the submerged personality. His history revealed how autonomous ego skills were discouraged and inhibited by his father. He learned early on to suppress his feelings and impulses, and to incorporate the ego demands of his father, responding to him defensively with compliance and rebellion. He viewed men as dictatorial and abusive if you didn't comply with them.

In reviewing work with this patient, we became sensitive to the issue of how much structure and interpretation a therapist needs to provide for individuals with borderline pathology, and how little with submerged personality. This dilemma is best illustrated by Kernberg's work with borderline patients, and Wolf and Kutash's work with submerged patients. Kernberg (1975) indicates that confrontation or interpretation of primitive, split-off self and object representations strengthens the ego and brings about structural intrapsychic change with borderline patients.

Wolf and Kutash (1985), on the other hand, discourage the therapist from using interpretation early in treatment with submergence. They explain that the submerged patient does not have the capacity to use the information in a constructive manner. The patient is more likely to ambivalate.

Thus, the therapist working with patients whose pathology falls within these two diagnostic categories has to consider the impact of being too structured and interpretive, causing the patient to view the therapist as the "secondary parent" and defensively complying and rebelling. In contrast, the lack of structure and interpretive work may have a disorganizing effect on the patient. The patient has, in effect, submerged the damaged split ego of the borderline, and unlike the "pure" submerged personality, does not have an intact submerged ego as the result of two years of early nurturant mothering.

A case seen individually by Dranoff and in group by Kutash and discussed by the two authors is presented in this chapter. It describes an individual who has significant ego impairment, which was expressed through difficulties in reality testing, drive regulation, and object relations. One alternative way of viewing the patient, as Kutash formulated it, is that in addition to the individual exhibiting borderline features, his ego functions have been partially submerged, resulting in an arrest of further ego development. Accordingly, the parent, in this case the father, experienced the child's striving for autonomy as a separation from him. In his fear of losing the child's symbiotic support, he demanded homogeneity and conformity. This conflict, as can be seen, does not have to be limited to the mother's involvement. In fact, as described by Wolf and Kutash in Chapter 1, the father can take on characteristics of the secondary mother. In the case to be presented, the patient's mixed pathology was explained by Kutash to result from his identification and interaction with an inconsistent "borderlinogenic" mother and a father who was, in the first two years of the patient's life, nurturing. As his son took steps towards individuation, the father became uninterested and less available unless his son met some need of his own. In addition, after age two and independence strivings by the patient, the pathogenic father became demanding, controlling, and abusive—"the secondary father, and the patient submerged his borderline ego."

THE PATIENT

Mr. M. was 29 years old, white, and Jewish. He requested psychotherapy because he was having difficulty maintaining a relationship with his 35-year-old girl friend with whom he had had a relationship for one year. She had two children and was, at the time he entered treatment, in the process of a divorce. Mr. M. described her as controlling their relationship and undermining whatever Mr. M. wanted to do. In giving his history, Mr. M. described his father as controlling and his choice of a girl friend who was controlling him in part reflected his relationship with his father. When Mr. M.'s girl friend would be controlling, Mr. M. would become accommodating and then rebellious. For example, Mr. M. might go along with his girl friend's requests and demands even if he thought they were unrealistic, foolish, or annoying. He felt, at those times, that if he didn't comply he would lose her. This would then be followed by rebellion in which he would storm out of his girl friend's house, destroy her property, pout, or withdraw by smoking pot.

Mr. M. was also seeking treatment to stop his habitual "pot smoking" and periodic use of Quaalude, Ativan, and cocaine. He noted that these drugs kept his destructiveness and violent rage under control, but left him alienated and isolated from people.

During the initial evaluation Mr. M. told the therapist he completely understood his problems and dynamics and wanted to know what the therapist thought about his problems. In retrospect, this was an effort to draw the therapist out so he could have a position to comply compulsively and then rebel against. He had been "shopping around" for a therapist, and by the time he had arrived, he had interviewed five others, all of whom he criticized. They were, in his opinion, either too directive, too distant, or, in the case of the therapist he liked, did not have any time to see him. He seemed to be telling the therapist, based on material that emerged subsequently, that there were very few people who were legitimately able to join his club, and the therapist was entitled to be proud of himself.

PREVIOUS TREATMENT

During the initial interview Mr. M. indicated that he had been in treatment four other times. Two of his therapies had been initiated by his parents when Mr. M. was 15 and 16 because of his drug involvement. After one and a half years and six months respectively, Mr. M. terminated these therapies because he felt they were for his parents. The third therapy was initiated by Mr. M.'s mother. In fact, the mother had at one point been in treatment with this particular therapist. Mr. M. saw this therapist on and off for two years, but felt this therapist was too directive. He wanted Mr. M. to do whatever he said—causing Mr. M. to rebel. Mr. M.'s refusal to abstain from drugs led the therapist to terminate treatment.

The fourth therapy lasted only six months. The therapist was confrontive, sometimes extending the sessions to one and a half hours. Mr. M. would leave sessions shaking because he would feel overwhelmed with fear about what he had learned. He discontinued treatment after his therapist suffered a heart attack. In some way, all of these therapists had become transferential extensions of the "directive" father; each therapist made demands like Mr. M.'s father, which Mr. M. felt he had to comply with and eventually rebel against.

PATIENT'S BACKGROUND

While only a modest amount of information was gathered in the initial sessions, Mr. M.'s personal history unfolded throughout treatment. The highlights are presented.

Mr. M. described growing up for the first two and a half years of his life in a small, suburban, predominantly middle-class community. He lived with his mother, father, a brother fifteen years his senior, and a sister nine years older.

Mr. M.'s father owned his own business and was described as a workaholic who apparently spent very little time with his family. He died of a heart attack when Mr. M. was 17 years old. Mr. M. described him as dictatorial, dogmatic, and relying on a lot of rules. For example, he would insist, "You have to be strong and not show emotion." As a result, Mr. M. felt he could never expose himself, be upset, or cry because he would be ridiculed and made to feel unacceptable. Mr. M. remembered thinking how he idolized his father, viewing him as strong and powerful. He loved his father but felt he never got much from him. When Mr. M.'s father was home, there was a lot of tension and fighting between the parents, with anger often directed at Mr. M. and his sister.

According to Mr. M., his mother viewed herself as a second-class citizen, a reflection of how she was treated as a child. Her husband also treated her in this manner, discouraging her from being herself. As a result of the parents' difficult and stormy relationship, Mr. M.'s mother would often seek affection from Mr. M. She would confide seductively in him, often telling him his father was abusive but good in bed. When Mr. M.'s father would come home, however, his mother would ignore Mr. M. and cater to her husband. This would be upsetting to Mr. M., who would feel abandoned. He would become intensely angry and competitive with his father, attempting to vie for his mother's attention. Mr. M. remembered being a preschooler and seeing his father slap his mother across the face. She had yelled to Mr. M., "Do you see what he did to me?" This experience heightened Mr. M.'s oedipal feelings of wanting to rescue his mother and defeat his father. These oedipal feelings were played out similarly with his older brother and sister. His older brother, like the father, wasn't around much and, as a result, did not have much involvement with Mr. M. On the other hand, Mr. M. was close to his sister. When he was younger, Mr. M. would cling to his sister when he was feeling sad and lonely. He would also confide in her. She would console him but discouraged his being autonomous in much the same way as their father did. And like the father, his sister would often ignore him and spend time with their mother.

Mr. M. recalled an early memory from the time he was 2 years old: "I remember being about 2 years old and sitting in a chair on my father's lap and looking out the window, and everything looked great."

He described his home as "warm, happy, and supportive" with his father being quite attentive to him. "There was a real feeling of family. A number of my relatives lived in the neighborhood too, and would visit often."

However, by age 2½ Mr. M. noted the atmosphere at home had changed dramatically. The family had moved from close quarters, where people were constantly in contact, to large quarters where he was left alone a lot of the time. He felt lonely and isolated much of the time. Mr. M.'s mother was spending more time shopping, being indifferent to Mr. M., and for the first time leaving many of the caretaking responsibilities to hired help. While Mr. M. continued to experience symbiotic strivings, his mother would be attuned to him only when it conformed to her needs. Mr. M. described his relationship with his father changing in much the same way that Wolf (1980) has described the submerged personality's "primary mother" becoming the "secondary mother."

Mr. M. was taken care of and toilet trained by a nursemaid who reportedly had been abusive. Although disappointed and angry about the nursemaid's treatment of him, Mr. M. reported wondering what he had done to cause his mother to leave him with this woman. The nursemaid was later dismissed.

After the abusive nursemaid left, Mr. M. had a Polish nursemaid whom he loved. He remembered her as being quite playful, telling him about "mushrooms and fairies, and magical stuff," and recalled how he loved to mimic her Polish accent. On one occasion, his father overheard Mr. M. mimicking the nursemaid's accent, and in a burst of anger fired the nursemaid. After this incident, Mr. M. remembered spending a great deal of time by himself. The family later employed a black couple, whose many responsibilities included taking care of Mr. M. He saw them as warm and consistent and became very attached to them. While the first nursemaid suggested for Mr. M. that he wasn't acceptable and couldn't trust people, the black couple seemed to have instilled in Mr. M. a sense of hope.

When Mr. M. entered school he had difficulty. He lisped and was dyslexic and overweight. He attended private school until the fourth grade. In addition, over the next few years, he had physical problems that required surgery. At age 7, he was operated on for a hernia and an undescended testicle. At 9, he went for a corrective surgical operation for strabysmus. At 10, Mr. M.'s family moved to the South where he attended a public school. He remembered being fat, shorter than the other children, and rejected or picked on by his peers —more experiences that left him feeling there was something wrong with him.

By the onset of adolescence, Mr. M.'s growing rage and disappointment with his father led to an intense conflict. He did everything possible, including taking drugs, to get back at his father. By age 11 he had found some ways to neutralize his aggression, suggesting some important residual resources in this man. For example, he discovered how to make gunpowder and by age 12 began building rockets with explosives that could blow them up. At the same age, Mr. M., attending Hebrew school in preparation for his bar mitzvah, locked a male teacher in the bathroom. He was expelled and was placed on home instruction. The rabbi who visited him at home seduced Mr. M. into a one-time homosexual experience. Mr. M. remembered how this experience made him feel a deep need for closeness with a father figure. It was the first time he had an orgasm and was both excited and frightened by the experience. He discussed with his family the rabbi's approaching him, and their horrified reaction made him feel ashamed and guilty. Mr. M. felt this experience further contributed to his thinking something was wrong with him and intensified his ambivalence about trusting men.

By 13, Mr. M. began dating, and by 14, he was getting high on LSD. Mr. M. confided to his mother that he had been taking LSD, and at the suggestion of her therapist, she told Mr. M.'s father. In Mr. M.'s eyes, his father became angry and abusive, and forced Mr. M. to see two psychiatrists. However, his father had little faith in these therapists and arranged for Mr. M. to go to a military academy in the South. At the military academy interview, Mr. M. indicated that if he was accepted, he would cause trouble—even blow up the school. He was not accepted into the school. Instead, Mr. M. attended public school in the South and found it very difficult. He felt inadequate, he had difficulty with the schoolwork, and his peers made fun of him. After six months, Mr. M. and his family moved north again.

By the time Mr. M. was 17, his mother and father were having even more serious marital difficulties. His mother decided to take a vacation by herself, leaving Mr. M. and his father together at home. Mr. M. felt once again that his father was responsible for the mother's not being available to him.

Mr. M. and his father were spending time together, and for the first time, they were beginning to appreciate each other. It was Mr. M.'s perception that their developing appreciation for each other was actually something that evolved at this time, even though this is difficult to imagine, given Mr. M.'s intense rage and disappointment with his father. One night Mr. M.'s father complained of feeling ill, and Mr. M. told him to get some rest and not to worry about it. That night Mr. M.'s father went to sleep and died of a heart attack. Mr. M. felt extremely guilty for not being able to save his father. This was compounded by the fact that he took money from his father's wallet when he heard of his father's death, using the money to buy drugs and get high. Mr. M. remembered being at the funeral parlor the next day and getting in touch with very loving feelings toward his father and wishing things could have been different. At this point, Mr. M. began trying to step into his father's shoes. He tried controlling his mother the way his father had done by making demands, telling her what to do, and being disrespectful. After much fighting, his mother locked up his motorcycle and threw him out of the house. Mr. M. remembered taking an apartment in a neighboring town and feeling "ugly, disturbed, crazy, and wanting to hide."

After Mr. M. had been using drugs for several years, he began taking heroin. This lasted for eight months. He finally admitted himself into a methadone program. After his detoxification, he attended one college for six months and then transferred to another college for three years, never getting a degree. He then returned home where he had continued to be involved peripherally in the family business. All the while he had continued taking drugs such as Quaalude, marijuana, and cocaine. His taking drugs, while serving the purpose of helping him contain his feelings, also helped him perpetuate the old stance of feeling detached and isolated, and being an outsider.

THE TREATMENT

Excerpts from the treatment have been selected to illustrate the interplay of borderline and submergence features in this patient.

At the end of the first session, it was suggested to Mr. M. that we meet for three consultative sessions to evaluate together how well the work was going. This was an effort to allow him to feel his part in the choice. It was explained that it would be helpful to learn more about his problems and why he felt this treatment would be different from his other therapy experiences. The object was to make a statement to Mr. M. that there was a purpose to therapy; he could understand himself and learn about what he wanted.

At the third session, Mr. M. indicated that he wanted to continue working together, noting, "I haven't used my prior therapies because I wasn't ready. I saw shrinks because my parents wanted me to, not for myself." It was difficult to determine if Mr. M. was being accommodating, viewing the therapist as the transferential "secondary father." However, he decided to enter psychoanalytically oriented psychotherapy on a twice-a-week basis, later increasing his sessions to three times a week. He was treated for a period of five years.

The approach to treating Mr. M. was to establish a "good-enough holding environment" described by Winnicott (1958) and Chessick (1974, 1977). It was the consistent, predictable, structured approach, that is, meeting at the same times each week, strict start and finish, and a realistic and consistent dedication to the work. This allowed for the development of the working alliance, in spite of Mr. M.'s serious submerged ego affects on a day-to-day basis. For example, Mr. M. would miss appointments, come quite late to sessions, be stoned during many of his sessions, and refuse to pay his bills.

Mr. M.'s preoccupation with his emotional ups and downs with his girl friend characterized the first three years of his therapy. On the one hand, he wanted her to be the "primary parent," being constantly available and tuned in to what he wanted. At these times he would feel excited and confident. When his girl friend was not available, critical, or undermining, Mr. M. would view her as the "secondary parent" and become intensely angry and destructive, and would then retreat. In one session, he noted that he needed his girl friend because he couldn't function without her. This was followed by two dreams: "I'm in school and I'm not making it. I had this dream several times this past week. I've been in school and one memory is I would start off failing with Fs and then I pulled an A and ended up with a final grade of C." He associated: "In school I never quite made it and somehow something always got in the way. I would always stop working or give up. I had another dream this morning. I'm in school, English class, and a woman teacher tells me I'm going to have to go to summer school. I've failed and I ask why. She says, 'Because you haven't been here,' and she says, 'Bring in your girl friend and her son and let's have a meeting.'" He began associating to the dream. "I felt anxious driving to therapy. I wasn't sure what I would have to talk about." He described his many discussions between him and his girl friend. Their relationship seemed to be improving and now he was feeling at a loss as to what to talk about. He felt he didn't have an "English paper" to present. "I'm not feeling like a whole person and I'd like to have someone, like my girl friend, around to help me. When I was coming to therapy I even asked my girl friend kiddingly if she wanted to come to my session."

While it is possible on some level that Mr. M. was wanting to make his girl friend a gift to the therapist, his associative material suggested that he was having to function more on his own in therapy. This was stirring up old painful feelings of Mr. M. not having his mother available to him. He was used to picking up cues from others, especially his mother, as to what would be acceptable for him to say and do. However, he was not able to do this with the therapist. At this point his acting out behavior increased. These behaviors were designed to make the transferential parent feel anxious, angry, and frustrated, and to seduce the therapist into becoming the secondary parent and the oedipal father. Mr. M.'s acting out behavior eventually led the therapist to feel anxious, frustrated, and angry. The therapist was slowly being seduced, as a countertransference response, to Mr. M.'s appeals for him to become the secondary father who would scold him. The therapist began confronting Mr. M. about his behavior, somewhat roughly in retrospect. For example, the therapist made use of Mr. M.'s smiling, laughing, taking a cigarette, or changing his posture to bring him more in touch with his feelings. Mr. M., of course, would become resentful. He noted in one session, "I feel like you are monitoring my smoking or trying to control me." These periods of confrontation increased Mr. M.'s fear that the therapist would be like all the other disappointing people in his life. However, the more Mr. M. would talk about his behavior, the more he was able to understand that underneath the "dance" as he called it, referring to his acting-out behavior, were feelings.

By the end of the second year of treatment, Mr. M. noted, "You've stopped taking a hard line with me. I feel you care about me. I'm going to give this [the therapy] a chance, but I'm very frightened that I'll be disappointed and you'll turn on me again."

The Middle Phase of Treatment

The middle phase of treatment was marked by a dream: "I dreamed of being in a sanitarium with a lot of animals around, kindly animals, and I was swimming upstream toward new construction. The animals are kindly animals, there's a feeling of family or home. The one animal swimming away is a woodchuck."

He noted how frightened he was of venturing out of his therapy, "of leaving the protection of the sanitarium. I've felt crazy all my life, it's like I've been in a sanitarium, and I'm beginning to feel less crazy. But it feels dangerous to venture out, to be more myself." He noted that he had learned to hold back his thoughts and feelings from everyone, out of fear that they would see and confirm for him that he had irreparable damage from his extensive drug use. This appeared to be a screen for the intense castration anxiety he experienced. For years he had been fearful there was something wrong with him, and that he might die at any time. He began to trace these concerns about his health to his childhood physical problems and surgery. Mr. M. became intrigued that such old feelings could have such an impact on him. Shortly after presenting this dream, Mr. M. took a physical exam and found out he was in excellent health. He began feeling more comfortable with the therapist, but these feelings of attachment made him feel like a child. At this point, he presented another dream: "There's a tiger, not full grown, it's myself, with a powerful head, looks like it could be strong, nasty, and angry. I like cats. I pat its head, and the tiger says, 'You're very brave, you hardly know me.'" He associated: "When I think of a tiger, I think of double-edged, beautiful, magnificent, and unpredictable."

Mr. M. noted he wasn't feeling like a whole person and had to have someone around to help him. The dilemma for Mr. M. was that whoever he had reached out to in the past had either "taken over" or "disappointed" him. He thought of his experience with the rabbi and worried that the therapist might betray him as the rabbi did. It seemed that the more therapy provided an opportunity for genuine intimacy for Mr. M., the more dangerous it became for him—stirring up homoerotic feelings that frightened him.

In the next session, he presented the following dream: "There is this guy my age building my house, which frees me up from my responsibilities. I'm with him at the building, it's a big gamble. Three weeks go by and I'm away. The house is all built, or rather three-fourths built, and I'm shocked. If this guy can build them so quickly I can do it faster. I see things aren't the way they should be and I get anxious. I don't know any of the contractors. I don't have any sense of what I'm doing. I'm freaked out. I drive away, and the house is horribly ugly and I haven't sold it. The elevation is horrible and I have tremendous anxiety." He begins to associate. "It's hard for me to rely on anyone because I've been hurt so much in my life." He thought of his experience with the rabbi, of being "erect," and how this experience hurt him. He wondered if "here too I'll be hurt. The other thought I have is that maybe I think I can build my house better if I do it myself, even though I'd like your help."

No matter how much we were able to explore his feelings about being hurt and betrayed, he continued to feel that to rely on the therapist meant he had to respond in a passive, submissive, and feminine way. He continued to feel as if he were once again in the hands of the rabbi/father/castrator. The negative transference continued to intensify, with Mr. M. becoming more and more angry. Moreover, he was convinced that if he talked about his feelings, he would hurt the therapist. This omnipotence could be seen in many of his dreams, in which he saw himself as a "werewolf stalking people" and a "killer dog with big jaws." He was feeling trapped inside himself, characteristic of the submerged personality, and wanted desperately to be freed of these feelings. He noted jokingly in one session, "If I'm really honest with you, you'll send me away or you'll end up getting a heart attack like my father and my last therapist." He was gradually becoming more disappointed with me and feeling as though I wouldn't be able to help him.

He presented another dream: "It's a mummy, a dead mummy. There were like a lot of people, a live mummy chasing me, and other people. I'm gonna let the mummy chase me. I go to the cellar and the mummy catches me. He grabs my arm and says, 'Please release me.' He has horrible eyes. Me or someone sprays water on the mummy. He's dissolved. Mummy said, 'Release me, let me go.'" He began associating to the dream. He thought of death, "a dead mummy that is living, moving, and it has eyes. I was disgusted and horrified that he would find me, and there was the excitement of him to find me." He thought of his old house (the one he had moved to when he was 2½ years old). "It was a magical place. I was scared when I was little. I was playing games with someone bigger than me, it was dangerous." He thought of his father and how frightened he had been of him. "I could never count on him."

Mr. M. was becoming more aware of his fear of men and how disappointing they have been for him. He began to see that the only ways he could respond to men would be either passive and compliant or angry and rebellious. Despite his growing awareness of his attitude toward men, he continued to view our relationship as dangerous and intruding upon his relationship with his girl friend.

Outside of Mr. M.'s sessions he was making strides in following his "map." He had stopped using drugs, was developing his business, making new friends, all of which were creating distance between him and his girl friend. She continued to be critical of his growing independence. He blamed therapy for his predicament. "I'll probably lose my girl friend because of this." He realized that he experienced these feelings with his father, who he felt was always taking his mother away from him.

The therapist's move to another office around this time precipitated more anger and resistance from Mr. M. He liked the old office in much the same way he liked his first house. He felt sad, and remembered losing his "crib" when his family moved to the big house. Many sessions were spent with Mr. M. talking about the emotional losses he experienced with his family, the loss of his home, his fear that he would lose his girl friend.

It appeared that this patient experienced listening and being neutral as not being there for him. In addition, his anger and feelings of loss of his "crib," both from the past and the present, and his "embarrassing sexual feelings" towards the therapist now as mother resulted in his fleeing from therapy. He had purchased a small cottage and wanted the opportunity to be more on his own. He seemed to understand that buying the cottage was a way to master the old trauma of his moving at the age of 2½. While this was adaptive, he was running away from his therapy. At one level he was disappointed and angry that he wasn't freed to be really more on his own and still be able to maintain his relationship with his girl friend/father. He felt that without his girl friend, he couldn't survive. At another level, by leaving his therapy, he was once again killing the transferential mother and going off with the transferential father. Mr. M., after much discussion about the premature termination, noted, "For right now I need to try living in my own place, following my map." He was later able to return because the therapist hadn't tried to stop him and thus stopped being father in the negative transference.

DISCUSSION

It was realized in consultation between the authors that with this patient, enough initial structure was provided for his borderline pseudo-ego, his introjected mother's ego, to allow him to appear to improve initially but only at the cost of a strong transference with the therapist seen as his controlling secondary father. It was only after a more neutral, less confrontational stance was taken that the real submerged ego began to emerge as he was encouraged in following his own "map." Furthermore, upon its emergence, it was found that the early experience with the borderlinogenic mother had created a borderline ego, submerged when the father became the secondary father. His years as the primary father could not overcome the early mothering by the mother, perhaps because he was so rarely present. After the patient returned to therapy, having tested that the therapist was not the father since he hadn't tried to stop the termination, his own ego was ready to emerge. He could now be treated for the damage in his own real ego as he now trusted the therapist. With these realizations, his therapy is progressing and he has recently been added to the group described in Chapter 3.

Therefore, our solution to the dilemma of this dual diagnosis of whether to provide confrontation and structure for the borderline or unintrusive neutrality for the submerged personality is first to facilitate the emergence of the true ego through a safe, neutral environment and then to treat whatever the true emerged ego is suffering from—in this case, borderline pathology.

References

Abend, S., Porder, M., and Willick, M. (1983). *Borderline Patients: Psychoanalytic Perspectives*. New York: International Universities Press.

Agee, J. (1965). *A Death in the Family*. New York: Avon Books.

Ainsworth, M., and Bell, S. (1969). Some contemporary patterns of mother-infant interaction in the feeding situation. In *Stimulation in Early Infancy*, ed. A. Ambrose, pp. 133–170. London: Academic Press.

Atwood, G. E., and Stolorow, R. D. (1984). *Structures of Subjectivity: Explorations in Psychoanalytic Phenomenology*. Hillsdale, NJ: The Analytic Press.

Bellak, L., and Faithorn, P. (1978). Ego function assessment, parts 1, 2, 3. *Weekly Psychiatry Update Series*, vol. 2, lessons 34, 35, 36. Princeton, NJ: Biomedia.

Bergler, E. (1944). Eight prerequisites for psychoanalytic treatment of homosexuality. *Psychoanalytic Review* 31:253–286.

——— (1949a). *The Basic Neurosis*. New York: Grune & Stratton.

——— (1949b). *Counterfeit Sex*. New York: Grune & Stratton.

Blanck, G., and Blanck, R. (1979). *Ego Psychology II: Psychoanalytic Developmental Psychology*. New York: Columbia University Press.

Bowlby, J. (1969). *Attachment and Loss*. Vol. 1: *Attachment*. New York: Basic Books.

Boyer, B. (1961). Provisional evaluation of psychoanalysis with few parameters employed in the treatment of schizophrenia. *International Journal of Psycho-Analysis* 42:389–403.

—— (1980a). Introduction. In *Psychoanalytic Treatment of Schizophrenic, Borderline and Characterological Disorders*, ed. B. Boyer and P. Giovacchini, pp. 1–35. New York: Jason Aronson.

—— (1980b). Office treatment of schizophrenic patients: the use of psychoanalytic therapy with few parameters. In *Psychoanalytic Treatment of Schizophrenic, Borderline and Characterological Disorders*, ed. B. Boyer, and P. Giovacchini, pp. 129–170. New York: Jason Aronson.

—— (1982). Analytic experiences in work with regressed patients. In *Technical Factors in Treatment of the Severely Regressed Patient*, ed. P. Giovacchini, and B. Boyer, pp. 65–106. New York: Jason Aronson.

Brombert, V. (1967). *The Novels of Flaubert: A Study of Themes and Techniques*. Princeton, NJ: Princeton University Press.

Capponi, A. (1979). Origins and evolution in the borderline patient. In *Advances in Psychotherapy of the Borderline Patient*, ed. J. Leboit and A. Capponi, pp. 63–148. New York: Jason Aronson.

Chessick, R. (1974). *The Technique and Practice of Intensive Psychotherapy*. New York: Jason Aronson.

—— (1977). *Intensive Psychotherapy of the Borderline Patient*. New York: Jason Aronson.

Deutsch, H. (1932). Homosexuality in women. *International Journal of Psycho-Analysis* 14:34–56.

Diagnostic and Statistical Manual of Mental Disorders, 3rd ed. (*DSM-III*) (1986). Washington, DC: American Psychiatric Association.

Dickinson, E. (1924). *The Poems of Emily Dickinson*. New York: Modern Library.

Eissler, K. R. (1953). The effect of the structure of the ego on psychoanalytic technique. *Journal of the American Psychoanalytic Association* 1:104–143.

Ferenczi, S. (1928). The elasticity of psychoanalytic technique. In *Final Contributions to the Problems and Methods of Psychoanalysis*, vol. II, pp. 1–27. New York: Basic Books, 1955.

Freud, S. (1912). Recommendations to physicians practising psychoanalysis. *Standard Edition* 12:109–121, 1958.

—— (1920). *Beyond the Pleasure Principle*. New York: Liverwright.

—— (1923). The ego and the id. *Standard Edition* 19:1–66.

Gardner, L. (1972). *Fat City*. New York: Dell.

Giovacchini, P. (1979a). The many sides of helplessness: the borderline patient. In *Advances in Psychotherapy of the Borderline Patient*, ed. J. Leboit and A. Capponi, pp. 227–279. New York: Jason Aronson.

—— (1979b). *Treatment of Primitive Mental States*. New York: Jason Aronson.

Gluzman, S. (1982). Fear of freedom. *American Journal of Psychiatry* 139:57–61.

Greenberg, J. R., and Mitchell, S. (1983). *Object Relations in Psychoanalytic Theory.* Cambridge, MA: Harvard University Press.

Harlow, H. (1958). The nature of love. *American Psychologist* 13:673–685.

Hartmann, H. (1958). *Ego Psychology and the Problem of Adaptation.* New York: International Universities Press. (originally published 1937.)

—— (1964). *Essays on Ego Psychology: Selected Problems in Psychoanalytic Theory.* New York: International Universities Press.

Horner, A. (1973). Ego boundaries: the line of resistance in psychotherapy. *Psychotherapy: Theory, Research and Practice* 10:83–86.

—— (1979). *Object Relations and the Developing Ego in Therapy.* New York: Jason Aronson.

—— (1984). *Object Relations and the Developing Ego in Therapy.* 2nd ed. New York: Jason Aronson.

Jones, E. (1927). Early development of female homosexuality. *International Journal of Psycho-Analysis* 8:459–472.

Juda, D. P. (1983). Exorcising Freud's "daemonic" compulsion to repeat: repetition compulsion as part of the adaptational/maturational process. *Journal of the American Academy of Psychoanalysis* 11:353–375.

Kahn, E., Kohut, H., and Rogers, C. (1985). A timely comparison. *American Psychologist* 40:893–904.

Kernberg, O. (1972). Early integration and object relations. *Annals of the New York Academy of Science* 193:233–247.

—— (1975). *Borderline Conditions and Pathological Narcisissism.* New York: Jason Aronson.

—— (1979a). Technical considerations in treatment of borderline personality organization. In *Advances in Psychotherapy of the Borderline Patient,* ed. J. Leboit and A. Capponi, pp. 269–308. New York: Jason Aronson.

—— (1979b). Some implications of object relations theory for psychoanalytic technique. *Journal of the American Psychoanalytic Association* 27:207–239.

—— (1982). The theory of psychoanalytic psychotherapy. In *Curative Factors in Dynamic Psychotherapy,* ed. S. Slipp, pp. 21–44. New York: McGraw Hill.

—— (1984). *Object Relations Theory and Clinical Psycho-Analysis.* New York: Jason Aronson.

Knight, R. (1953a). Borderline patients. *Bulletin of the Menninger Clinic* 1:1–12.

—— (1953b). Management and psychotherapy of the borderline patient. *Bulletin of the Menninger Clinic* 17:139–150.

Kohut, H. (1971). *The Analysis of the Self.* New York: International Universities Press.

——— (1977). *The Restoration of the Self.* New York: International Universities Press.

——— (1984a). *How Does Analysis Cure?* Chicago, IL: University of Chicago Press.

——— (1984b). The curative effect of psychoanalysis: a preliminary statement based on findings of self psychology. In *How Does Analysis Cure?*, ed. A. Goldberg, pp. 64–79. Chicago, IL: University of Chicago Press.

——— (1984c). The role of empathy in psychoanalytic cure. In *How Does Analysis Cure?*, ed. A. Goldberg, pp. 172–191. Chicago, IL: University of Chicago Press.

Kutash, I. L. (1980). Prevention and equilibrium–disequilibrium theory. In *The Handbook on Stress and Anxiety*, ed. I. L. Kutash and L. B. Schlesinger, pp. 463–473. San Francisco: Jossey Bass.

——— (1984a). Anxiety. In *Encyclopedia of Psychology*, ed. R. A. Corsini, pp. 78–79. New York: John Wiley.

——— (1984b). Comments on psychoanalysis in groups: creativity in diegophrenia and treatment methods with case material. *Group* 8:23–26.

——— (1984c). Psychoanalysis in groups: the primacy of the individual. *Current Issues in Psychoanalytic Practice* 1:29–42.

——— (1985). *Pseudo-egoality and the personality disorders.* Paper presented at the American Group Psychotherapy Convention, Washington, DC.

——— (1988a). Group composition. *The Group Psychotherapist* 1:9–11.

——— (1988b). A mini article on "a mini group." *The Group Psychotherapist* 1:19.

Kutash, I. L., and Greenberg, J. C. (1986). Psychoanalytic psychotherapy. In *Psychotherapist's Casebook*, ed. I. L. Kutash and A. Wolf, pp. 22–42. San Francisco: Jossey Bass.

——— (1989). The remote patient as a symptom of personality disorder. *The Psychotherapy Patient* 6:115–123.

Kutash, I. L., Kutash, S. B., and Schlesinger, L. B. (1978). *Violence, Perspectives on Murder and Aggression.* San Francisco: Jossey Bass.

Kutash, I. L., and Schlesinger, L. B. (1980). *Handbook on Stress and Anxiety.* San Francisco: Jossey Bass.

Kutash, I. L., and Wolf, A. (1983). Recent advances in psychoanalysis in groups. In *Comprehensive Group Psychotherapy*, ed. H. I. Kaplan and B. J. Sadock, pp. 132–138. Baltimore, MD: Williams & Wilkins.

——— (1984). Psychoanalysis in groups: the primacy of the individual. In *Inhibitions in Work and Love: Psychoanalytic Approaches to Problems in Creativity*, ed. H. S. Strean, pp. 29–42. New York: Haworth Press.

—— (1986). *Psychotherapist's Casebook.* San Francisco: Jossey Bass.

—— (1989). Equilibrium, disequilibrium and malequilibrium in groups. *The Group Psychotherapist* 2:20–25.

—— (1990). *Group Psychotherapists' Handbook.* New York: Columbia University Press.

Laing, R. D. (1959). *The Divided Self.* Baltimore, MD: Penguin Books.

Langs, R. (1973). *The Technique of Psychoanalytic Psychotherapy.* Vols. 1 and 2. New York: Jason Aronson.

Laplanche, J., and Pontalis, J. -B. (1973). *The Language of Psychoanalysis.* Trans. D. Nicholson-Smith. New York: Norton.

Leboit, J. (1979). The technical problem with the borderline patient. In *Advances in Psychotherapy of the Borderline Patient,* ed. J. Leboit and A. Capponi, pp. 3–62. New York: Jason Aronson.

Leboit, J., and Capponi, A. (1979). *Advances in Psychotherapy of the Borderline Patient.* New York: Jason Aronson.

Lichtenstein, H. (1961). Identity and sexuality: a study of their interrelationship in man. *Journal of the American Psychiatric Association* 9:179–260.

Mahler, M. S. (1952). On child psychosis and schizophrenia. *Psychoanalytic Study of the Child* 7:286–305. New York: International Universities Press.

—— (1979). *The Selected Papers of Margaret S. Mahler.* New York: Jason Aronson.

Mahler, M. S., Pine, F., and Bergman, A. (1975). *The Psychological Birth of the Human Infant.* New York: Basic Books.

Masterson, J. F. (1976). *Psychotherapy of the Borderline Adult: A Developmental Approach.* New York: Brunner/Mazel.

—— (1981). *The Narcissistic and Borderline Disorders: An Integrated Developmental Approach.* New York: Brunner/Mazel.

Meissner, W. W. (1984). *The Borderline Spectrum.* New York: Jason Aronson.

Miller, A. (1979). *Prisoners of Childhood.* New York: Basic Books.

Mintz, E. (1971). *Marathon Groups: Reality and Symbol.* New York: Appleton-Century-Crofts.

Modell, A. (1975). The ego and the id, fifty years later. *International Journal of Psycho-Analysis* 56:57–68.

Nelson, R. (1974). *Van Wyck Brooks: A Writer's Life.* New York: Dutton.

Ornstein, A. (1974). The dread to repeat and the new beginning. *Annals of Psychoanalysis* 2:231–248.

Pasternak, B. (1958). *Dr. Zhivago.* London: William Collins.

Phillipson, H. (1955). *The Object Relations Technique.* London: Tavistock.

Pressman, M. D. (1960). *On the analytic situation: the analyst is silent.* Paper presented at the midwinter meeting of the American Psychiatric Association, New York City, December 9, 1960.

Rachman, A. W. (1976). *Humanistic analysis with an individual in a group setting.* Paper presented at the meeting of the International Congress of Group Psychotherapy, Philadelphia, PA, August.

—— (1977). Self-disclosure, self-analysis and self-actualization for the group psychotherapist. In *Group Therapy 1977: An Overview*, ed. L. R. Wolberg and M. L. Aronson, pp. 146-150. New York: Stratton Intercontinental Medical Books.

—— (1979). Active psychoanalysis and the group encounter. In *Group Therapy 1979: An Overview*, ed. L. R. Wolberg and M. Aronson, pp. 75-88. New York: Stratton Intercontinental Medical Book Group.

—— (1981). Humanistic analysis in groups. *Psychotherapy: Theory, Research and Practice* 18:457-477.

—— (1987). Ferenczi's contributions to the evolution of a self psychology framework in psychoanalysis. In *Self-Psychology: Comparison and Contrast*, ed. D. W. Detrick and S. P. Detrick, pp. 89-109. Hillsdale, NJ: The Analytic Press.

Rachman, A. W., and Wayne, M. (1986). *The emergence of the concept of empathy in psychoanalysis: from Ferenczi to Kohut.* Paper presented at the meeting of the Seminar Society for the Advancement of Self Psychology, New York, September.

—— (1988). The rule of empathy: Sandor Ferenczi's pioneering contributions to the empathic method in psychoanalysis. *Journal of the American Academy of Psychoanalysis* 16:1-27.

Rinsley, D. B. (1980). *Treatment of the Severely Disturbed Adolescent.* New York: Jason Aronson.

Rogers, C. R. (1951). *Client-Centered Therapy: Its Current Practice, Implications and Theory.* Boston, MA: Houghton Mifflin.

—— (1959). Client-Centered Therapy. In *American Handbook of Psychiatry*, vol. 3, ed. S. Arieti, pp. 183-200. New York: Basic Books.

—— (1961). *On Becoming a Person.* Boston, MA: Houghton Mifflin.

—— (1967). Client-centered therapy. In *Comprehensive Textbook of Psychiatry*, ed. A. M. Freedman and H. I. Kaplan, pp. 1225-1228. Baltimore, MD: Williams & Wilkins.

—— (1975). Empathetic: an unappreciated way of being. *The Counseling Psychologist* 5:2-10.

—— (1978). The formative tendency. *Journal of Humanistic Psychology* 18:23-26.

————— (1979). *On Encounter Groups*. New York: Harper & Row.

————— (1980). *A Way of Being*. Boston, MA: Houghton Mifflin.

————— (1986). Client-centered therapy. In *Psychotherapist's Casebook*, ed. I. L. Kutash and A. Wolf, pp. 197–208. San Francisco, CA: Jossey-Bass.

Sandler, J., and Sandler, A. (1978). On the development of object relationships and affects. *International Journal of Psycho-Analysis* 59:285–296.

Searles, H. F. (1965). The place of the neutral therapist response in psychotherapy with the schizophrenic patient. In *Collected Papers on Schizophrenia and Related Subjects*, ed. H. F. Searles. New York: International Universities Press.

————— (1979). The countertransference with the borderline patient. In *Advances in Psychotherapy of the Borderline Patient*, ed. J. Leboit and A. Capponi, pp. 309–346. New York: Jason Aronson.

Shapiro, E. R. (1978). The psychodynamics and developmental psychology of the borderline patient: a review of the literature. *American Journal of Psychiatry* 135:1305–1315.

Shneidman, E. S. (1980). *Voices of Death*. New York: Harper & Row.

————— (1960). The theory of the parent-infant relationship. *International Journal of Psycho-Analysis* 41:585–595.

Silverberg, W. (1948). The concept of transference. *Psychoanalytic Quarterly* 17:303–321.

Spitz, R. (1965). *The First Year of Life*. New York: International Universities Press.

Stolorow, R. D. (1976). Psychoanalytic reflections on client-centered therapy in the light of modern conceptions of narcissism. *Psychotherapy: Theory, Research, and Practice* 13:26–29.

Stolorow, R. D., and Lachman, F. M. (1980). *Psychoanalysis of Developmental Arrests: Theory and Treatment*. New York: International Universities Press.

Stolorow, R. D., Brandchaft, B., and Atwood, G. (1987). *Psychoanalytic Treatment: An Intersubjective Approach*. Hillsdale, NJ: The Analytic Press.

Truax, C. B. (1966). Therapist empathy, warmth and genuineness and patient personality change in group psychotherapy. *Journal of Clinical Psychology* 22:225–229.

Truax, C. B., Wittmer, J., and Wargo, D. G. (1971). Effect of the therapeutic conditions of accurate empathy, nonpossessive warmth and genuineness on hospitalized mental patients during therapy groups. *Journal of Clinical Psychology* 27:137–142.

Weiss, J., and Sampson, H. (1986). Testing alternative psychoanalytic explanations of the therapeutic process. In *Empirical Studies of Psychoanalytic Theories*, vol. 2, ed. J. Masling, pp. 1–26. Hillsdale, NJ: Analytic Press.

Winnicott, D. W. (1958). *Collected Papers*. New York: Basic Books.

—— (1960). Ego distortion in terms of true and false self. In *The Maturational Processes and the Facilitating Environment*, pp. 140-152. Madison, CT: International Universities Press, 1965.

—— (1963). The development of the capacity for concern. In *The Maturational Process and the Facilitating Environment*, pp. 73-82. New York: International Universities Press.

—— (1965). *The Maturational Processes and Facilitating Environment*. Madison, CT: International Universities Press.

Wolf, A. (1949). The psychoanalysis of groups. *American Journal of Psychotherapy* 3:525-558.

—— (1950). The psychoanalysis of groups. *American Journal of Psychotherapy* 4:16-50.

—— (1957). Discussion of *Psychic Structure and Therapy of Latent Schizophrenia* by Gustave Bychowsky. In *Psychoanalytic Office Practice*, ed. A. H. Rifkin, pp. 135-139. New York: Grune & Stratton.

—— (1967). Group psychotherapy. In *Comprehensive Textbook of Psychiatry*, ed. A. M. Freedman and H. I. Kaplan, pp. 1234-1241. Baltimore, MD: Williams & Wilkins.

—— (1974). Psychoanalysis in groups. In *The Challenge for Group Psychotherapy: Present and Future*, ed. S. DeSchill, pp. 120-172. New York: International Universities Press.

—— (1980). Di-egophrenia and genius. *American Journal of Psychoanalysis* 40:213-226.

—— (1983). Psychoanalysis in groups. In *Comprehensive Group Psychotherapy*, ed. H. I. Kaplan and B. J. Sadock, pp. 113-132. Baltimore, MD: Williams & Wilkins.

Wolf, A., and Kutash, I. L. (1980). Psychoanalysis in groups: dealing with the roots of aggression. *International Journal of Group Tensions* 10:1-4.

—— (1982). Book review of *Psychoanalytic Group Dynamics*, ed. S. Scheidlinger. *Journal of the American Academy of Psychoanalysis* 10:632-635.

—— (1984a). Psychoanalysis in groups: creativity in di-egophrenia. *Group* 1:12-22.

—— (1984b). Psychoanalysis in groups: dealing with difficult patients. In *Psychoanalytic Approaches to the Resistant and Difficult Patient*, ed. H. Strean, pp. 107-127. New York: Haworth Press.

—— (1985). Di-egophrenia and its treatment through psychoanalysis in groups. *International Journal of Group Psychotherapy* 35:519-530.

—— (1988). Treating creative di-egophrenics in psychoanalysis in groups.

In *Borderline and Narcissistic Patients in Therapy*, ed. Slavinska-Holy, pp. 283–308. New York: International Universities Press.

—— (1989). Psychoanalysis in groups: dealing with resistance. *The Group Psychotherapist* 2:5–10.

Wolf, A., and Schwartz, E. K. (1960). Psychoanalysis in groups: the alternate session. *American Imago* 17:101–108.

—— (1962). *Psychoanalysis in Groups*. New York: Grune & Stratton.

Wolf, A., Schwartz, E. K., McCarty, G., and Goldberg, I. (1970). *Beyond the Couch: Dialogues in Teaching and Learning Psychoanalysis in Groups*. New York: Science House.

Zetzel, E. R. (1971). A developmental approach to the borderline patient. *American Journal of Psychiatry* 127:867–871.

Index

267

DATE DUE